D1257668

DE WITT CLINTON

EMPIRE STATE HISTORICAL PUBLICATIONS

I *THE EVOLUTION OF LONG ISLAND*
Ralph Henry Gabriel

II *THE INDIANS OF MANHATTAN ISLAND AND VICINITY*
Alanson Skinner

III *A HISTORY OF THE NEW YORK IROQUOIS*
William M. Beauchamp

IV *LONG ISLAND'S STORY* and its sequel *THE REST OF THE STORY 1929-1961*
Jacqueline Overton — Bernice Marshall

V *HISTORY OF LONG ISLAND* Third Edition, 3 volumes
Benjamin F. Thompson and Charles Werner

VI *THE INDIAN PLACE NAMES ON LONG ISLAND AND ISLANDS ADJACENT*
William W. Tooker

VII *MYTHS AND LEGENDS OF THE NEW YORK IROQUOIS*
Harriet M. Converse

VIII *NEW YORK IN THE AMERICAN REVOLUTION*
Wilbur C. Abbott

IX *COLONIAL HEMPSTEAD: LONG ISLAND LIFE UNDER THE DUTCH AND ENGLISH*
Bernice Marshall

X *THE MILLS OF LONG ISLAND;THE WINDMILLS AND THE WATER MILLS*
Compiled by Cornell Jaray

XI *DE WITT CLINTON*
Dorothie Bobbé

XII *HISTORY OF THE ADIRONDACKS,* 2 vols.
Alfred C. Donaldson

XIII *MEMORIALS OF BRIDGEHAMPTON*
James Truslow Adams

XIV *HISTORY OF THE TOWN OF SOUTHAMPTON*
James Truslow Adams

XV *LONG ISLAND BEFORE THE REVOLUTION.* A Colonial Study
(originally published under title "Early Long Island")
Martha B. Flint

XVI *COLONIAL DAYS IN OLD NEW YORK*
Alice Morse Earle

XVII *HISTORICAL AND DESCRIPTIVE SKETCHES OF SUFFOLK COUNTY*
Richard M. Bayles

XVIII *HISTORY OF THE STATE OF NEW YORK,* 10 volumes in 5
Edited by Alexander C. Flick

Published and Distributed Exclusively by
IRA J. FRIEDMAN, INC.
PORT WASHINGTON, LONG ISLAND, N.Y.

EMPIRE STATE HISTORICAL PUBLICATION XI

DE WITT CLINTON

By

Dorothie Bobbé

A New Edition
With an Introduction
By
HENRY STEELE COMMAGER

IRA J. FRIEDMAN, INC.
Port Washington, Long Island, N. Y.
1962

Manufactured in the United States of America

Library of Congress Catalog Card No. 62-19668

Printed by Nassau Lithographers, Inc., Mineola, L.I., N.Y.

Respectfully,

to

FRANKLIN D. ROOSEVELT,

This Story of

Another Distinguished Son of New York

DE WITT CLINTON
By John Trumbull

AUTHOR'S FOREWORD TO THE NEW EDITION

When the idea was first conceived of confining within a single volume the innumerable interests and accomplishments of De Witt Clinton, the aim was to present a comprehensive view of the man; something never attempted before (or, it may be said, since). So varied were those interests, so insatiable his intellectual curiosity, so many and widely differing his achievements, that phases of his character and career had previously sufficed as subjects of complete books. James Renwick, for instance, a contemporary and friend of his, wrote of his educational contribution in a mood of understandable admiration. David Hosack, another intimate, made a study of his scientific experiments, and told something of his part in the project of the Erie Canal. William W. Campbell showed him in a different, but to himself, no less important light - - as a family man - - at the same time reproducing a number of his public speeches and writings. What follows is the first and only work, to date, that narrates the whole story.

The research involved was naturally complex, but a number of generous people and institutions made it less onerous than it would otherwise have been: the faculty and librarians of Columbia University, who gave access to Clinton's Manuscript letter-books and journals in their care; a great-great grandson of John Pintard, Clinton's friend as boy and man, who placed at the author's disposal Pintard's correspondence, diaries and other papers, also in manuscript; the Rev. Scott King of Little Britain, New York, and the Rev. Elwood Corning of Newburg, New York, who were both of the greatest help in pinpointing the birthplace and tracing locales and details of the early years; the staff of the State Museum at Newburgh, who were lavish with assistance;

Morton K. Pennypacker, now deceased, then a willing, entertaining and knowledgeable guide to his inimitable library at East Hampton; the Manuscript Divisions of the State Library, Albany, and the New York Public Library, as always unstinting with their aid; and the late Justice Phoenix Ingraham, who permitted a photograph to be made of the striking portrait by Jarvis, reproduced in these pages.

The involutions of New York politics in Clinton's day remain unmatched, even in the modern maelstrom of the giant State which owes so much to his efforts. No pre-election tussles of our own time, no rivalries between State and City officials, between the Federal Government and the State, are half as fierce or as devious, or as riddled with slander and self-seeking. Government in his time, and particularly in his native region, was an almost impenetrable maze of double-dealing, in which an honest man found it hard not to lose his way; and this has given rise to so great a mass of commentary and analysis, in published volumes and manuscript collections, that the very numbers of the sources consulted swiftly overran the practicality of any unabridged list. A condensed bibliography therefore appears at the end of this study, with some leads to complementary works used.

In the hope that her book will continue to be of assistance to students and others, the author salutes the readers of the new edition.

DB

New York, 1962

CONTENTS

ILLUSTRATIONS

INTRODUCTION

The United States was born the largest nation in the Western world. But size was not thought to be an asset, politically or philosophically. Montesquieu had laid it down as a law of history that only military despotisms could be large; Republics must be small, or they would go under. Great territorial extent meant fragmentation, and in the eighteenth century the forces making for fragmentation were far stronger than the forces making for unity. How turn size into an asset? How bind together into a single nation such far-flung and disjoined territory as the new United States inherited? "To the patriotic American of 1800, struggling for the continued existence of an embryo nation, with machinery so inadequate", wrote Henry Adams, "the idea of ever bringing the Mississippi River either by land or water into close contact with New England must have seemed wild." Yet, he added, "physical contact alone could make one country of these isolated empires."

To this problem of binding together an immense and disparate nation the leading statesmen of the early Republic bent their minds and their talents: Washington, with his lifelong interest in the Ohio country; Jefferson, indefatigably concerned with acquiring a western empire, holding it, exploring it, opening it up to the American farmer; his friend Albert Gallatin, who was responsible for the first great comprehensive program of internal improvements; John Quincy Adams, who carried on where Gallatin left off, and whose luminous mind saw the possibilities of science and invention as a cement to the Union. To this distinguished group of nation-makers must be added the name of De Witt Clinton of New York. For it was Clinton's vision, tenacity, and courage that were most largely responsible for joining the waters of the Atlantic with those of the Great Lakes, through the Erie Canal. It was, indubitably, the greatest engineering project of its day; what is not so commonly recognized is that it was also one of the greatest nationalizing enterprises of its day. As Clinton's secretary, Charles G. Haines, wrote in 1821. "paramount to all other considerations is the influence to be anticipated from the western canal in giving strength and durability to our national confederacy. We must bring north and south, the east and the west, nearer each other by the attractions of interest."

De Witt Clinton himself occupies a curious and almost an ambiguous place in American history. He was a bundle of contradictions, and his career was full of paradoxes. Democratic by principle--and a strong supporter of General Jackson-he was an aristocrat by inheritance, and by preference. Of unimpeachable integrity--he died poor, after a lifetime of public service--he was one of the creators of the spoils system, and his name is irretrievably linked with that feature of the American political party. Agrarian in his way of life, and deeply interested in scientific farming, he was sensitive to the demands of business, commerce and banking, closely associated with the great merchant families of New York City. A national figure--he served in the United States Senate, and was twice candidate for the Presidency-he is remembered rather as Mayor of New York and Governor of New York State. By conviction committed to states rights, he made far-reaching contributions to nationalism. His positions puzzled even his contemporaries: he has what may well be the unique distinction of being nominated for the Presidency by both a Federalist caucus and a Republican convention in New York, at the same time. He was, moreover, a scholar and scientist, one of the most variously learned public men of his day.

Clinton belonged to that age which thought it right for men to devote their lives to the public service and to learning. Nephew of the famous George Clinton, Governor of New York and leader of the anti-Federalist forces, De Witt found himself at an immature age one of the budding politicians of his state. Ten years later he was a dominant figure in New York Republicanism, busily thwarting the unhappy Governor Jay, and just as busy disputing with the masterly Aaron Burr for control of his own party. Elected to the United States Senate, Clinton withdrew within two years to accept the mayoralty of New York, and for over a decade he gave that city the best administration it was to enjoy until the advent of Fiorello La Guardia. Not content with being Republican mayor of New York and (at the same time) lieutenant-governor of the State, Clinton allowed himself to be the Federalist candidate for the Presidency. Had Pennsylvania conveniently gone the other way, Clinton would have landed in the White House, in time to witness its burning. It is perhaps no wonder that his followers grew not only confused but resentful, and ousted him from both of his jobs in 1815. Nothing daunted, he turned his energies to what was to be the crowning work of his life: the Erie Canal. In 1816 the legislature adopted his scheme for a canal from the Hudson to Lake Erie, and the following year an appreciative electorate placed him in the governor's chair at Albany. He had, then, the opportunity to build the canal as he thought it should be built, and the happiness to preside, as governor, over its formal opening in 1825.

This was Clinton's most significant contribution to his country's welfare, but it represented only one aspect of his affluent character. He was, like so many of the statesmen of the early years of the Republic, a man of wide-spreading interests and talents: historical, literary, cultural, religious and humanitarian. He founded the Public School Society of New York and was one of the pioneers of American public education. He was deeply versed in history; helped organize the New York Historical Society, and himself made important contributions both to the preservation of historical materials and to their interpretation. He was one of the founders, too, of the Academy of Art, and of the Literary and Philosophical Society of New York. And as a humanitarian reformer he anticipated many of the reforms that were to triumph in the next generation.

Curiously enough, this attractive, colorful and significant figure has been persistently neglected by American historians. Mrs. Bobbe's biography, originally published in 1933, was the first full-length study of the man. Nor have the past thirty years added anything of significance to the Clinton literature. It is therefore highly gratifying that this admirable book is once more available to a generation which can profit greatly from its drama and its moral.

Henry Steele Commager

Amherst, Massachusetts

DE WITT CLINTON

1

HERITAGE

THERE WERE Clintons who went to America to serve the British king; and Clintons who went there, in a way, to avoid him. The two branches were related by blood, but hardly in spirit. There had been a Clinton, true, of the second-named group whose loyalty to King Charles I had been complete to the point of self-sacrifice. But those who supported Charles I were rendered exiles by those who overthrew his kingdom, and the banishment endured to the third and fourth generations. A William Clinton had rallied, for his own undoing, to Royal Charles' standard. A Charles Clinton, his grandson, finding himself still barred from his ancestral demesne, finally fled from the British Isles, and chartered a vessel, and sailed in it for America.

Between, the family had wandered. To France first; thence to Spain; and finally to join a number of their fellow-supporters of the former monarch in Scotland. Here William Clinton married a Miss Kennedy, kin to the Earl of Cassillis, and became a pillar of the Presbyterian Church. But circumstances, composed in equal parts of politics and religion, uprooted Clinton somewhat violently once more, and it was in Northern Ireland that James, son of William, was born.

This James grew to manhood in the reign of James II, when Presbyterianism was like to be crushed in Ireland between the whirling millstones of Protestantism on the one hand and the Church of Rome on the other. Spurred doubtless by this and other more prideful considerations, he journeyed into England, to plead for the return of the family estates. But the Royal Courts invoked the Statute of Limitations, and the plea was in vain. Young Clinton lingered long enough to marry an English girl named Elizabeth Smith, the daughter of one of Cromwell's former henchmen, and in due course carried her back with him to Ireland. There he found himself serving a presently conquering William of Orange by bearing arms in support of that monarch at Enniskillen and elsewhere, and was rewarded by a grant of land in County Longford.

And so, in County Longford, in 1690, Charles, son of James, was born. There he grew up, a Presbyterian and therefore an outcast inevitably, whether Protestants triumphed or Catholics arose in Ireland, and through all the changes in the English rule and in the English Established Church. Ownership of land in Ireland in that day did not necessarily denote ease of circumstances. There were seizures and levies by presumable overlords, and it was naturally on those made more or less voiceless by reason of dissent that such oppressions fell the hardest. Likewise when the local heads of the Established Church were computing their tithes, it was somehow on dissenters that the burden frequently fell the most severely.

Moreover, there was the unarguable matter of British trade, with which Irish trade could certainly not be allowed to conflict. William of Orange had brought olive-branches from Holland, and the last-named country forthwith became a market for which England was greedy, and vice versa. Dutch flax ousted Irish, and British woolens did likewise, until what with restrictions on faith and on trade, and levies from both spiritual and temporal heads, an Irish gentleman farmer knew less and less which way to turn.

In increasing numbers these and also humbler yeomen of nonconformist leanings sought to solve their difficulties by turning toward the West. They fled to the American colonies, an obvious haven for such as they. In so great numbers they fled, indeed, that their defection grew in time to be a menace that had both Ireland and England dismayed, while their mass appearance on the other side of the Atlantic was no less a matter for perplexity there.

In the year 1729, when George II was king, Charles Clinton, having arrived at man's estate; having married, moreover, and founded a family of his own, made up his mind to join this exodus. It was a mind trained to encompass such momentous decisions. Charles was a man of culture as well as a farmer.

With four coreligionists, relatives and friends, he therefore sought a ship that could be chartered. No need to worry about loading it with companions for the voyage. Seventy passengers, men, women and children, boarded the frigate that Clinton and his associates hired—the Dublin frigate *George and Anne,* of a burden of ninety tons. Family records recount that Charles leased his County Longford estate to the Earl of Granard for a matter of ninety-nine years. And on the twentieth of May, 1729, he sailed, with his wife and children, his two sisters and their families, and his sizable company of friends.

Their destination was Philadelphia, already the refuge of the greatest number of the Presbyterian Scotch-Irish. And their hopes were high and roseate.

But they did not reach Philadelphia, on that utterly terrifying voyage. Charles Clinton, wealthy enough, with the aid of those who accompanied him, to charter this vessel and its captain, saw in the captain's eye, before the ship was many days out from land, something he did not like. Thoughts of his wife (she had been Elizabeth Denniston), his two small daughters and his son, in the cabin below; of his numerous relatives and friends and their families with them, must have made him tremble.

And tremble he might. All had paid for the passage before the frigate left Dublin. All had seen that provisions for man, woman and child were laid aboard—sufficient and to spare for any normal voyage of a month or so. And all who could had read the ship's papers, binding the ship's company to its passengers for faithful performance.

But this was to be no normal voyage; no faithful performance. The Captain—his name was Rymer; a brute of a man—proved soon to have a vastly different plan, and proceeded to exact the support of his officers and crew by the means best suited to his nature and purpose. Briefly, the first man who defied Captain Rymer on that strange trans-Atlantic voyage he laid out, dead, with a pipe-stave. After that it was plain sailing—for the captain.

As for the passengers, they began to learn a number of horrifying things. In the first place, the curious lapse of time transformed their provisions into something one ought to conserve, as much as it was possible to do so. Then the crew grew singularly and increasingly uncommunicative. The days continued to pass without change in the limitless watery scene around them; the weeks. And then an amazing climax, a crisis, was reached. They came in sight of land.

"Virginia," said the boatswain, promptly. "I know it well. I have sailed that coast on many a voyage."

But Captain Rymer did not acknowledge that the far-off smudge was any Virginia seaport, any land at all. He damned the boatswain for a "lying, skulking dog," and ordered the ship put about. . . .

Then, at last, his purpose became quite plain—plainer as the awful weeks passed. The daily ration dwindled almost to vanishing point. Starved, in a ship that was headed for nowhere in particular, save, perhaps, perdition, two of Charles Clinton's babies among others, infants and adults, sickened, the infants of an unchecked epidemic of the measles; their elders of a malnutrition that was the death-knell of the infants too.

Appeals, threats, supplications failed. The two children, a boy and a girl, died, and were buried at sea, and a tragically large number of their fellow-passengers followed them in the weary days that ensued. Parents and guardians, wives and husbands (such as were left) faced the immediate future. It was simple enough, if appalling. The man in command, with the enforced connivance of his crew, had apparently decided to starve all his passengers to death, and take, not the consequences, which he doubtless knew how to avoid, but the booty. Indeed he could plead patriotism in pursuing such a course. There were those among his passengers who were to believe to their dying day that he had been bribed to punish paying Irish farmers for fleeing Irish terrain, and to discourage others from following in their tracks.

But whatever his purpose, one fact was clear. Men of substance, aboard ship with all their worldly belongings, were much less valuable to an ambitious sea-captain than those same worldly belongings without their owners. . . .

Now it has been observed that Charles Clinton was an educated man. He was, among other things, a practiced surveyor and a scholarly mathematician. In consultation with his brothers in distress, he now offered, with their assistance, to seize the master, to take over the vessel and the crew, and to navigate the ship himself, which he was confident of being able to do. It was an excellent plan, save for one flaw: the attitude of the crew themselves. Fear still ruled those men of the sea, chaining them irrevocably to their chief. And the plan died, for without their acquiescence it came under the head of piracy.

For almost five whole months that voyage endured; but those who managed to endure likewise remained unbeaten at the end of it. Food shrank to a half-biscuit and a half-pint of water per day, per person. But fortunately there was still the money, the magnet for cupidity; and ultimately the money, that once had threatened to be the emigrants' ruination, turned out to be their salvation.

They managed to compound with the master of the ship: so much of the wealth and belongings of each of them for him; so much (a sufficiency) for them.

And thus the first Clinton came, with one remaining child, with a sorrowing wife and a sadly depleted fortune, to America on the 4th of October, 1729.[1]

It was, strangely, in America that the two long divergent branches, already alluded to, of that ancient family were to meet. Their kinship had to do with the earlier Earls of Lincoln. It extended back to a certain cousin and military cohort of William the Conqueror, and through him is romantically linked with the story of ancient Kenilworth Castle. Sir Walter Scott, in the twenty-fifth chapter of "Kenilworth," says:

"On the exterior walls frowned the escutcheon of the Clintons, by whom they were founded in the reign of Henry I."

Yet the same England that William had conquered, that Kenilworth adorned, was ultimately to vanquish this Clinton family tie.

Charles Clinton prospered in America. He had one daughter, Catherine, remaining, and four sons were born to him and his wife in the new country. He dwelt till the spring of the year 1731 in a temporary sort of way near Cape Cod, where the

[1] The diary of Charles Clinton lists the dead, but makes no mention of the reasons for the abnormal length of the voyage. A narrative written by the son of John Young, a fellow-passenger on the journey, is the source of most of the above details; while the family sketch written by Charles A. Clinton, son of the subject of this biography, shows that the foregoing account of the voyage was that which the family recognized. Perhaps secrecy as well as money figured in the bargain with the captain!

black-hearted captain had set them down; but in 1731 he moved into the province of New York, which was kind to the sort of religious dissenter he was. And he settled down at last in the county of Ulster, with the remnant of his company, on a tract of land which the elders among them were able to buy, eight miles from the banks of the upper Hudson, behind Newburgh. A kinsman of one of their number, John Little, had preceded them here, and awaited them in what was still a wilderness. Under a sheltering tree in that wilderness Clinton made his temporary home, while he and his fellows, after several abortive attempts, managed to throw up a group of rude but sturdy stone houses, and formed a settlement worthy to be christened as such. A settlement and also, necessarily, in some respects a fortress. Theirs was an outpost of civilization indeed, an easy prey, unless stockaded, to wild men and wild animals as well. They called it, for all they were voluntary refugees, Little Britain. . . . .

With the years, Charles Clinton, at the head of his family and his community, became an honored figure in upper New York. He was a man of handsome and commanding presence, well-liked by young and old, and respected by all. Bookish, he engendered awe where books were few. Master of the contents of the volumes he had carried with him from the old country, he possessed the key to the friendship of the local pastoral leaders and the old Dutch landed gentry of those parts. For education, with those who had fled, or whose ancestors had fled, for freedom of mind and of spirit, was king.

Also he was possessed of another rare and valuable possession—a wife with a highly cultivated intelligence. Girls were suffered to bother little with books and quills and numbers in those days, but this daughter of the Irish Dennistons had Irish charm and wit, and set some of it down on paper—letters for her grandchildren to cherish; and they did. She had also an ever-increasing establishment in that busy settlement, primitive of aspect but shining in physical and spiritual attainment, that nestled among the hills. This was the theater for her indubitable abilities as housewife, social leader (which in her small rural way she could not have helped being) and parent.

Mr. Clinton farmed his land; he did a little surveying; he dealt out local justice, unofficially at first, but later under the seal of the Province, as Justice of the Peace and eventually as a Judge of the Court of Common Pleas for the Precinct of the Highlands, as his more or less immediate neighborhood was then called. The greater Britons of the Government posts hobnobbed with him and his, and when a George Clinton came out from England to become Governor of the Province of New York in 1743, the two men discovered the diluted consanguinity (George was youngest son of the sixth Earl of Lincoln; Charles was directly descended from a younger son of the second Earl) and also a more tangible fraternity. There is a fable that such friends did Charles Clinton and the new British Governor become, that one of the former's sons—the youngest—was christened George by request, and as a direct tribute. Dates, however, give the lie to this story, and if the boy was christened George for any family reason, it was possibly the same one—pride of lineage, custom, honor—that had probably prompted the royal Governor's own parents. This pride Charles had, and revealed it to the end.

The Governor, however, does seem to have had a partiality for George, and to have expressed it on many occasions. The veil of the future was closed. Not thus early would he have credited the prophecy that this lad, who bore the same name as he, would one day rule in his stead, as the head of a free and sovereign State. Was not his own youngster, Henry, here, and of an age with the youngest of his cousins? Were not the futures, the interests of the American and the English Clinton boys identical, and did they not center round the glory of the King's domains? As Charles' sons grew old enough, they joined the local militia. As the Governor's boy went into his 'teens, he became a fellow-recruit in the selfsame army. How, then, could companions under arms in training be anything but companions on the same side of any actual affray? Young Henry Clinton, in 1750, was a novitiate in the British army; so was Cousin Charles, and so were his boys.

It was through the medium of the royal Governor that Charles Clinton was tendered the office of High Sheriff of the City and County of New York, "or any other commission within his power" under the Crown. Mr. Clinton declined, as he was "in good business" and preferred "the charms of retirement and the cultivation of literature to the cares of public life." (There were Clintons-to-be who would wish, at times, that they had emulated his example.)

The Governor, nothing daunted, turned his favors upon young George, giving the latter a commission as Clerk of the Court of Common Pleas of Ulster County "upon the death of John Crook, then Clerk." As the Governor was upon the eve of retiring to England, and was moreover an extremely unpopular executive, some of his council ventured the opinion that he could not bestow such a commission. He said he would try it, and "if you fail to get the post on the death of Crook," he said to George, aged 14, "I will see that you get a better one."

Nor was he the only royal Governor who would wish to do the older Clinton honor. Sir Charles Hardy made the latter a Lieutenant-Colonel of the second regiment of Ulster County militia in 1756, and two years later he was placed in command of a battalion of one of the Provincial regiments, under Colonel Oliver Delancey. It was in this command, in the days of fighting Frenchmen and Indians, when Britain and her American colonies stood embattled side by side, that Charles Clinton saw active service under the British flag, winning laurels under Bradstreet at the capture of Fort Frontenac. Also his sons, now grown and ready to have families of their own, were soldiers, or army surgeons, alongside him.

Alexander, the eldest surviving son, had been educated at Princeton College under President Burr. He was the poet and musician of the family, and a master in the use of the broadsword. By profession he was a doctor, and a successful one. He married one Maria Kane, but died when still a young man.

Charles, the second son, followed the same profession, distinguished himself as a surgeon in the King's army, and lived to see his nephews grown to manhood.

James, the third son, was born at Little Britain in 1736. "He was," as a modern commentator [1] remarks, "like David, a warrior from his youth." In his youth, indeed, there was fighting to be done, and James, as has been remarked, won his spurs in company with his father as a captain of militia at Fort Frontenac. He, too, was a well-educated youth, having, with Charles and George, received a thorough grounding in mathematics and the classics at the hands of a certain brilliant young redemptioner whom for-

[1] Arthur Pound, in "Native Stock." The Macmillan Company, New York, 1931.

tune had brought to Little Britain. But James' heart had ever yearned after soldiering; and so, although he had pretensions to skill in mathematics, and was a surveyor of actual experience under his father, he did not emulate that father in treating military training and service as a mere sideline, but elected, and was allowed, to make it his career. In Colonial days he served as captain in command of the four companies of provincial troops raised for the defense of the western frontier of Orange and Ulster counties—against the Indians, primarily; and later became a Lieutenant-Colonel in the Ulster County militia.

It was when the French war was five years over, and an English cloud was already threatening by reason of the Stamp Act, that he married Mary, the only daughter of Egbert De Witt, a gentleman whose family had helped make the history of Holland and the history of America too. The first De Witt to journey to America was the captain of a Dutch ship, the *Little Fox,* who, in 1613 (seven years before the Pilgrims landed at Plymouth Rock; thirteen before Minuit purchased Manhattan Island) brought his vessel into Long Island Sound in company with that of Adriaan Block. The earliest of Mary De Witt's direct line was Tjerck Classen De Witt, who came to New Amsterdam from Grootholdt in Zunderlandt in the early 1630's; settled eventually at Wiltwyck, or Esopus, or Kingston, as the place was successively named; and thus was long in America when the Clintons began fighting for King Charles. He was, says a family genealogist, "a man of considerable means.... Affairs seemed to prosper with him.... In 1689 he was one of the magistrates of Ulster County, and had held other offices." He married and became the father of twelve children, the eldest of whom, Andries, duly married one Annetje Jans and in turn was a dozen times a father. Andries' tenth child, Egbert, settled in Napanoch, Warwarsing, Ulster County, and in 1726 married Mary Nottingham, whose mother was Dutch, whose father English. She duly presented Egbert De Witt with a family of ten—nine sons and one daughter; and the last-named was the girl called Mary, who married Colonel James Clinton.

She was born in 1737, and the English strain in her which came to her through her mother mingled with Dutch blood undiluted for centuries.

"The Hollanders," says the Rev. William Walsh, of Newburgh, in his genealogical story of the De Witts, "loved music and art; had organs in their churches and the violin and flute in their homes; loved fun and amusement; enjoyed the *kermiss* and made Sunday a day of innocent enjoyment and rest, as well as of prayer and divine services."

Mary, being a girl, enjoyed but little schooling. Nevertheless she was endowed with qualities which might perhaps be ticketed as British common sense and the lighter Dutch brands of humor and charm. She was married to James Clinton in 1765, and handed the intelligence, the humor and the charm, with a considerable heritage of beauty, down to the four sons and three daughters with whom she and the Colonel were blessed. The Clinton side provided courage and an uncomplicated faith. The family was a happy one.

As for George, the former Governor's young favorite, born at the homestead on July 26th, 1739, he duly forged upwards in the local militia, commissioned at 19 a subaltern in his father's regiment, and playing his part in the French war. After the peace he studied for a while in the office of William Smith, the noted historian and lawyer, but duly obtained and entered into the duties of the office of Clerk of the Court of Common Pleas which his somewhat high-handed English kinsman had so blandly bequeathed to him. While still a youth, he married Cornelia Tappen of Kingston, a lady as Dutch in blood as the De Witts, and as long devoted by blood to the Province of New York. George, a young man of brilliant intellect and infinite personal charm, was admitted to the Bar in 1764, and was a lawyer until he was twenty-seven, serving for a year as Surrogate of Ulster County. In 1766 he was elected by the popular vote a member of the colonial Assembly from his county, and thus was launched on what was to be his life-work. A successful New York legislator from the first, George Clinton, in the sense that from the first he was on the side of the people. The people did not forget that fact when the time for recognition came.

But indeed a fateful moment was already arriving. The British colony that had basked in the warmth of the more paternal attitudes of English Kings and Queens and the broad statesmanship of certain English ministers; that had long enjoyed the complaisance of governing bodies which had often found it profitable to close an eye to infringements and infractions, was already a changed entity when George Clinton first took his seat in the royal colonial legislature. George III had come to the throne of England. George Grenville had succeeded Pitt as Prime Minister. And a certain principle of self-taxation, which had long been a bulwark in defense of Colonial freedom and Colonial trade as well, came into jeopardy and fell under the new administration.

Thus it came about that a strange upheaval, symbolic of wider fissures, took place within the circle of the Clintons. When the royal Governor of that name had gone home with his family in 1753, it had been to carry on his services to the King. Becoming Governor of Newfoundland, he died in that office in 1761, a servant of the Crown to the end. His colonial kinsmen, whose immediate and personal history did not point toward any blind acceptance of a royal check-rein, weighed their loyalties, their past and their future, and deemed it the wiser part to stay faithful to the principle of liberty for the land of their adoption.

Colonel Charles Clinton was ancient by this time. His sons had growing families of their own. When the old man lay on his deathbed in 1773, little De Witt, the third son of James, was more than four years old. His memories of his grandfather, though he was too young as yet to comprehend the sentiment behind the words, would be of an enfeebled patriarch, murmuring to those around him, "Preserve your country's freedom." And by "your country" Charles Clinton did not mean England.

So Charles' sons prepared to play their part on the patriot side of current affairs. George, the youngest, was increasingly prominent in public life; James, his older brother, was growingly significant in military circles. Even Catherine, sole surviving child of the tragic voyage from Ireland, had married a man of military pretensions—a certain James McClaughry.

The old man died, full of honors, and even full of hope, on November nineteenth, 1773. And at this, the end of his vicissitudinous existence of eighty-two years, the heart of Charles Clinton proved to have clung sufficiently to the land and the blood of his forefathers to render a little racial pride irresistible. In his will he requested that a family graveyard be established in Little Britain from the proceeds of his estate; also that on his stone be marked the time of his death, his age, and the Clinton coat-of-arms.

"I hope," said he, "that they will indulge me in this last piece of vanity."

None the less were his roots embedded deep in the new country. He died, it is said, with the word "Freedom" still lingering on his lips; and two years later, his sons put his spoken principles into practice. George was chosen, in April, 1775, one of New York's delegates to the second Continental Congress—the Congress which ultimately drafted and passed the Declaration of Independence. On July 2nd, 1776, George Clinton cast his vote for Independence, and immediately went home to assume a new Congressional appointment as Brigadier-General in George Washington's army. This was not the highest honor that lay in store for him, but it serves to account for the fact that George Clinton's name does not appear as one of the Signers of the Declaration.

James had continued up to this moment the military representative of the family. In 1775 he had been appointed by the Congress Colonel of the Third Regiment of New York Militia; and in this capacity James, son of Charles, great-grandson of Carlist William, marched against the King of England under the banner of a free America—a British America if possible, but a free one, whatever might portend. In 1775 he had led his regiment into Canada with Montgomery's army—the tragic army whose defeat was in a measure due to the loss of the heroic Montgomery himself. In 1776 both Clinton brothers were fighting, both in a high command. In 1777, when the first State Constitution was adopted, George, the younger, heard the voice of the people in unmistakable terms. In the face of other excellent claims, the people voted him not only New York State's first Governor, but Lieutenant-Governor also, and automatically the commanding officer of its forces. James, whose pride in George was always immeasurable, accepted the rôle of Colonel and later Brigadier-General under him.

And so it came about that in the year 1777, a certain final family foregathering took place. Sir Henry Clinton, the son of the former Governor, was back from England in the land of his boyhood days. Then, he had been a unit in New York's militia in company with the young colonials. Now, he came, first to Boston and Bunker Hill; later to New York State, as a commander in Britain's punitive army—ultimately the Commander-in-Chief, succeeding Howe. A confident General—and indeed, he had reason to be....

They met, the three Clintons, at a group of fortresses on the Hudson—the upper Hudson, the key to that which the King could still call his Colonial domains. James was in command of the fort named Clinton; George had taken charge of the defense of Fort Montgomery, having prorogued the State Legislature for the purpose. They had in all a force of five hundred men, of whom but one company was artillery. Sir Henry, with his headquarters in an already conquered New York City, with an army four thousand strong, swooped upon the forts by landing lower down and deploying through the mountains; and with dispatch, though not without an obstinate fight, captured them both; both fortresses, that is, and very nearly both men. He remembered his cousins well, and, like his father, had a partiality for George. George, however, at that moment, was escaping by the skin of his teeth, hardily and at the last moment, as befitted his reputation for unbounded courage. James, suffering a bayonet wound, had jumped into the branches of a tree under a volley from the British that killed the men who attended him. He managed to make good his escape from there, aided like his brother by an intimate knowledge of the region. And all that remained were the forts, the prisoners, the dead, and two lone officers who stood back to back, ready to resist with hands denuded of weapons, or die in the attempt. One was Colonel McClaughry, the widower husband of Catherine Clinton, who had died in 1762; the other was a gentleman named Humphrey. Saved by a Briton who admired their pluck, these two were haled before the General.

He recognized McClaughry, and asked of him,

"Where is my good friend George?"

"Safe," said McClaughry, with an Irish sharpness, "thank God, beyond the reach of your friendship."

So it was. A new generation of Clintons was to come into an entirely new inheritance. The American George's one son and his several young daughters were no longer to be sprigs of an ancient aristocracy, but buds on a Republican tree. James' four small boys, Alexander, Charles, De Witt and George, would follow no magnificence in scarlet and gold, but had already learned a very specialized regard for the still somewhat sketchy uniform of Washington's army. Some local historians hold that De Witt had actually been born to the trappings of war, in the fort named De Witt, at Deerpark, while his mother was snowbound on a visit to her brother Jacob, who commanded there. Others insist that he came into the world amid more peaceful surroundings, at the pleasant homestead which his grandfather Charles had bestowed on James at the latter's marriage. It was situated close to the Hudson, in territory that was then still embraced by the village called Little Britain. It became a part of New Windsor later, and the house still stands, and is pointed out as De Witt Clinton's birthplace.

Be that as it may, he had first seen the light of day on March 2nd, 1769, as the first rumbles of discontent were sounding. Certainly he had spent his babyhood in the balconied frame house by the river that he was always to love so well—a river that so soon now was to echo none the less with fear. For it was amid the very real reverberations of the guns of the opposing forces that De Witt Clinton learned his lessons.

His tutor was the Rev. John Moffat, pastor of one of the more Republican-minded Presbyterian churches close by his home. Time was when the Clintons had sat under pastors intensely loyal to the King; but no more. Under the patriot Moffat's care the boy De Witt remained until he was thirteen years old. At Mr. Moffat's hands he received the beginnings of a sound classical education. And when he passed from elementary studies into the preparatory halls for the higher learning, the guns of war were still noisy, and tides had swollen and receded again, and an American congress still sat in Philadelphia, presiding over a group of thirteen commonwealths whose only true wealth was still courage.

Sir Henry Clinton had beaten his cousins by sheer force of superior numbers in the little affray at Forts Montgomery and Clinton, hastily-erected, and buttressed by an impeding chain in the river; keys, such as they were, to the fastnesses of the upper Hudson. And the upper Hudson, had Sir Henry pursued his advantage as planned, might well have served as a weapon to sever the infant States, keeping them from inter-communication, and stifling their hopes for all time.

He did not pursue it. He did not, as he was expected to do, push on to the aid of his colleague Burgoyne, hard-pressed in the wild land to the North. Ultimately he went home to try to explain why it was he had not done so. In the meanwhile New York was, and remained for weary years, a conquered territory.

De Witt Clinton's father, however, now Brigadier-General, was proving his worth to Washington and the main army in the capacity of second-in-command to General Sullivan in the hazardous but completely successful expedition against the Six Nations of Indians. His letters of this period to his wife portray a soldier intent on his job—the loving husband and father (which he never failed to be) transformed into a ruthless and a merciless fighting man, engaged on a desperately punitive job. James' task was to prove to the Indians that their partisanship of the British cause was mistaken, and he performed it thoroughly.

De Witt Clinton's uncle George, Governor of New York and Commander-in-Chief of the State Militia, had established his headquarters at Mrs. Falls' Tavern above Newburgh, and was fighting too, both for his official domain and for his country.

The scene of the second stage of De Witt Clinton's education was John Addison's academy at Kingston, where the young men, in the spirit of the hour, formed a club and gravely debated such questions of moment as "Whether war on a country is a blessing or a curse," and "Whether is revenge the effect of courage or cowardice." The school was a justly famous institution that had the added distinction of being the sole survivor of the general scholastic devastation caused by the local and general tactics of the army of occupation.

But times were already changing for that army of occupation itself. The long, hard winters and the summers of despair that their adversaries had faced were soon to end. General James Clinton, now kicking his heels in command of the Northern Department at Albany, while the British waited, warily, for Washington, was suddenly summoned to start a march to the southward. It ended at Yorktown, as did a great many other things. It was General Clinton's brigade that had the honor of receiving the surrendered colors of a defeated enemy. . . .

So it came about that when young De Witt Clinton had been a student at the Kingston Academy for almost a year—on the 25th day of November, 1783—his father and his uncle, recently returned, took him on a visit to New York. Bells were ringing that day in New York, and flags would be flying soon. But not, save at each last outpost of the British, the royal Union Jack.

Near the Dove Tavern, four miles from the city, a frail barrier had been erected. And down past this barrier rode General Washington, with a remnant of his army, that day, in token of reclamation, as the British commander and his remaining troops left the spot.

"A tavern a little above," writes John Pintard, who was to be De Witt Clinton's lifelong friend, "had a sign of 7 stars. Early in the morning, a painter added six more—the number contained in the field of 13 stripes, red and white, being the flag of the United States."

The Revolution had proved worth the fighting. The splendid story of redemption, new hope, new glory against odds; the final chapter, in which James Clinton and his men had played such a conspicuous part, was told. Now came the true Independence Day, as far as New York was concerned. Down from the tavern so appropriately named rode the victorious American army, or marched behind the horses, resplendent in new uniform or picturesque in tattered old one, or in rags more nondescript still, but with banners flying. And hard on the heels of the fighting men, along the dirt roads by the farms and the redeemed ruins that were the homesteads of the Americans, came men—a civilian troop of horse, four abreast. At Queen Street, according to plan, the civilians dismounted, and broke up as a guard of honor. But most of them, afoot, joined the men and women and children, in winter attire of drab great-coat or homespun cloak, deep bonnet or hard three-cornered hat, but all bedecked like the troops—thousands, cheering and crying, running—running down to the Fort.

Governor Clinton rode beside General Washington. General James, his brother, rode with Knox and the staff. For seven years this group of men had been comrades in arms, and in the hearts of all was a mingling of joy in triumph, sadness in the moment of parting.

Amid the shouting, excited throng walked General Clinton's boys, the fourteen-year-old De Witt among them. With the rest they had marched and cheered for miles, down the winding Bouerie road to the little, cobble-stoned city of New York; past the battered but still colorful small houses of Dutch burghers and the greyer ruins of the English cottages; between the throngs that packed the rude and war-torn streets. Down around Queen

Street, shortly to be renamed Pearl Sreet, by the water's edge they surged, to the fort at the foot of Manhattan. And once there, they whooped and hooted with the rest of the lads when it was discovered that the British, lately in possession of the fort, but now taking to the boats in the waters of the bay below it, had left the Union Jack still flying in the strong breeze of a wintry day, and moreover had cut the halyard and greased the pole from which it flew.

A patriot mariner with spikes to his shoes settled that; and down went the last of the King's emblems in New York, and up went the stars and stripes, and three mighty cheers with it.

"This was about noon," says Pintard, "and the bay was covered with seven British ships of war and an innumerable number of transports—having on board families of refugees bound to Nova Scotia. It was a rueful day to them, leaving friends and home to wander in an inhospitable clime, where they all arrived safe...."

That night, in Fraunces' Tavern, Governor Clinton was host at a dinner to General Washington and his staff, in the Long Room upstairs. And in that same already historic chamber, two days later, Washington's officers clasped their commanding officer in farewell. And all shed tears, it is said, for the years of comradeship in danger that were over. George Washington went home, imagining that he was to be a country gentleman for the remainder of his days. Governor Clinton retired to the more peaceful of his executive duties, and to the almost superhuman task of local reconstruction, at this the real beginning of his great career of statesmanship.

And Governor Clinton's brother, General James, found himself free at last to demonstrate to his boys and girls that their education, as far as his part in it was concerned, was not to be composed entirely of a lesson in Independence.

2

EDUCATION

1775-1786

IN COMMON with other lads destined to rise to the front ranks in America with the coming of the nineteenth century, De Witt Clinton paid in advance for future greatness. Danger had overshadowed his childhood—danger and a necessarily inculcated sense of duty; for in a new nation that had had no time for self-organization, none was too young to serve in some capacity or other.

Family records say that in 1775, when the news came that his father had been wounded in the siege of Quebec, a six-year-old De Witt demanded that his mother supply him with a gun. At the age of nine he possessed a uniform, and wore it, gravely parading with his brother George. He appears to have been an affectionate child, devoted to his mother, and incessantly anxious for the safety of his father; praying at his nightly devotions that this terrifying war might end. He was fond of flowers and curious rocks and stones, of birds and fishes, even at that tender age; and books were already his joy.

His days for studying such things as botany and natural history in the abstract were, nevertheless, still in the great future. At the moment in question he must perforce have been starting the practical application of the elements and the allies of these sciences. The children were doing the farm work, the men's work, then, while their fathers went out to war. And when those fathers were leaders in the fight, the sternness of the children's duty, the nearness of their danger, was proportionate. The danger which brooded over his youth made De Witt Clinton permanently fearless. The duty impressed on him by word and circumstance robbed him of both the opportunity and the ability to play. His father was a leader. Stationed with his regiment in New Windsor in the ripening days of the war, James Clinton's presence had been a comfort even while his allotted task was a constant reminder to wife and children of what they might reasonably expect. He had helped survey the river valley and the heights, to lay out the forts and, with his brother and their associates in arms, presently to build them. He had seen to the making, and the placing, of the great chain that barred the Hudson River below Popolopen's Kill. Clintons, De Witts and Tappens of all ages were in command of New York regiments then, or serving in the ranks. George Clinton's *ex-officio* command of the New York State militia was in itself no mean task, since the militia generally had formed the habit of simply going home when it happened to feel dissatisfied.

There had been travail. Food was scarce, and certain Tory-minded farmers in the neighborhood had made it scarcer by smuggling it through to the British. Also the British themselves, be it repeated, had been no further away, from 1776 onward, than New York City. After Bunker Hill had come New York's purgatory—the forced abandonment and the subsequent burning of the town; the weary retreat as Harlem Heights was lost, as Fort Washington fell, as White Plains was gallantly defended, but in vain; as General Washington and the main army were slowly pushed across into New Jersey, and out of New Jersey still further, into Pennsylvania.

What of the New York women, the New York children, alone on the farms, then? While George Clinton was fighting back in the losing battle of White Plains; while James was bringing strength, puny enough, to the river banks, their families were huddled together at that too significant spot—the Highlands of New York. Fear rode the Highlands from 1776 onward. Burgoyne came down to below Saratoga before he was stopped by Gates and Schuyler. Westchester, Jersey, fell into British hands, and marauding parties kept the Hudson valley in continuous terror, landing where they chose, pillaging, burning as they chose. And overshadowing it all was the royal plan which those New Yorkers who were in rebellion against royalty could not fail to learn: the King's military advisers had selected as the objective and the meeting-point of the three strategic branches of the royal army—Albany! With Albany and New York in British hands, the conquered Hudson would break in twain not merely the unmanageable colonies, but the hitherto unquenchable hearts that beat along its banks. That, indeed, was why St. Leger had his orders to advance from the region of the Mohawk and the Lakes, aided by the willing warriors of the Six Nations; why Burgoyne was to battle his way down from Canada; why Sir Henry Clinton—

There had been really so little to stop Sir Henry, even after Washington and Putnam fortified West Point in 1778 and placed a second chain there. The Hudson was to be his triumphal path. . . . That none of these British plans bore fruit did not lessen the years-long agony of the women and the children of the Highlands. On the contrary, disaffection and desertions from the cause were added to it, and terror of the Indians, the allies of the British, afforded the crowning touch. De Witt Clinton was eight years old when the forts below West Point fell, and father and uncle came to their homes in uniforms soaked with blood. He was almost ten when his mother journeyed briefly and fearfully up to Albany to join her husband, then preparing to unite forces with Sullivan in the West, where the Indians were turning the Lakes into similarly gory pools. . . .

"Polly" Clinton, as they called her, did not linger long in Albany. The fear of the red men and the fear of the redcoats, too, was, as the family records show, too real and far too close. It was one thing to fight the Indians, with all their peculiar modes of warfare; and quite another to dwell defenseless against them. While Mrs. Clinton was gone, her brother Andries De Witt, who lived not many miles away, wrote to the General:

> . . . We have had a troublesome time last Summer, as you without Doubt have heard; continuelly expected to be attacted by the Savages and their Bloody Associates but have been preserved by Him who governs all. . . .

That fair expanse was no man's land—an easy if not a happy hunting-ground. In unofficial raid and with terrifying audacity the redcoats, eluding scattered battalions, thus struck terror at the hearts of the families on the farms and in the homesteads. In horrifying stealth the redskin came down like a wolf on the fold, often unobstructed because the men of the farms were further afield, with their muskets.

Which is why the letters of Generals George and James Clinton, and the letters to them, speak of their ladies' health, of their ladies' fears and fortitude, of the stealthy journeys the families took, as matters for uncommon congratulation or special sympathy. Two letters from James, written to his wife, the first on the eve of his departure for the West, the second on his arrival there, are worthy of note for the perfect picture they afford of the two sides to the character of De Witt Clinton's father. De Witt happens to have inherited them both. In the first letter, dated June 13th, 1779, James tells his wife that he is sending her and the children gifts from Albany; that he has made an inventory of his belongings, and he sends her that too; that he has made his will....

> ...I have done the best I could for all of you (he writes), and if I did not, I would be ungrateful, for you have done everything in your power to serve me....

And he tells her he wanted her there to consult with over his will, and that he hopes it will please her, as that was all that was in his mind when he drew it. And he sends her and all of his children his love and his prayers.

Three weeks later he writes from the head of Otsego Lake, where he is sitting impatiently through a great drought, having moved his two thousand men with their two hundred odd *bateaux* by land and water thither. And he tells her in some detail how he has caught and hanged two Tories.... His impatience comes from having to wait for another wing of the army, when he is due to join Sullivan at the headwaters of the Susquehanna. Lake Otsego, through which his boats must pass, is getting low by reason of the drought, and by the time the General is ready to move, the small channel through which it feeds the great river is choked and shallow and, it would almost seem, impassable.

Not quite. James Clinton was not a surveyor for nothing. He dammed up that end of Otsego Lake, raising the tide three feet. He ordered his boats into line, and broke the dam, and floated them all successfully down into the river.

> ...We burned all the Indian towns on our way down the river (he wrote calmly to his wife), which were too many to name in this letter as I am in haste, being ordered to march tomorrow morning for the Seneca Country....

But a woman of that day and that hour would see a more lurid picture behind the casual words. In obeying General Washington's order for the destruction of the encampments of the tribes who had wrought such havoc in New York, General Clinton had been both clever and fortunate to escape with (as he called it) his "sculp."

At home meanwhile, the families foregathered. De Witt children were taken to visit their Clinton relations in New Windsor, and the length of their stay depended largely on the proximity or otherwise of men in scarlet coats. Those men had reached Kingston once, and sent it up in flames. It was not the first time that Mary Clinton's family had faced fire and terror there. Her ancestors, in the old Dutch days, had helped build a stockade on the very spot where the same burned village and burned De Witt houses now stood. Her great-aunt had been carried off thence, in violence, a prisoner, by the Indians. Tappens, too, had built Esopus, and now lost their homes in the holocaust. Tappens and De Witts were to help it rise again, and to serve long in its future history. And a Clinton, as has been observed, was to add his small meed to the town's fame by preparing for college there.

In 1777, however, British torches had ravaged every house in the village, including Mr. Addison's Academy building. It was a beacon plain enough to set New Windsor among many other villages, on both sides of the river, packing and waiting with bated breath for news of the coming of those unappeasable torches.

Thus these people had longed for peace in a completely literal sense. As more and more men had been drawn off for military service, so the fear had grown. Washington and the main army came to New Windsor for most of 1781, but conjecture dwelt with them there, and fear took their place once more when they departed. When Washington came back, his glorious march to Yorktown, and his history-making there, were done. His final headquarters were in Newburgh, New Windsor's neighbor, where the peace declaration was signed.

It will be seen that the life of a small boy in New Windsor in the 1770's was a kaleidoscope whose colors were sometimes somber, sometimes blinding, always, it must have been, bewildering. The end of the war brought De Witt Clinton's father back to the bosom of his family. It sent his uncle George to New York City—gratefully it must have been, for hitherto he had pursued his problematical duties as Governor at Poughkeepsie, at Kingston, at Albany—wherever a besieged Legislature could contrive to find a meeting place or muster a quorum; attending to his military duties assiduously meanwhile, and snatching up his family where he could. The McClaughry uncle was out of the fight, a prisoner since the siege of Fort Montgomery. De Witt uncles were still at their various posts.

And of Mary Clinton's seven children, only six had stayed at her side. The eldest son, Alexander, had gone into the Continental Army as an ensign at the age of fifteen, and rose to a lieutenantship. His father, in a letter on the occasion, expressed a brief regret that the lad could not finish his schooling. His mother, doubtless, wondered whether the war would last long enough to take the three others boys too. But neither complained. The General was not alone of his household in quality of courage. His wife had kept hers too, and her beauty, and even her sense of humor, as her few letters of the period show. They show also a background of matter-of-fact awareness that the home was the woman's fortress, and in time of siege a place to be protected by her as such. That her particular fortress was left unharmed throughout the occupation of New York by the British does not mean that her soul escaped equally scatheless. The women who, while their babies slept, had listened for the Indians of nights could not soon forget it. This one, with husband and brothers in the field—in the forefront of the field—had known life at its most poignant.

But all things end. When De Witt, aged thirteen, went to the restored Academy in a phoenix-like Kingston, the actual fighting was already over. When his father decided to send him to Princeton, the peace was one year old.

Picture, then, a tall, handsome boy of fifteen, dressed in a lively-hued, tall-collared, wide-faced coat and neat small-clothes of fine homespun, the length of his stylish waistcoat accentuating his already striking stature, the snowy ruffles at throat and wrist proclaiming him a careful mother's son; three corners to the hat upon his curling brown hair, which would be bound at his neck in the fashion of the day; shining buckles to the shoes at the extremities of a pair of shapely stockinged legs; and you have

De Witt Clinton on his way to college under the chaperonage of his father, on a May day in 1784. A young New Yorker in the broadest and oldest sense of the term, enjoying the fun of a flying visit to the reawakening town that nestled in one small corner of Manhattan Island.

For a flying visit it was intended that it should be. New York had not yet recovered herself to the extent of restoring that seat of the higher learning, King's College, which the King's soldiers had treated with such scant respect that none of its halls, to say nothing of its students or its professors, remained in condition for the purposes of instruction. It had, as a matter of fact, been in a bad way for years before the Revolution. There were not very many young men to be put out of an education when King's College closed its doors in 1776, though what was lacking in numbers was made up in quality. Robert R. Livingston, Gouverneur Morris, John Jay are names that adorn the rosters of King's College as well as those of American history. Alexander Hamilton was among those, matriculating in 1774, who left the fields of learning for those of war before the completion of their college courses. The committee of safety had closed the doors of the College after them, and only outside the building did King's College operate spasmodically for a couple of years, till it ceased, as King's College, its brief existence. The equipment and the library books were carried to the City Hall when the British invasion threatened. Thence the books found their way, in the subsequent stress of reconstruction, to an unused room in St. Paul's Chapel, where they were to remain undiscovered for some thirty years; and the College building became a patriot hospital; and later on, a British....

But now, with New York once again in his countrymen's possession, De Witt Clinton was going to Princeton, because such members of his family as had received a college education had sought and found it there. The organization and the more liberal phase of the religious policy of the governors of King's College had come a little too late for that generation. A good Presbyterian hesitated then to send his son to that institution. The College had owed its foundation and its buildings both to the English Episcopal Church, and the Dutch and Presbyterian churches had only edged their way in after insistence. Affiliation with its prescribed form of worship remained an essential qualification for its president and faculty. And good dissenters meanwhile mostly went elsewhere, Nassau Hall being the logical educational haven for a Presbyterian.

Now, King's College was no more; but the sons of dissenters were mostly still able, as it happened, to go where their fathers had gone before them. Hence De Witt Clinton, destined for Princeton.

Meanwhile, however, the city of New York was enthralling. Last year, when Washington rode through, he had seen burned houses, ravaged churches, devastated roads,—a little city rising at last above despair, but rising only in spirit. Now, New York was beginning to emerge physically as well. There was building going on everywhere; there was road-mending and road-making; business was reviving under a revived Chamber of Commerce; and thrift was going hand in hand with shrewd expenditure. James Duane, whom George Clinton, by popular request, had recently appointed Mayor, was a busy man, but not too busy to entertain a distinguished visitor from up-State. Richard Varick, Recorder, aged thirty, renewed with pleasure a military friendship in the midst of strange civil duties. And Roosevelts, Phenixes, l'Hommedieus, Rutgerses, Van Cortlandts were only a few of the myriad friends of the General in the reorganized public life of New York. While De Witt roamed with young cronies from the Fort at the southern extremity of the city to the Common at its northernmost limits, tramping the cobblestones in the few paved streets, traversing the dirt and dodging the central Dutch gutters of others, his father was welcomed into the convivial circles that met at the few surviving hostelries where gentlemen foregathered, and into the more gracious atmosphere of the restored parlors of Manhattan, over whose practices Aunt Cornelia Clinton, as the Governor's lady, was beginning to hold sway. The State Legislature was in session; and where the Legislature sat, already there was social flutter a-plenty. A little too much, perhaps, for the soldier James.

James emerges as one of the less popular members of a large and well-known family, in spite of the breadth of his acquaintance. Always a soldier first and foremost, he had really enjoyed no great time for cultivating the social arts of which his brother George now revealed himself completely and gracefully the master. It is perhaps matter for regret that De Witt, who later emulated George in so many of the shapings of his life, was always to resemble his own father in this, one of the less attractive and desirable of James Clinton's characteristics. De Witt, too, was to have many friends, and was to enjoy the devoted affection of a few of them. But on his own part he was never to master the art of popularity as practiced so skillfully in the New York of his day.

New York, however, was proud of the General. Its people knew his history as they knew their own. And as to what little they did not know, he brought them up to date. He told them, for instance, that he was taking his boy to the college in New Jersey.... And that was a piece of information that stuck in New York's throat, that grated on State pride. Was one of the State's own heroes to be permitted to send his son, the nephew of New York's Governor, afield for an education, for want of the facilities for learning at home? Could not something perhaps be done about that?

It seemed, with a little investigation, that something could. The question of education had greatly exercised the Legislature since the beginning of its current session; and one of the most recent pieces of legislation in which it had indulged had been the passing, on May 1st of that year, of "an act for granting certain privileges to the College heretofore called King's College, for altering the name and charter thereof and erecting an University within this State." A Board, entitled "the Regents of the University of the State of New York," was created, with the Governor, the Lieutenant-Governor, the Speaker of the Assembly, the Mayors of Albany and New York, the Attorney-General and the Secretary of State as *ex-officio* members, and twenty-four citizens and representatives of the various religious denominations in the State completing the personnel. Their mission was to supervise a State-wide University, to be composed of different and strategically-placed college units, all under the Regents' direct jurisdiction, with "all the rights, privileges and immunities heretofore vested in the Corporation of King's College," but minus restrictions or distinctions as to religious affiliations or procedure.

The Regents had met on the 5th of May at John Simmons' tavern in Wall Street, and elected Governor Clinton as Chancellor, Lieutenant-Governor Pierre Van Cortlandt (long since unofficially chosen to fill the second of the offices to which the Governor had been so generously elected) as Vice-Chancellor; Brockholst Livingston as Treasurer; and Robert Harpur as Secretary. John Peter Tetard, a French clerical veteran of the American Revolution, was made Professor of his native language, and committees were appointed to continue the organization of a faculty and the raising of funds, etc. James Clinton's name appears in the list of this first Board of Regents, but it would appear that the completion of De Witt's education seemed too urgent for his father to wait upon results from that quarter. There were too many public questions that were more immediately pressing. Mayor Duane, for instance, as one of the committee appointed to do the work of assembling a college faculty, was finding the exigencies of his and his colleagues' present multifarious duties in connection with other aspects of reconstruction such as to cause the committee's duties to be temporarily shelved. Likewise, funds were urgently needed, but were more vital to other causes.

The arrival of the Governor's nephew, however, galvanized the townsfolk into action. The Mayor and his committee were besought to form a class, a faculty and a curriculum forthwith. Duane in turn sought out an Irish divine named William Cochrane, a master of the classics and a graduate of Trinity College, Dublin, who had already established a modest grammar school. This gentleman he begged to take young De Witt Clinton and such others as might apply into his tutorial charge as the nucleus of a State-controlled institute of learning, until the official appointments for a faculty could be made; and it was in this manner that the former King's College came into existence, on the 15th of May, 1784, under the new and appropriate name, Columbia. The Chancellor, the Vice-Chancellor, two of the Regents, and Professors Tetard and Cochrane duly held the first entrance examination on the 17th, and De Witt Clinton, aged fifteen, came before them, the first college entrant, and matriculated with ease.

The class of 1786—for other youths, among them two young members of the Livingston family and a boy named Abraham Hun, who was to be the chief intimate of Clinton's college days, were enrolled in the weeks that followed—went into session in a temporary room in the old City Hall in Wall Street, with the Common Council conducting the city's business in another part of the building. This last was, incidentally, important business, for it included not only the restoration of the city, but the increasing of its citizenry. Two hundred immigrants, Irish, French and German, had been naturalized in the city in the preceding year, among them a young man named John Jacob Astor, who was to leave his mark on the city and to bestow his friendship on De Witt Clinton. From other sections and other States had come even greater numbers. And those who desired to live and to vote in the city and the State of New York continued to multiply.

Nor was the preliminary business in connection with Columbia College itself yet completed. The act constituting the Regents did not work, and was amended in November, 1784, to extend their number and to take in certain provisions found to be necessary since its passing. Also the mission of one Colonel Matthew Clarkson, who had gone to France and Holland to solicit contributions, and to purchase "philosophical apparatus," had not proved productive. The Regents were therefore kept busy raising temporary funds by Legislative and private grants, and of necessity the appointment of additional professors languished till the fall, when Clinton and the half-dozen or so of his classmates began officially to take Rhetoric from the Rev. Benjamin Moore, Geography from the Rev. John D. Gross, Natural Philosophy and Astronomy from Dr. Samuel Bard, and Chemistry from the blind Dr. Henry Moyes, together with natural history. As yet the College boasted no President, for want of sufficient money to compensate him. One important addition to the staff was made in the following spring, however. The subject of mathematics still lacking a professor, Mayor Duane found a young Scotsman, a distinguished graduate of the University of Aberdeen, who happened to be returning from an abortive educational mission to Virginia and to be regretfully contemplating the necessity for going home. His name was John Kemp, and he duly accepted Duane's offer of the professorship of mathematics, and thus entered upon a connection with Columbia that was to endure for twenty-eight years. These were De Witt Clinton's teachers. Kemp, who had absorbed some then novel views on the practicability and desirability of a national debt, and the workings thereof, handed them down to this apt pupil to store away till the day when he could adapt them to State requirements for the purposes of a most important State venture. Kemp taught him "natural philosophy" too, including for purposes of practical illustration the principles and characteristics of inland navigation....

Of Dr. Cochrane's opinion of Clinton as a student, we have an expression in his own words:[1]

> ...He did everything well; upon the whole, he seemed likely to me to prove, as he did prove, a highly useful and practical man; what the Romans called *civilis*...a useful citizen, and qualified to counsel and direct his fellow-citizens to honour and happiness....

Some one, years later (it may have been James Renwick, for he calls attention to it in his life of Clinton), told Dr. Cochrane that Mr. Clinton's political opponents, sneering at his looks and his dignity and his magnificent bearing, called him "Magnus Apollo."

"...If he have not degenerated from what I knew him as a boy," said Cochrane, "he is well entitled to the appellation as a title of honour."

In 1785, however, he was a rather gravely happy boy. He lodged with one Mr. Gano, and spent his off hours, considerably supervised by the indefatigable Professor Kemp, in companionable rides and walks and talks with Hun and with young Francis Sylvester, another classmate, who was later to adorn the Church. And they aped their masters' attitudes and decried their eccentricities, as schoolboys have from time immemorial. De Witt, indeed, once acted directly for himself and his young associates in penning a protest against the aforementioned extracurricular supervision by the master Kemp, and presenting it to the Regents. The side of Professor Kemp was sustained, but De Witt seems to have lost no prestige and suffered no hurt by thus taking the initiative in behalf of the aggrieved.

His college life was pleasant. The benevolent Dr. Gross, who was revolutionary enough to combine world political history with his doses of geography, was beloved by all the boys, and from letters that passed between Clinton and Sylvester and Hun, Kemp's super-vigilance was the only thing that bothered them. Further, there was companionship outside for young Clinton. His brother Alexander had come to New York to act as the Governor's secretary, and his brother Charles was also in the city, preparing to take up seriously the business of a surveyor. There was thus no great opportunity to indulge in nostalgic or even, it

[1] From a letter addressed to Dr. Hosack after Clinton's death, and included in Hosack's Memoir.

seems, the more dutiful thoughts. His mother wrote complaining that Alexander was punctual with his letters home, and Charles, but not De Witt.

> ...I beg that in future you will not miss one opportunity of informing me of your welfare and other matters, which, however trifling they may be, you may be sure cannot fail being agreeable to me (she wrote on the 22nd of February, 1785). Your father and myself would have been down in the slay, but we feared the snow's failing which would undoubtedly have been the case. Inform me in your next what progress you make in your studies, whether your present situation is agreeable, and what manner yourself and your brothers spend your leasure hours. Your father, brother and sisters are all well and desires to be remmembered to you. Katy desires me to send you a kiss. My compliments to Mr. and Mrs. Gano. I am, dear De Witt,
>
> Your most affectionate mother,
>
> MARY CLINTON.
>
> P.S. Your sister Polly is at N. Windsor, at Mr. Furman's, larning to sing....

He had news enough to tell her of his College. The old and handsome buildings that had formerly housed King's College, close by the Broad Way, as the name was still written, and facing on the river to the southwest of the Common, were placed under repair. There was a great deal to be done, and far too little money, still, to do it with. A certain Major Edward Clarke left £1,000 in 1785 for books for the college library, but other contributions seem to have been conspicuous by their absence. The fact remained that the wounded, the sick and the dying, first of the patriots and later of the British, had been sheltered here, and the bare needs of a military hospital of the eighteenth century had ripped out the softer and, by comparison, more luxurious college furnishings and decorations. If Columbia was to regain its natural home, that home must be rehabilitated somehow. The reconstruction that began in consequence was a symbol of the city and the hour. Down in the cobbled streets around, the burghers and the merchants and the artisans had flocked back to what was left of their houses. That is, if they had rallied to the patriot side of the fray they were suffered to come back in numbers. And eventually a great many of those to whom the epithet "Loyalist" had seemed worth enduring were, finding exile from their lifelong haunts both expensive and unendurable, to be allowed to return.

Many of them, who had gone away men of wealth, drifted back in need, to find their homes and belongings forfeited. But New York, which had banished the Tories, received them again with sufficient warmth, and the triumphant Sons of Liberty insisted only that the newcomers be voiceless in public affairs. So it was—for a time. . . .

As far as De Witt Clinton was concerned, the desirability of New York City as a place in which to be completing one's education surely did not wane. The population was continually shifting, with great influxes of strangers settling in, and big contingents of residents moving on to pastures new. The remains of ruined buildings still stood in many parts of the town; cows and orchards and potters' fields still distinguished the landscape beyond the Common where the almshouse and the prison stood. The population of the city was twenty-four thousand. The lawyers—whose numbers seem to have been disproportionately large—were busy settling land fights, or failing to settle them. The royal newspapers were dropping the King's name from their columns in the name of good business. There was one bank—the Bank of New York, established in 1784; but the first insurance company, the Mutual Fire Assurance Co., was not to make its appearance until 1787. There was one theater—the old, primitive playhouse on John Street, reopened, in the face of considerable moral protest on the part of those depressed by the rigors of reconstruction and oppressed by the qualms of heredity, in 1785. And there was the whole commercial, social, political, religious and scientific world to conquer. John Jay had come home from his peace-making in 1784, and that was a field-day for New York. Then in December the Continental Congress had moved in from New Jersey, and Wall Street and the City Hall there had become the central point of the new Capital of the United States. New York City buzzed with public affairs.

"While I am in this place I hear nothing but politics," wrote another lad, a youth of eighteen, who in 1785 was briefly the house guest of the President of the Congress, Richard Henry Lee, and the dinner guest of Governor George Clinton. The boy's name was John Quincy Adams, and he was on his way home from France to take up his studies at Harvard. His picture of New York at the moment is of a capital tremendously exercised by the British delay in complying with the terms of the peace which he had lately seen his father help to make in Paris. The Canadian fur trade was jealous of the northern posts that had to be relinquished. The tariff barriers by which the various States were endeavoring to protect their new-born trade were alarming nobody so much as the natives of those States themselves. The United States was poor in terms of cash; the Colonies had always relied on England, on Europe, for credit. American merchants, and even more American legislators, needed support, confidence from without and from within. The Articles of Confederation of 1777 had bound together a league of independent sovereignties, very loosely, without power save from their several home governments. And a variable and uncertain currency completed the picture of fading hopes of a strong and lasting Union. Yet Union meant life to all. The only differences then beginning to show themselves between embryo American statesmen were differences in interpretation. Increasingly this new world, this independence, was urging upon them all the need for a united front. But some men—Hamilton, Jay, Livingston and a small group, as far as New York was concerned—translated Union into the doctrine of Federalism. Others—and notably George Clinton, New York's Governor—were girding up their loins to fight for that which was theirs, hard won, in the sense of a patriotism bounded by the limits of their individual States as members of a related group, and not of any consciousness of one nationhood....

Thus affairs of the utmost moment closely touched the life of De Witt Clinton in New York City. It is therefore perhaps the more creditable to him that his college career was in the nature of a triumphal progress. The first Commencement exercises at Columbia were held in April, 1786. The first graduate of Columbia College was a seventeen-year-old De Witt Clinton.

> On Tuesday last (11th) (says the *New York Journal and Weekly Register* for April 13th of that year) was held the first Commencement of Columbia College, and the public, with equal surprise and pleasure, received the first fruits of reviving learning, after a lamented interval of many years.
>
> The Honorable the Continental Congress, and both Houses of the Legislature, suspended the public business, to support the important interests of Education by their countenance, and grace the ceremony by their august presence. The procession moved from College Hall about an half an hour after eleven in the forenoon....

> When they arrived at St. Paul's Church, the place appointed for their graduation, the Reverend Mr. Provoost introduced the solemnity of the day by performing Divine Service.
>
> Mr. Cochran, Professor of the Greek and Latin Languages, was appointed to call up the speakers in their proper order.
>
> Mr. De Witt Clinton, the first candidate who spoke, addressed the audience in an elegant Latin oration, *De utilitate et necessitate studiorum artium liberalium,* which he finished with a polite and well-adapted salutation, in the same language, to the Members of Congress and of the Legislature; to the Regents and Professors, and to the audience at large....

He emerged as a Bachelor of Arts, with a temporary certificate, bearing the seal of the Corporation, promising him his official diploma "as soon as a President shall be appointed for Columbia College."

There now arose the question of his future. His uncle the Governor, who had lately been occupied upstate in helping to make peace with the Six Nations, was extremely interested in that future. He had a small son of his own named George Washington Clinton, but for the moment his grown nephews seem to have loomed larger in his view of events. There were farmers and soldiers, statesmen and lawyers in the family, and some, indeed, who had been a blending of all four. The time was to come when De Witt himself would be numbered among these more versatile of his kin, but for the present he imagined that his was the choice of pursuing a single bent.

He had joined, at College, a literary and debating circle known as the Uranian Society, as a member of which he had been outstanding, in spite of his youth. In rapid exchange of views, in reasoning power, in summation and oratory and composition, early records say, he shone. It was, of course, the legal profession which lured him, and his father, his uncle and most of his friends encouraged him in the choice.

They began (though they did not put it that way to De Witt) to look for a tutor worthy of such material.

3

NOVITIATE

1786 - 1789

THE CITY was rich enough, indeed, in lawyers. Alexander Hamilton had entered into practice in 1784, with his office and his elegant home at No. 58 Wall Street, and had speedily added courtroom luster to his military fame. Aaron Burr, having won his brilliant and irresistible way to admission, was established at 10 Little Queen Street, "rarely," as Mrs. Lamb remarks, "losing a case." Melancthon Smith and Egbert Benson were leading legal luminaries. Samuel Jones was solidly earning the title "Father of the New York Bar," that was later to be bestowed on him by professional acclaim. Brockholst and Edward Livingston, Morgan Lewis, John Cozine, Robert Troup, Josiah Ogden Hoffman, John Lawrence, John Rutherford, John McKesson, Jacob Morton, Robert Benson, John Watts, William Wickham and Daniel Crommelin Verplanck composed the younger fry, all busy, all well-known.

De Witt Clinton thus had experience and brilliance to choose from. And choose he must. Not for a number of years were the colleges of the United States to include legal courses in their curricula. A young man who wished to become a member of the Bar must still seek a reputable member of the Bar to coach him and ultimately to present him. Thus there were law-clerks whose potentialities were not to be confined within the limits of their principals' attainments. Had the Clintons decided to place De Witt in the care of Egbert Benson, for instance, they would have been affording him the scholastic company of a youth named James Kent, who was one day to rise to the head of the profession in the State. The choice was not a likely one, however. Benson must already have stood more or less committed to the views he was for some years to share with Jay and Hamilton and Livingston. At any rate, De Witt went into the office of Samuel Jones—which was excellent for Mr. Jones as well as for De Witt Clinton.

It was an office that had, as a matter of fact, remained open through the Revolutionary War. The distinguished lawyer, from acting as a member of the Committee of One Hundred and lending his voice to the early patriotic protests, had later taken the line of least resistance and elected to remain quietly on in the occupied city of New York. That his sympathies meanwhile had not been "violently loyalist," as some historians assert, however, seems to be proved by the fact that he was elected to the State Assembly in 1786, and at that date took up again his political career in the interests of the new country, as well as continuing to be much sought out for his legal advice. He himself had studied law in the office of William Smith, the sometime preceptor of De Witt Clinton's uncle George—which fact may possibly have contributed to the present choice.

Samuel Jones carried on his practice, and gave his lessons, in his house at No. 34 Broadway—that quiet main street along whose pleasantness a number of gentlemen were reëstablishing their mansions. A Broad Way then, but not a very long way. Its southernmost limit, the somewhat dilapidated Bowling Green, was also being fringed with fine residences, though the most fashionable quarter lay along Wall and Cherry Streets. Its northern end came at the Common or Park, where the Bridewell and the charity buildings remained. From Mr. Jones the Broadwayite, De Witt derived an extremely sound knowledge of the laws governing real estate—important particularly at that moment. Also a close and worthy acquaintance with the English common law, with Blackstone and the weightier authorities. The first of these was to stand him in immediate good stead. The second was to equip him for that special service to American jurisprudence which he was destined to perform. He lodged at the Governor's house in Pearl Street, where his brother Alexander, a clever and popular young man, a member of the Society of the Cincinnati by virtue of service in the Revolution at such an amazingly tender age, was still occupied as the Governor's private secretary. Here it was that De Witt heard increasing talk of the sovereign State of New

York, and of the vital necessity of keeping New York a sovereign State. . . . Not for George Clinton the word of his colleague and friend John Jay, who cherished as "one of the first wishes of my heart, to see the people of America become one nation in every respect." Not for Clinton the highly centralized vision of the youthful Alexander Hamilton, whose ideas for a Federal Constitution were in process of being formulated and presented. Governor Clinton, as ardent a patriot, certainly, as ever drew breath, was indeed no Federalist. New York had suffered very sorely in the war, by reason of seven years of British military occupation and other woes. New York was now beginning to come back in no debatable fashion, and the Governor was passionately opposed to New York's becoming fettered by a constitutional and a centralized governmental association with twelve other states and their problematical fortunes. He had voted warmly to give the Congress war powers over the United States. But he did not subscribe to the growing sentiment that the Union would best be preserved by consolidating and enlarging those powers and extending them in peace-time.

So it was that De Witt imbibed anti-Federalism together with the social graces, in the intervals of studying law. His father, who had lately been serving with his nephew-by-marriage, Simeon De Witt, and with General Philip Schuyler, on a commission to fix the boundary between New York and Pennsylvania, was constantly urging him by letter to observe and to absorb, and also to report. He need not, it seems, have urged. Life was full for young De Witt Clinton, and life did not pass him by.

Life was fair, for the most part; but the first deep shadow came in the spring of 1787. His brother Alexander was drowned while crossing in a ferry-boat from Paulus Hook [1] to New York City.

> I had the information (wrote James to De Witt on the 20th of June, 1787) of the remains of poor Alexander being found, I think the second day after it happened. I am glad he was decently buried, which is all can be done for him in this world, except you get a head and foot stone for him with something cut on it as you and your uncle thinks fit. This day he would have been 22 years old if he had lived.
>
> In regard to your last letter concerning your practicing in the county courts, it would be agreeable to me if it would answer

[1] Now Jersey City.

> in every respect. I know it would be an advantage to George, but as you are young, if you have to stay the three years with Mr. Jones it will be no loss to you if you behave with prudence and œconomy, and adhere to the principles of virtue, which I hope will be the case. I will endeavor to support you with credit while in town, if it be in my power. Do keep an account of all your experiences, and be careful about contracting any debts unless absolutely necessary....

Nor was his father the only one who offered him good advice. His uncle Charles, the doctor, wrote to him from Walkill in November of 1787,

> ...You know there is Improvement to be obtained from Men as well as Books; and blending them properly, the one will serve as an agreeable Relaxation to the other; when I say Men, I do not exclude Women, if they are your choice also, but I leave that matter solely to yourself, as you appear to be circumspect in your Conduct about them....

De Witt's study of Man, however, does seem to have been confined to the masculine for the time being. With the death of his brother, he became, to an extent, his uncle's confidant, and his uncle's views on current affairs he adopted whole-heartedly as his own. So, for the moment, did his tutor, Samuel Jones.

It may here be pertinent to point out that New York State, as well as George Clinton, its Governor, had long since acquired a history of anti-Federalism. Since 1783 it had been fighting jealously against the collection of a revenue by Congress on the increasing wealth of commerce that flowed in at the port of New York. Congress had fought as avidly for what it considered its due, but Governor Clinton, in the most dignified way, had refused to be compliant. In the winter of 1786, Congress acted on the recommendation of a commercial convention of the States, then lately gathered at Annapolis, and requested that delegates from all sections of the Union meet at Philadelphia in the following May, to consider changes in the Articles of Confederation. It did so in the face of a growingly obvious impotence and an increasing need for economic and political discussion of its future powers.

In April, 1787, the Federal-minded in New York managed to send Alexander Hamilton to the State Assembly as a member from New York City. Around him the nationalists in the Assembly promptly rallied. Around his father-in-law, General Philip

Schuyler, then a State Senator, the Senate pros were likewise gathered. The Governor's chief henchman, on the other hand, was none other than Samuel Jones, and the fight, as far as New York was concerned, in the beginning was largely put into somewhat fiery words by these two opposed pairs.

Hamilton, however, achieved a coup that year by a successful effort to have the political disabilities that had been placed on those whose sentiments had favored the Crown in the late war removed by legislative enactment. This ultimately led to an upheaval in the southern district, including particularly New York City, which since the Revolution had been dominated by the former local Sons of Liberty, a group distinctly of the people and also distinctly for George Clinton. Hamilton's successful move in behalf of the Tories meant a Hamiltonian sweep in New York City. By the State Constitution, only freeholders could vote, and there proved to be so many former Tories who still owned or had been suffered to retrieve at least a portion of their former lands, and so many Liberty Boys who owned no land at all, that, naturally combining with the Federalists, the reinstated Tories insured control of the district to Mr. Hamilton. And control of the district was, even thus early, spelling control of a great many things outside.

In the result, New York State finally voted to send delegates to the general convention, with the proviso, inserted by the great strength of the antis, that the delegation was merely empowered to aid in the amendment of the existing Articles of Confederation —nothing more. The three who composed the New York delegation were Robert Yates, John Lansing, Jr. (both, at the moment, Clintonians to the last ditch)—and Alexander Hamilton.

It is familiar history that that convention, meeting in Philadelphia, speedily progressed so far toward abandoning the Articles of Confederation for a new Federal Constitution that Yates and Lansing, of the New York delegation, empowered to amend but by no means to abandon, promptly withdrew from the scene. Hamilton remained, on his own responsibility, and played his great part in the creation of the new Constitution. In convention it was argued and bitterly fought over and finally approved. The convention made its recommendation to the States, and Alexander Hamilton came home to fight the battle all over again in New York.

Meanwhile De Witt Clinton, aged eighteen years, had actually put his own views on record. In November and December of 1787 (the two months immediately following the final report of the convention) the *New York Journal and Weekly Register* published a series of letters under the signature "A Countryman." These attacked the "Federalist" letters of Hamilton, Jay and Madison, then current in the *New York Advertiser* and other strongly Federalist papers. They attacked the veteran Benjamin Franklin for his speeches in convention. And they artfully marveled that men who were willing to throw overboard the good old Articles of Confederation should be given the title "Federalists," while an "Anti-Federalist" was one who had faith in those articles and wished to preserve them and strengthen them.... The letters damned "aristocracy," and boldly presented the cause as that of the rights of the common many as against the power of the loftier few. They adverted to that freedom for which Americans had so recently fought and died. Was that freedom, asked "A Countryman," in effect, to have been wrested from the clutch of one autocracy, only to be sacrificed blindly to another?

The letters were credited to older heads than De Witt Clinton's, but they are well identified as his, and on December 22, 1787, we have the young George, his brother, writing to him: "Your Countryman's letters... I think better adapted to the understanding of the common people than any piece in the newspapers...." No mean praise, this. A survey of the newspapers of the period reveals little else but "pieces" for and against the Constitution.

In the spring of 1788, the various state conventions assembled to debate the question of a general government versus a continued alliance of autonomous state sovereignties—in other words the adoption or non-adoption of the Federal Constitution. And when New York's convention—somewhat reluctantly, such was the local popularity of the Governor's point of view—gathered at Poughkeepsie, De Witt Clinton found himself already grown politician enough to be unable to remain behind while his uncle, and also his father (now a duly-elected member of the New York State Assembly, and a chosen delegate to this meeting), set forth to take part in the affray. He went along. He sat enthralled in the convention chamber through all those fierce and splendid debates.

Contention was rife. In the Federalist press of the State, George Clinton was now represented as lustful for power and jealous for his monopoly of local patronage, etc. Up to that time, it is true, the State had been his, and while the word "patronage" had no such meaning as it was later to assume, the power was his too. Nevertheless there is no shadow of doubt that it was his State, and not his power, that he was fighting for at the moment —his State which now emerged clearly divided over this question of the Constitution. The north and the central counties were almost solidly against it. The southern, including the city of New York, were as solidly in its favor. The last-named city sent Jay, Hamilton, R. R. Livingston, Richard Harrison, John Sloss Hobart, Nicholas Low, Isaac Roosevelt, James Duane and Robert Morris as its delegates to the Convention. Ulster County sent the Governor and his brother James at the head of its group. Dutchess sent Melancthon Smith, John De Witt, Jacobus Swartwout and Gilbert Livingston among others. The division between the ruling views of these groups of men symbolizes the opposing sentiments of their general sectors. Up-State, the Governor's following stood firm. In the City—but the glamorous City delegation speaks for itself. Suffice it to say that in the State of New York the two main parties came to be known as "Federalists" and "Clintonians."

De Witt sat in his lofty perch, a tablet of paper upon his knee, and wrote his impressions for that same newspaper, Thomas Greenleaf's *New York Journal,* which had printed his "Countryman" letters.

He sent his news to Greenleaf by way of a mutual friend, Charles Tillinghast. Not all of it was published. Some of it, indeed, remained in draft within the confines of his letter-books. A great deal reached Greenleaf but did not find space in his paper. It will serve, however, as eloquent testimony to the mental stature of the youthful Clinton. The Convention met on the 17th of June, 1788, and appointed the Governor as its President. On the 19th, with Henry Oothoudt of Albany in the chair, the gathering heard Chancellor Robert R. Livingston, who advanced the proposition, unanimously agreed to, that no question should be taken till the whole draft Constitution had been debated by paragraphs. All went well until the paragraph concerning the ancient sore point of direct taxation arose. Melancthon Smith, ally of the Governor, then had his say in opposition; criticized Livingston's speech, and was answered—"eloquently," as the young Clinton remarks,—by Mr. Hamilton. Mr. Smith was ready with an amendment, and Lansing lent him his support.

The debate occupied several days, in the course of which the Governor on the one hand and John Jay on the other were among those who took the floor. These were the chief protagonists in New York of that drama which first placed in conflict the rights of the individual and the rights vested in a constitutional government. On the 27th, De Witt Clinton wrote to Greenleaf:

> The Convention are now debating upon the power of taxation, etc., lodged in Congress.... Judge Smith opened the debate today and with his usual good sense proved clearly the danger resulting to the liberties of the people from the depositing of such essential and individual powers into the hands of men so little responsible as the Congress under the new Constitution will be....

On July 2nd, the signs of a possible crisis are to be noticed:

> Dear Sir,
>
> The Convention have now moved to the 2nd article. Several amendments have been proposed this day, and none dissented. This conduct in the other party is somewhat singular. Yesterday the news of the Virginian... adoption arrived here from New York by Bill Livingston. He came in 9 hours he says. It has made in my opinion no impression upon the Republican members.... The Chancellor the day before yesterday attempted to ridicule the opposition out of their arguments, but yesterday he was severely attacked by G. Livingston, Williams and M. Smith. He, however, acquitted himself with great address. One remark of Judge Smith's was so apropos to the Chancellor's character that I cannot help setting it down. The Chancellor had ridiculed the notion of being afraid to lodge the purse and the sword in Congress in an able manner. Judge Smith in answer observed that he had no objections to giving the Congress the sword, but he was for restricting their power over the purse because the honorable gentleman very well knew that some people who had no great inclination to handle the sword were notwithstanding very fond of thrusting their hands into the purse. This observation Mr. Chancellor in reply passed over....

On the 12th he reports that the business of the Convention was in fact wound up to a crisis, and describes the amendments offered by the antis, and their anxiety for another convention of the States for the purposes of altering the document accordingly.

Momentous amendments, some of them to prove in the immediate future that the Constitution-makers might well have listened with less impatience to the words of their adversaries as the latter prepared to give ground.

The battle meanwhile had been waged with vigor by Hamilton, Jay, Livingston and Robert Morris on the one hand, and by Smith, the Governor and Lansing on the other.

> ...The first (remarks De Witt) insist that Congress can never receive us into the Union in this manner. I have, however, no doubt but what they will, and then our representatives in Congress can be of service in calling another convention.

For that was still the hope of the antis. A change, it will be observed, had come into the quality of their opposition: "Adoption," for reasons that will shortly be made clear, had crept into their vocabulary in spite of themselves. To the last they fought to make adoption conditional upon the inclusion of the most important, at least, of their amendments. Jay was for "recommending" these amendments, but for ratifying meanwhile. The antis fought on. They had been selected by their constituents in the confidence that they would sign no ratification unless the document framed at Philadelphia was at least radically altered —sufficiently altered to preserve State rights and to limit centralized power in a degree which they, eternally shy of autocracy, thought essential. But in spite of their efforts, a considerable weight had, by the end of June, been added to the Federal side of the scale. In the general convention it had been agreed that if nine or more States ratified, the Constitution should be considered as adopted, and non-ratifying States should thereupon be considered as seceding from the Union....

While the fight on the amendments was still young in New York, word had come that a ninth State—New Hampshire—had ratified. The fight took on from that moment an entirely new aspect. "Feds" in Albany began annoying their neighbors by firing off guns in rounds of ten....

> ...I have been informed (wrote De Witt Clinton) that the quarrel between Antis and Feds at Albany has not entirely subsided—that the latter persevere in firing 10 cannon and that the country people are much enraged at it.... I have no fear but that the Antis will keep together now.... I have seen some extracts

of letters and other statements in some of the New York Federal papers that are not true. To use an expression of Hume, a man of sense will lend a very academic faith to them and others similar.

Thus the nineteen-year-old. He reported more than once that the end was in sight, but his prognostications of "a few days more" were repeatedly disappointed. The news from Virginia had brought the tally of ratifying States up to ten; but on the 18th of July he was still writing in a vein of wonder:

To detail the complicated proceedings and political manœuvers at this place would be inconsistent with the brevity of a letter. The proposal I mentioned in my last (and which for distinction's sake I shall call Smith's I proposal) was violently opposed by the Federal party. A few days ago, Hamilton introduced a proposition with explanatory and recommendatory amendments. The next day... Judge Hobart moved for an adjournment until the 2 day of next September, at this place. The ostensible reason was that as a change of circumstances had taken place since the election of the members, it would be proper that they should go home and consult their constituents, but the real design was I believe different. This motion was opposed by Lansing, Bray and Harper, and advocated by the Chancellor and Duane principally. The question upon it was taken the next day, and there appeared 22 for and 40 against it, Jones, Schenck and Havens voting with the 19 Feds....

The "Jones" is here significant. That legal luminary, much to his pupil's disgust, was weakening. So, it will have already become apparent, were others. In the end, even Melancthon Smith, after urging "a new proposal, the substance of which was a censure upon the Constitution and the reasons notwithstanding of the accession of this State; a bill of rights and explanatory amendments; the writing a circular letter to all the States entreating them to join in calling another convention; and a condition that if a general convention does not take place in — years, then this State shall be at liberty to recede;" put his name to the ratification of the Federal Constitution.

...I look forward with anxiety (De Witt Clinton had written on July 18th). The Scylla and Charybdis I would wish to avoid are non-conditional adoption and a disunion of the opposition....

But that disunion inevitably came to pass. The most prominent anti-Feds parted company, those who signed serene in the belief that by doing so "*in full confidence* that the amendments proposed by this convention will be adopted," they had insured the calling of another convention forthwith. The Federalist Jay himself drew up the circular letter to the other States of the Union, praying that this should be done, and both sides signed it; but it was not until the first Congress of the United States under the Federal Constitution actually went into session that some, at least, of the amendments for which the antis had fought were debated, recommended and adopted, ultimately to become in themselves the very heart of the document.

The Constitution of the United States was adopted by the State of New York on July 26, 1788, by a majority of three. Samuel Jones, Melancthon Smith and Gilbert Livingston were among the former antis signing, the first proposing the "in full confidence" motion; the last-named pronouncing an eloquent discourse on his reasons for being convinced that adoption was the wiser course. James Clinton voted doggedly anti to the last. His brother, as President of the convention, did not vote. Their county stood behind them to a man.

It now became Governor Clinton's duty to uphold the Constitution by carrying out its enactments as they effected his domain. Simultaneously, it became his nephew's duty to return to the narrower paths of legal learning.

De Witt had not wasted his time at Poughkeepsie. His newspaper contributions had added their meed of fuel to the anti-Federalist fires, and also, it may be inferred, to Governor Clinton's esteem of his second surviving nephew. But most significantly they had placed that nephew irrevocably in what would later come to be known as the Jeffersonian ranks. That is, they had committed him to anti-Federalist principles for as long as New York had remained aloof. And when, in spite of the Clintons, New York adopted the Constitution, though he promptly expressed himself as sharing his uncle's view that good Americans must uphold the new order of things, his essential ideas and ideals had not changed. He still stood committed to anti-Federalism in its altered connotation, and found himself devoted for life to republican principles and the sovereignty of the people, as against Hamilton's aristocracy of brain and power and right.

John Fiske has said, "All American history has since run along the lines marked out by the antagonism of Jefferson and

Hamilton." The beginnings of that particular antagonism were to come a little later on. Jefferson at the moment was still in France. But here were Clintons of New York, already starring in the anti-Federalist drama. No Hamilton, no Adams would ever love a Clinton, though Federalists there were to be who would admire De Witt. The battle was on. The future Democratic party, which in Jefferson's time and long afterwards was to be termed the Republican party as opposed to that of the Federalists, had its true beginnings in the "anti-Feds." The Jefferson-Hamilton battle ground was ready.

De Witt was very much a man. His mother, that simple soul and loving spirit, put more pride than hurt into the letter she wrote from the farm at this time to her husband, in which appears the plaint, "I suppose De Witt has forgot us all." But he had not forgotten his mother or his home. He wrote, and lovingly, whenever he could find the time—which simply was not often enough for Mary.

Pride in the young man, however, was of course not confined to Mary Clinton. Late in the year 1789 the Governor wrote a letter from New York to his brother James. James' son meanwhile had learned a truth that would be useful in later life: that political differences had no place in his private existence. He had sat again under Samuel Jones, and the love and respect he had felt for his teacher had flowed again sufficiently strongly to make politics a thing apart. It had been well, as the Governor's letter goes to prove:

> ...De Witt passed his examination very respectably, and I believe he excelled, which I hardly expected as to the practice, which I did not believe he had paid as much attention to as to the principles of law, which is the more substantial part and better suited to his genius. He says it is your opinion he ought to settle in the country, and that his brother Georgie ought to study with him there. I differ with you in sentiment. I think he ought to settle in this city, for various reasons, and particularly as his brother is to study with him, as his advantages here will be much greater than in the country. De Witt is young. His parts are uncommonly good. He has attended more to books than men and manners, and should he settle in the country, he will instead of acquiring those accomplishments which he has hitherto neglected, and very wisely, for more substantial knowledge, become more rusticated and have less chance of distinguishing himself as a man of eminence in his profession. If he can the

> first year or two barely maintain himself, it is sufficient; at his period of life he ought to look for nothing further. I believe (I) can be of service to him here. But I will not advise....

Nevertheless his advice was taken. And "for several reasons," as he said, his advice was good. Not the least of these was the aspect of New York in 1789. For in 1789 George Washington, first President of the United States, was proudly installed in office. And the city of New York, the scene of his inauguration and the prospective theater of his labors, forthwith blazed into a prominence and an activity unheard of.

4

SECRETARY

1789 - 1795

SO DE WITT CLINTON hung up his shingle, not in a mere battered city struggling to revive itself, but at the headquarters of a new and quite glorious nation.

To be sure, the gentlemen who had lately arrived to take their seats in Congress found it primitive—"not half as large as Philadelphia, nor in any manner to be compared to it for elegance." The former Dutch houses of stone had given way to frame buildings with brick fronts. Tea and drinking water still came around, and was to do so for many a year, in barrels. Water for household purposes was carried by hand from the pump in Chatham Street, fed by the Collect Pond. Watchmen did the policing of the town, and the duties of the Common Council had lately ranged from fining farmers for letting pigs run in the mud of the city streets to making ready a building fit to house the inauguration of a President.

Columbia College, St. Paul's Church and the Hospital were the three buildings meanwhile entitled, according to the visiting legislators, to be classed as "elegant." The chief diversions were excursions to Murray Hill, to Gracie's Point—a ride of several hours. Harlem Heights was a mecca for the patriotic sightseer, but to get there took a whole day, and cost thirty-eight shillings in a hired coach.

But now all travelers, all the State, converged upon New York. Great and elaborate were the preparations for the coming of President Washington. De Witt Clinton saw him, in his triumphal barge, with its thirteen oarsmen dressed in white, arrive at the foot of Wall Street. He saw the banners that draped the many-paned windows of freshly-painted houses, the flowers that had been cast on the cobbles to bedeck the hero's path. He saw his uncle, the Governor, resplendent, alight from his carriage to welcome an old friend and a new leader, and make to escort him back to its padded and flower-strewn seat. But Washington elected to walk, through the packed lanes of vociferously-shouting citizens, to the Governor's Pearl Street house. There a collation awaited, and all the *corps diplomatique* and the President's official "family" (Mrs. Washington being not yet arrived), and the distinguished members of both houses were assembled to do him honor.

De Witt saw it all. He saw Washington installed as a New York resident in the house which the Quaker merchant, Walter Franklin, had built at the corner of Cherry and Pearl Streets. Since Walter Franklin's death in 1780, his widow, inheriting a very large fortune and a choice of houses from him, had allowed this city mansion to be used by the presidents of Congress. She had recently remarried, her bridegroom being Samuel Osgood, who had held military office under Washington throughout the war. And when Washington, coming to New York and the Presidency, refused the permanent hospitality of the Governor and others who offered, Osgood and his lady, by request, made ready the Franklin house as a Presidential mansion. Young Clinton was to know that attractive white house well, in a very special relation to one of the Franklin family. But for the moment he was more patriotically drawn, with the mass of his fellow-citizens, to a familiar yet unfamiliar building in Wall Street—the Federal Hall, on whose balcony the resounding inauguration of the first President of the United States took place. Before the men of means in the city had raised their thirty-two thousand dollars for the purpose of remodeling it, and Major L'Enfant had done his excellent job of redesigning, and the powers had equipped it with its appropriate new name, it had been that same old City Hall in whose chambers young Clinton had begun his college career.

New York now became social as never before. Edmund Randolph came to take office as Attorney-General, sighing a little for Virginia, and renting a mansion in the neighboring village called Greenwich, a mile and a half to the north of the Federal Hall. Chancellor Livingston had his town residence at No. 3 Broadway; John Jay his at No. 133. Vice-President John Adams and his family came to live at the pleasant estate named Richmond Hill, a mile or so from the city, also in the Greenwich region, where Washington had formerly had his headquarters. Alexander Hamilton entertained lavishly in his Wall Street mansion. Mrs. Bingham, of Philadelphia, acknowledged queen of Federalist hostesses; "Lady" Kitty Duer; and Sarah Livingston, the wife of John Jay, were the reigning beauties of the day. Gouverneur Morris was the frequent host of the great at Morrisania, which he had lately purchased; and these, and the Presidential mansion, and the Governor's house, and those of a score of other political leaders, were the centers at which New York society now came into its own. After Mrs. Washington's arrival there were Presidential levees twice a week. There were social gatherings of the lesser lights nightly. At New Year there was a veritable blaze of entertainment, for the old Dutch custom of visiting round on New Year's Day still clung to New York, and President Washington not only expressed his delight with such simple sociability on the occasion, but threw his house open to gay parties, cake-laden in the good Dutch manner, all that day.

A young man therefore need not be at a loss to break into whatever circles he fancied—particularly a young man who stood in such close relationship as did De Witt to the Governor, New York's official host.

But there was an even closer relationship to the Governor in store for De Witt. He was working hard for a practice, and was meeting with a certain meed of success. His father and his uncles and their military friends kept him busy enough with land matters. Soldiers and their officers had been paid for their services, partly at least, in land—land in the undeveloped center of the State, land confiscated from Tories in town and country. This was still proving a harvest for the lawyers in straightening out titles, proving claims, fixing boundary-lines. De Witt, with such a wealth of relatives and friends thus owning lands, inheriting others, purchasing more when the Government found them a little cash to make up their compensation, was kept busy and was able to put his best knowledge to highly practical uses. Also he was coaching his eighteen-year-old brother George, whose chief ambition, *vide* his letters, seems to have been to prove worthy of this his tutor.... Charles, aged 22, had settled down to his business as a surveyor, and was aide to his father in that capacity. De Witt remained the Governor's *protégé* and confidant in this somewhat difficult year....

It happened that George Clinton was being markedly left out of the Federal appointments as handed out by Alexander Hamilton, the Secretary of the Treasury and the wielder of power at the seat of government; and was even experiencing a little doubt about his own current reëlection to the high office he had held for the past twelve years. His former sentiments were coming home to roost. Hamilton was craftily running Robert Yates, the former ardent anti-Federalist and Clintonian, as a candidate for the Governorship against him, in the obvious hope of dividing the Clintonian vote and adding it to that of the Federalists....

In the event, George Clinton proved still too popular, particularly in his own region, his record still too great, for him to fail this time. He was reëlected, but by a bare four hundred majority, and subsequently found himself sufficiently at leisure to look around for a likely young man to fill the post of confidential secretary left vacant by the death of his nephew Alexander.

It had become a post of rather greater trust than ever, in view of the current germination of political animosities and disappointments. The former antis, in spite of Governor Clinton's personal success, had gone down like flies before the assault of the Hamiltonians throughout the State. The Governor would face no friendly majority when he took up his duties again.... Logical, then, to keep the private secretaryship in the family, and to look among the three remaining sons of his brother for the incumbent, his own son not having as yet emerged from childhood. Young Charles, of course, with his career well chosen and well-launched, was not very likely material. George was too young. And even had he not been, was there not, most patently, De Witt—De Witt who had already demonstrated such a remarkable aptitude for politics and legislation as well as for scholarship?

In scholarship he continued to shine. Columbia's Commencement exercises of 1789 were graced by the presence of President

Washington—his first public appearance in his official capacity. The occasion was also marked by the bestowal of an M.A. degree on Columbia's already distinguished alumnus, De Witt Clinton. Incidentally there were official diplomas now. In 1787 the Board of Regents had undergone another organic change, and direct administration of Columbia College as a unit of the State University had been vested in a Board of Trustees of its own. William Samuel Johnson became Columbia's first President, and the temporary certificates of De Witt Clinton and his colleagues of the early classes were replaced by official documents in 1788.

But as the law had beckoned Clinton the student, now politics began to crook a highly persuasive finger at Clinton the attorney.

> ... The city is at present filled with legislatures and law courts (he wrote to his uncle in February, 1790). The Supreme Court of the United States is now in session, and has done no other business than admitting a few counselors and making a few rules. One of their orders: "That all process shall run in the name of the President," though apparently unimportant, smells strongly of monarchy. You know that in Great Britain some writs are prefaced with "George the Third, by the Grace of God, etc." A Federal process beginning with "George Washington, by the Grace of God, etc." will make the American President as important in law forms as the British King.
>
> Our State Legislature has transacted no business of very great consequence, unless the adoption of the trivial and equivocal amendments may be so styled, and the rejection of a lame bill for the manumission of the future offspring of the negroes, which neither provided for the support of their infant years or the protection of their rights.
>
> Two plans of the last importance to the welfare of the Union have been laid before the Congress. One is a report from the Secretary of the Treasury, which states the importance of public credit, the injustice of discriminating between the original holders and purchasers of public securities, the propriety of assuming the State debts and the necessity of constituting a funding system.
>
> The foreign debt is calculated at eleven millions, 710 thousand and 378 dollars. The domestic debt at near 43 millions of dollars. The unliquidated debt of the Union, 2 millions. The State debts, 25 millions. The annual expenses of government, 6 hundred thousand dollars. In the whole, 32 millions of pounds. The whole resources of the Union will hardly pay the interest of the debt and the necessary expenses. To fund such an immense debt at its normal value will be mortgaging to perpetuity all the

> revenues of the States for the payment of its interest, and if an emergency happens, which will necessitate an increase of the revenue, the people must either be borne down with heavy taxes or the States plunged deeper in debt. The sinking fund of Great Britain in eleven years of profound peace only extinguished ten millions of the principal—in a war of seven years their debt was augmented 100 millions. What effect then will the puny sinking fund of one hundred thousand dollars (the revenue of the post-office), proposed by the Secretary, have in the extinguishment of our debt? It is remarked that sinking funds have enfeebled like slow poison all the nations that have adopted them.
>
> The other plan is for the regulation of the militia. Gen[l]. Knox recommends the establishment of three different classes: The first or the legionary corps to consist of young men between 18 and 21, to be clothed by the people; to turn out 30 days every year; their officers to be paid and the men to be victualled during that time. This proposal is so palpably absurd and impolitic that I take it for granted it will meet with no success. It is not a little surprising that Gen[l]. Knox hints in his introductory letter, its being approved by the President....

Which proves, among other things, that the mantle of his uncle (making allowances for his own youth) was already enveloping De Witt Clinton. So it was. On April 24th, 1790, he signed the roll of attorneys sworn in to the Supreme Court of the State. But he did not, for the moment, make use of the official status thus attained. Instead, he left his law-books and his office and his young fraternal neophyte, and entered his uncle's family as Alexander's successor.

It was the very eve of the Jefferson-Hamilton struggle; the real beginning of the fight for survival of the Federalist Party. De Witt Clinton, a mere youth, was to live and work through the heyday of that combat, while men, from talking it out in the taverns, went to fighting it out in the streets; through the democracy vs. aristocracy phase; through the partisanship period which came out of the French Revolution, then in the birth-throes, and the subsequent struggle of England to overthrow it. His term of service as his uncle's secretary covered the whole of the early period of that upheaval and of the more local struggle that was so amazingly to grow from it. He was to be even nearer to the center of affairs when the latter attained to concrete results.

He took it all in, and many things absorbed him. In 1786, in the city of New York, a patriotic order had been born out of the hatred engendered in the hearts of the former Sons of Liberty against Mr. Hamilton's reinstated Tories. It was called the Tammany Society, after the Indian chief of that name, a lover of peace and of patriotism. And it was the antithesis of the somewhat aristocratic Cincinnati Society, composed though the latter was of Revolutionary officers. In view of the fact that "Tammany" was to have a very special and in fact a sinister significance in the life of De Witt Clinton, its aims and the changes in those aims have their special place a little later in the present narrative. Suffice it to say that in the beginning Tammany had all the attributes of a purely patriotic order, following the tribal titles and customs of the chieftain whom it honored. The unmoneyed of both political faiths were among its membership. In May, 1789, when it added "Columbian Order" to its title, President Washington was named honorary Grand Sachem, and Governor Clinton a Sachem in its council. John Pintard, a legislator of the popular party for a brief period in his youth, was its first Sagamore, and De Witt Clinton, at the age of 21, became its Scribe.

It was one of his minor occupations. His true career had begun. Being appointed secretary to the Board of Regents of the University, of which the Governor was presiding officer, and secretary to the Board of Fortifications, he blushed unseen in neither capacity. He was part of the new America. He was part, also, it may be mentioned, of that social swim which his uncle had long thought so desirable for him....

His personal appearance was, even thus early, striking. James Kent, called to the Bar in 1787, and more or less aligned with his former mentor Egbert Benson on the Hamiltonian bandwagon ever since, met Clinton first at this period of his life, and was struck with his stature and his mien. De Witt stood six foot three, and was slim then, and upright always. His face was Roman in its almost perfect beauty of feature—the mouth thin-lipped but generously curved, the eyes wide-set and frank, the nose generous and classic in line. His chin was bold, his curling hair a rich brown. It was not to be expected that such a youth would be left in the cold, either by New York's maidens or by their mothers. He was free of every city drawing-room, from Bowling Green to Great George Street, and of the many suburban drawing-rooms in the mansions dotting the verdant East River bank, and to the north. He sported with the sons, and he talked and walked and danced a little with the daughters. His uncle's daughters were all greatly attached to him. His own sisters, Mary, Elizabeth and Catherine, pretty and vivacious, descended on him from time to time, and shared his occasions and his friends. Mr. Jones, who had succeeded Richard Varick as Recorder of New York, had an agreeable young family. So had Chief Justice John Jay, and parents' politics had nothing whatever to do with young people's occasions. The theater in John Street saw them often. A flourishing theater, especially since its band-leader, Mr. Fayles, had achieved immortality by composing the air called Washington's March—or, more familiarly, "Hail Columbia."

And New York City itself continued its interesting course. New York City was making a bid for the permanent sheltering of the United States Government. Fort George, the historic symbol of defense at the foot of the island, had fallen into decay and become a stamping-ground for horses and a dump for odds and ends. It was now demolished, the land cleared, and a Government House, destined for the permanent official home of the President, was erected on its site. The Battery was reënforced and buttressed and made spick and span, the Bowling Green was enclosed in a wooden fence, and the south end of the island began to take on an air of very handsome respectability.

But in vain. Mr. Hamilton was greatly exercised over the sustained opposition to his scheme for funding the State debts. The Republicans, innately suspicious of a centralized money power, fought this supremely Federalist measure; and the agricultural interests suspected the mercantile interests of a plot to make agriculture pay for industrial speculation. However, it happened that the gentlemen planters from the South nourished hopes of locating the permanent capital of the nation nearer home—preferably on the banks of the Potomac.... They compromised. In March, Thomas Jefferson arrived from France to take up his duties as Secretary of State; and incidentally to show the Republicans of the United States that he was their foreordained leader. Hamilton sought him out. There was an interview between them—in the street, it is said, before Washington's house (President Washington had removed to the McComb mansion on Broadway, near the newly rebuilt Trinity Church, at the end of February). Hamilton pleaded the urgent necessity of the assumption of the debts by the Government, and informed Jefferson of the danger that some of the creditor States would secede if this measure was not taken. Jefferson heard him, and was convinced. The Union must be preserved at all costs. A dinner was arranged, to which the principal opponents were invited; and over their wine the gentlemen arrived at a workable understanding. Hamilton agreed to throw his political weight in opposition to his political home as the home of future Presidents. In return, sufficient votes would come from the South to insure the assumption of the debts by Congress....

And so, in July, Congress decided to build a new Capital City on the banks of the Potomac. And in August, Philadelphia became the temporary Capital of the United States, and the Government removed to that place.

Simultaneously, De Witt Clinton went to Albany with his uncle for the new session of the New York Legislature, and by the same token entered his school of political science—an experimental school still, but an adequate one.

The pity is that his political beginnings were so easy and so exalted. Not for him the venomous struggle of Burr against Schuyler, against Hamilton. Not for him the arduous fight of so many of his contemporaries. Not yet, that is.... His beginnings were all fair. In perspective he is to be seen intelligently watching the development of the Federalist party, and no less the machinations of the leaders of that party against the ancient power of his uncle in the State, the power of the State in the nation.

The Governor, under the enactments of the State Constitution of 1777, exercised the appointive power with the "concurrence and advice" of a Council of Appointment; the veto power with the aid of a Council of Revision. The former consisted of four Senators, one from each quarter or section of the State, chosen in caucus by the Assembly. These gentlemen had the right to vote on all nominees, the Governor having a casting vote but no other. It will be observed that everything was done with a view to curbing the power of the executive. It was not as yet a matter of patronage. In George Clinton's earlier unbroken tenancy of the Governorship, patronage in the modern sense had, obviously, been virtually non-existent. The first Governor of the State, by the voice of the people, he had no favors to do, no honors to bestow for benefits received. And even when his successive administrations had brought their State and national political complications, he had worked in harmony and mutual respect with his Councils of Appointment, whose personnel was changed, by law, each year. Even when the Council had been divided in politics, as it had in the more recent years, his had been a voice to be heeded, a character to be respected. He had never countenanced the removal of a man from office because of his political faith, and even when a man was to be ousted for misdemeanor, Governor Clinton had seen to it that he was given a chance to plead his own defense. Likewise when Federalism became a name for a party, he had remained impartial in the appointive power, and in those cases where he filled the office of a Federalist whose term had expired with a Clintonian friend of his own, the choice and the man were invariably unimpeachable.

The Council of Revision consisted of the Chancellor and the Justices of the Supreme Court, who exercised the veto power in conjunction with the Governor.

In 1792 Alexander Hamilton persuaded John Jay to run for the office of Governor against George Clinton in the forthcoming election. Clinton won that contest also, though not without a scandal over the canvass in certain counties of the State—a scandal that ultimately defiled both candidates, but redounded more to the discredit of their respective parties than to their own. Clinton, however, was losing ground in the State, and his party had met with unmistakable disaster once again. By 1794 the Federalists had so far gained the upper hand that three of the four members of the Council of Appointment were die-hards of that party, and a majority in both houses had been gained by it. The net result of this metamorphosis was a clean sweep, more or less, of Republican office-holders in city and State—mostly by means of a waiting policy with regard to the expiry of Republican terms, and in a couple of instances by ousting Republicans for highly problematical misdemeanors. The Federalist Council of Appointment, in other words, proceeded to play havoc with the Governor. It arrogated to itself the concurrent right to nominate candidates for office—a right which John Jay, as framer of the State Constitution, had never intended to bestow, as will also make itself apparent. And it proceeded to nominate Federalists exclusively for offices high and low, and to vote consistently against the nominees of Governor Clinton, or refuse to vote on them at all. This procedure rendered the Governor, to all intents and purposes, completely powerless, his party a nonentity. George Clinton, anxious for the right functioning of the Government at all costs, pursued a course of passive protest, but the weapon in the hands of the ruling party was irresistible. Only later was that weapon to rebound on the heads of the Federalists themselves, and Governor Clinton's nephew was to have no small part in the direction of its flight. . . .

The present, however, was De Witt's political lesson, and he learned his lesson well. Passionately attached to his uncle, he rapidly acquired that statesman's antagonisms, but without troubling a great deal to emulate his major graces. George Clinton had been a great Governor, and was yet to be. City and State had grown under his leadership. His service, civil and military, had been constant. His interest in internal improvements was even to lend fuel to the fires of his nephew's fame, as it brought credit to his own. His county, Ulster, loved him as a son. His friends, even after the division over the Constitution, were legion. It is neither necessary nor possible to particularize in this direction here. Only as it was to affect the life and career of his nephew and secretary is his record of moment to this work.

These early years showed De Witt Clinton a cross-section of party politics. They placed in his hand, incidentally, a rod in pickle for the "Feds," and in his heart a rancor against those who were opposed to his point of view politically. Integrity was ingrained in him, but he was already learning that it was not invariably appreciated. His family had fought and bled and slaved for the United States. Not for a subsequent losing view, they felt (and he with them), should they have been ostracized. Hamilton had punished them for disagreement with himself. He had refused them the chance to expiate their opposition to the Federal Constitution by working in the executive department of the nation. The previous record and present standing of George Clinton in national affairs obviously entitled him to this privilege. Military service, unaccompanied by public legislative service, on the part of other men was being nationally recognized. Moreover, there is no room for doubt, and there could have been none then, that George Clinton would have worked for country as honorably as he had worked for State, and would have been an asset in governmental office. The future, from whose fields Alexander Hamilton was to be so tragically removed, was to prove this. Above all, conciliating the Clintonians might have proved wiser, in the long run, than antagonizing them any further.

Hamilton, however, in the seventeen-nineties, pushed the Clintons and their friends inexorably back into the State for whose undisturbed preëminence they had fought, and then proceeded as inexorably, through his party, to rob them of the support of that State itself. Simultaneously, the pride, the hurt, of the Clintons became concentrated in the heart of De Witt. He became the symbol—the hostage to the future.

However, he was not all disillusion, even yet; nor, by any manner of means, all vengeance. His connection had given him prominence. His character, becoming known, was gaining him respect. His youth and his looks and brilliant intellect were winning him popularity. He was in demand.

That was the birthday, or at least the revival day, of many clubs and orders and secret societies. He was invited to join the Holland Lodge of Freemasons, which "performed its labors," according to the records of the time, "in the Low Dutch lenguage." He became its Senior Warden in 1792, and Master in 1793. It was here, in all probability, that he first met John Jacob Astor, then still a struggling merchant in furs among other commodities; for Astor was after a very brief interval his successor in both offices.

In November, 1794, he pronounced an oration on Benevolence before the charitable and social Society of the Black Friars, of which he had also recently become a member. This address, and also that which he made before the Holland Lodge upon his induction as Master in December, 1793, were both published and still exist in pamphlet form. They are noteworthy if only for the fact that they exhibit the earliest signs of that weakness for classical allusion and that strong leaning toward history which were to govern his oratory and other aspects of his career throughout his life.

That year he became a soldier. With war-clouds enveloping the nearer shores of the European continent, and American merchant shipping already beginning to suffer through inability to uphold its rights of neutrality in foreign waters; with partisanship hot and strong in the United States, and the memory of local battlefields too fresh, the militia took on new strength. In New

York De Witt Clinton joined with a group of young men to form a company in the regiment of artillery under Colonel Bowman's command, and, chosen Lieutenant, soon rose to the rank of Captain and later to that of Major. He drilled assiduously with his officers and men, and with them drew up a set of rules for deportment, action and behavior, with a system of fines for various shortcomings in the way of attendance at parades, etc., which singled them out for commendation as an exemplary military group.

De Witt was twenty-five, an army officer, bold and exceedingly handsome. On January 15th, 1794, his cousin Cornelia, one of the Governor's daughters, wrote him the following letter. He was at Albany; she with her mother in New York, and also with her *fiancé,* whose name was Edmond Charles Genêt . . . which explains the pretty Cornelia's extremely Jeffersonian politics:

> . . . We have the best news every Day from France. The papers I send with this will inform you how successful that Nation is. Our political affairs here take a favorable turn. The Tories are silent or if they speak it is no longer to abuse the Minister, but his Country—and he is only spoken of as having done what he was commanded to do. I hear everything goes well in Philadelphia. There are democratic meetings and resolutions which you will see in the Diary of this evening. I will not say that I am sorry Albany is not pleasing to you, as it may be the means of sending you to us sooner than you intended. I am not the only one who wishes for your return. I saw the Franklins at the concert last evening. Maria desired me to remember her to you, and Sally hoped you would be here before the next Assembly. Peg De Peyster sends you a kiss.
>
> Accept my respects.
>
> CORNELIA.

De Witt was very fond of his cousin the future bride of the somewhat tactless Minister from the French Republic. But of all the damsels who sent him charming messages to lure him back to New York City, there was really only one who had caused his heart to flutter.

This was Maria, the eldest daughter of the deceased Walter Franklin, whose house on Cherry Street had become a Presidential mansion; and of his wife, now Mrs. Osgood. Maria Franklin was nineteen, and bewitchingly pretty, and wealthy, and she was obviously swept away by the magnificent De Witt.

They loved. He came courting her when his duties did not call him to Albany, and when they did, doubtless his reputation, growing daily in the remnants of his uncle's Clintonian party, wafted its echoes her way. Maria had been brought up in the Quaker tradition, but her mother, after marrying the Presbyterian Osgood, does not appear to have clung to the more rigid observances and customs of that calling, and pretty clothes and music and dancing, and also crowds of the more distinguished of the New York young men, were as much a part of the life of her girls as was a most excellent training in common sense and housewifery.

In 1795, after eighteen years in office, Governor Clinton refused to run for reëlection, pleading ill-health (and indeed he was a martyr to rheumatism), but doubtless equally moved by the increasingly anomalous character of his position as head of the State. He retired, for the time being, to private life—a totally unaccustomed existence for him. His secretary perforce retired too. De Witt went back to the practice of the law, entering into a partnership with John McKesson, a young Clintonian legislator who had recently suffered for his beliefs, and whose admission to the Bar had preceded De Witt Clinton's by only a few years. He went back to his clubs and his societies and his books, and also to his squiring among the beckoning bevy of beauty which centered around a certain white house at Pearl and Cherry Streets.

For as far as his own affections went, they continued to be concentrated at that point. If competition there was for his heart and hand (and there appears to be more than a hint that this was so), the lovely Maria Franklin won with ease.

So, it would seem, did De Witt, whose existence continued to shine. For in 1795, Maria said yes.

MARIA FRANKLIN CLINTON
By St. Memin

5

SCHOLAR

1795 - 1796

IT WAS thus as a prospective bridegroom that De Witt Clinton labored to retrieve his legal practice. He worked hard, against a mingling background of happiness and sorrow. His mother died in September, 1795, at the age of fifty-eight, and left darkness where there had been a very special light for him. She had received, in his maturity, the unfailing devotion of his always domestically inclined nature. She had deliberately spurred him on to strive for success, and he strove now harder than ever. There was, of course, a promise in the future as well as to the past. His future wife, a girl of considerable means, does not appear to have presented herself to him as an excuse for any mere dalliance with the necessity for earning a livelihood on his own part. On the contrary, he was quite obviously desirous of establishing himself before he married her. His commonplace book shows him avid for work—all work, lucrative and otherwise. He was successful. Clients sought him out, and his relatives evidently also continued to find him able. It was no later than February 10th, 1796, that he and Maria were married.

His status now, through his lady, was that of a man of considerable property—his property to administer, when she came of age, said the law of his day. She was not of age until one year after her marriage. Meanwhile three uncles, Quakers,—Bownes and Franklins,—served as her guardians, and accounted to her husband for the administration of her lands at Newtown, Long Island, upon which stood the farm and the handsome house (now hers, subject to her mother's use) where her father had died. Also for the lots he had bequeathed to her in the so-called military patents north of Albany; a house and grounds in New York which her uncle Henry Bowne (her mother was of the Long Island Quaker family of that name) occupied; four thousand pounds in cash, and some plate and personal trinkets.

Maria was cultured and charming and good to look upon. What was equally pleasant, she now proved modestly retiring as became her Quaker upbringing, and domesticated withal. Their life together must have been idyllic for that single year of private existence (there were to be no more such, to speak of, for all their days). That year was a highlight. In summer, De Witt and his Quaker lady lived in her ancestral homestead at Newtown. In winter they dwelt in New York. And while Maria made a home for him, he made an excellent, if superfluous, living for her. While she cultivated, with the arts and the accomplishments of a modest American housewife, a warm-hearted care for the personal comfort of her husband, and a faculty for winning the approbation of his friends (she was always to do that), he went back to his studies. He encompassed the dream of many years by seriously taking up the science of botany, guided by his friend Dr. David Hosack of Columbia College. He delved into the mysteries of natural history, of chemistry and zoölogy (then an entirely new science as far as the United States was concerned) under the direction of Samuel L. Mitchill, who was presently officiating as Columbia's chemistry professor. These things fascinated him always. Education, for himself and for all, was ever to be his lodestar. His true acquaintance with flowers and birds and beasts, with rocks and stones, winds and tides, weather and wheat, began at this time. He extended his studies to sociology, conditions among the poor and conditions on the farms and in the country and the world at large; customs of the Indians, both friendly and antagonistic. He conceived an abiding love for the classics and for the newer literature; an enduring reverence for history and a realization of the need for its preservation, in that one priceless year.... Perhaps, as his critics charge, his love of the classics was greater than his ultimate mastery of them, and his quotations along that line, of which he was so fond, were sometimes superficial or even incorrect. The myriad other preoccupations that increasingly absorbed him, accounted for this. But his knowledge of history, of sociology and the sciences was not only deep but was put into practical application by him throughout his life, with equally practical results.

Meanwhile he remained, as ever, an interesting member of an interesting family. His brother Charles had married a girl from Little Britain, a descendant, like himself, of one of those hardy voyagers from Ireland on the frigate *George and Anne.* Her name was Elizabeth Mulliner. They were much in New York, and as often at De Witt's fireside. Young George was a lawyer, and was smitten greatly with Mrs. De Witt Clinton's sister Hannah. It was a pleasant existence. In the courts of a small circuit which an attorney must embrace in those days, Clinton continued to make a name by virtue of a broadening grasp of the law and a conscientious preparation of his cases. His professional connection continued to grow, while in the field of natural history he continued to lay the foundation for that unofficial reputation which his present preceptor, his friend for the rest of his life, Dr. Hosack, was later to bestow on him. The Doctor, in his memoir of Clinton, writes of him at the close of his life that he knew of no man who would have been better fitted to assume a professorship of that science in any college of his day. It was but another manifestation of his rich inheritance. His grandfather had sought knowledge, culture, in the midst of a hard struggle for existence. His father, the General, had sought them too, in the very toils of a struggle for liberty. De Witt's struggle was to be a little more complex, not so bloody, but every bit as real. Yet he never failed to find time, and zest and mind as well, for the closest study of mineralogy, of ichthyology and ornithology, besides the sciences already mentioned. "In mineralogy, including geology," says Hosack, "few persons possessed superior or more accurate knowledge.... In botany, he was intimately acquainted with the general principles of the Linnæan system, and had an extensive knowledge of those plants which are most useful, and are employed as the objects of agriculture, medicine and the arts...." He was to be a member of "most of the literary and philosophical societies of Philadelphia, Massachusetts, Connecticut, Charleston and New York." And before his course was run, his scientific researches and discoveries were to win him honor and recognition from the foremost European institutions and scientific circles. He was to become an honorary member of the Linnæan and the Horticultural Societies of London and the Wernerian Society of Edinburgh.

For although he has come down in history as a politician and often as purely a self-seeker, it is in his search for knowledge, for light, in his everlasting pursuit of education and his dissemination of it, that the surer key to his character lies. Those were the only uses to which he ever desired to put his achievements in the way of self-advancement. And wherever he went, and no matter what his immediate mission, he surveyed the path before him literally with a seeing eye, so that bird life, amphibia, plant and earth and atmosphere, and for the most part man, were books for him to read, revelations for him to wonder at, problems for him to solve. That was the real De Witt Clinton—scientist, student, something of a philosopher, something of a poet, with a little in him of genius and a very great deal of ambition. He sought to rise, but it was not merely the man De Witt Clinton that he wished to elevate. It was all that Clinton knew, all he hoped for, all the schemes for more prosperous living and more timely dying, that he felt he could advance and dispense if he rose. It will easily be observed that throughout his life his scientific predilections and his desire to apply them in the interests of his country went hand in hand.

Such a man was bound to rise. And if the fruits of success were almost invariably to be bitter in the mouth, there would still be the fruits of knowledge, proportionately sweet. He studied religion, metaphysics and the arts, and found time for them all. He rose very early; he was punctilious about his appointments —and his appointments, even thus early, were many. For all the years that he kept a diary, that diary is thronged with visitors' names—visitors for dinner, for supper, and often for breakfast; visitors between times, and a weighty and bulky correspondence always. He was destined to be in public life—in the thick of the fray—for almost all the total of his years. He was invariably accessible to all who wished to see him. And yet no day passed that, crowding the public man, precluded the scholar. His love of books was such that he could never, even in his least affluent moments, resist a prize or a find along that line. His papers, his private pen never lay long enough to gather dust. The diary itself is for the most part sparse, but occasionally it blooms with a poetic or a scientific flower; sometimes it bursts the bonds of reticence and caution that the politician Clinton was to set himself; sometimes it forgets that it is the diary of a public man at all, and goes off on a schoolboy story of a happy excursion. But only seldom does he seem to have had the time for more than a line and a note of the weather—for he was a student of that, too, and carried a pocket thermometer with him on his travels. It is significant that the only lengthy and discursive entries in his diary were made on the few occasions when he had time to spare on his later travels through the State. Appropriate, too, for it was then that his fame was to be inscribed on the scroll of the future.

But with all his varied pursuits and interests, the things that gave him the most joy of all were domestic pursuits. All who ever knew him—even those who found him cold in casual encounter—knew him for a gentle, tender family man. He loved to walk with his wife in the town, or in the field-lanes to the north. He liked his daily ride to market, in the manner of the man of his town and of his day. He was as fine a judge as there came of beef and mutton and poultry, vegetables and dairy produce. At Newtown, in the springtime, he farmed. He planted saplings and roots and seeds, corn for fodder and vegetables for his table. He fished, relishing the sport, in the nearby streams. He bought cows and pigs and chickens, and sold them too, and drove a good bargain.

He was content enough, but there was nothing static in his contentment. A successful farmer-lawyer, there was nevertheless no question of the fact that he was only at the beginning of his ambitions. Whether the year 1795 had or had not put a definite period to his uncle's political life (and as a matter of fact it had not), both his uncle and he still cherished schemes for his own immediate future; temporarily locked away, perhaps, but still clamorous.

With his record, he probably would not long have been left unmolested by political parties in any event, even had he personally eschewed the possibility of a public career. As it was, in the year 1796 the Democratic State leaders (now definitely identified as the leaders of what was to be known as the Republican party) approached him with the request that he run for the Assembly as a representative of the City of New York.

At once his multifarious other interests proceeded to take, comparatively, a back seat. It was, indeed, the only period in the whole of his life in which he allowed even politics to eclipse them to such an extent. This was his chance, and, as Hosack remarks,

> Political consideration was at that time his dominant motive of action. The germs of the two great parties were then just exhibiting themselves. De Witt Clinton, following the principles and examples of his uncle, from that time on devoted his pen and his faculties to the support of the Republican Party.

His uncle was still his hero—still, to him, a martyr to be vindicated. The lance De Witt Clinton carried to the political field was first tilted in behalf of Governor George, against the men who had wronged him.

But Federalism was already past its great heyday. Even Washington was no longer a god to all men. To a rising Jeffersonianism which was unreservedly pro-French, Washington was a symbol of aristocracy, of pro-British sentiment. De Witt Clinton was not pro-French. He was never, as it happened, anything but pro-American. But he was heart and soul for Jefferson, and for the voice of the people as against those who would quiet it—the doctrine that Jefferson was unremittingly preaching. And De Witt Clinton was headed, as Jefferson was, for the day of democracy.

6

LEGISLATOR

1796 - 1802

FEDERALISM WAS not yet dead, however, especially in the City of New York; and by the same token De Witt Clinton was not quite to succeed this time as a Republican at the polls. But there were signs and portents. John Jay, coming home from his new treaty-making mission to England in 1795, had been greeted with the news of his election as Governor of New York, and had resigned his office as Chief Justice of the Supreme Court of the United States to take up that which George Clinton had so recently relinquished.

Slightly more than one month later, the treaty Jay had lately made with England was revealed to the American public. He had been sent abroad to obtain pledges securing American shipping from seizure, American sailors from impressment. American-owned slaves, stolen by British soldiers, were to be paid for or returned. He obtained no such assurances. The forts to the northwest that had been held in violation of the treaty of peace would be vacated by the British. Trade would be a little freer—not much. And Jay had won a little redress for damages already caused at sea, conceding in return, however, that debts owed by private parties in America to British creditors would be paid.... An avalanche of maledictions forthwith fell upon his head—even in New York, where his accession to the chief executive office had only recently been vociferously acclaimed. Feeling against Jay was only exceeded by feeling against England. The Republican party had forthwith become an entity as such, and was reënforced by men high in office and high in public esteem; by officers of

Washington's cabinet who split with him and with each other over this question of the correct preservation of neutral rights; by some of the former rank and file of the Federalists, and above all, preeminently and officially, by Thomas Jefferson.

By 1796, however, the heat of this feeling had died down somewhat. A great many people were admitting that the treaty was probably the best that could have been obtained at the time. Forthwith, France, or her agents in America, redoubled the campaign already launched by Genêt (with somewhat disastrous personal results), and took to the most insidious courses to stir up anew the pro-French (and incidentally anti-English) feeling. But the methods raised alarm instead, in a great many instances; and when the elections for a successor to George Washington took place in 1796, the Federalist stand against French propaganda was once more receiving considerable support, amplified by the active sympathy of British immigrants and would-be citizens. Jay and his portion of the party in New York, though vilified the year before, were once more accorded honor in their own State; and De Witt Clinton among others of the Republican ticket was defeated at the polls.

John Adams succeeded George Washington in the Presidency in 1797. Thomas Jefferson became Vice-President of the United States. The two men, former friends, now represented the opposite poles of current party politics, signally swept asunder by the retirement of Washington, whose beneficent presence had welded incompatibilities together these many years. Jefferson stood for the French brand of liberty and the principles of Thomas Paine. Adams stood for most of the things that Washington had held by, and owned no partisanship for any foreign country, though his party as a whole was deemed to lean toward England. Moreover, Adams' hard-won and meager triumph over Jefferson signalized the real beginnings of the age-long regional rivalry: North vs. South, in its earlier and less tragic phase. His administration, progressively unpopular, though not entirely through faults or measures of his own, marks the final decline of the national power of the Federalists. The party of the future, from this time on, was increasingly that of the Vice-President. And the party of the Vice-President was no less progressively that of the New York neophyte De Witt Clinton, whose uncle had run in the recent Presidential race and been met with the bitterest opposition from Federalism in his State. De Witt, staunch through blood and through politics both, began his own true political career by hotly defending that of his uncle and patron. The gesture did not fail to win him personal recognition among New York Republicans, who at that moment were experiencing an unexpected and significant accession of local strength from another quarter. Robert R. Livingston, the Chancellor, had split with the Federalists. He now went over, with all his wealth and most of his powerful kin, to the Republican side. Some said he had failed to see eye to eye with Hamilton over the funding system. Others hinted that he was disgruntled because Jay had won high Federal office at the birth of the new republic, at a moment when Livingston himself was due for just such recognition. He had vigorously opposed the Clintons and their anti-Federal ideas, but, though powerful in New York (or perhaps because of that fact), he and his had been ostracized no less, and left out of the patronage.

Parton has remarked that New York politics at the time consisted of Clintons, Livingstons and Schuylers. "The Clintons," he says, "had power; the Livingstons had numbers; the Schuylers had Hamilton." There was now also Aaron Burr, lately a United States Senator, but now back in the political rank and file of New York; popular personally, ambitious beyond words, and an ardent worker for the Republican party. In the year 1797, New York City elected Aaron Burr, Samuel L. Mitchill and De Witt Clinton members of the State Assembly.

De Witt was still only twenty-eight years old when he took his seat in the New York Legislature on January 2nd, 1798, and listened to the New Year's address of Governor Jay. He had removed his wife and his infant son Walter, born in 1797, to Albany, and turned the work of a steadily growing law practice over to John McKesson, who soon relinquished it likewise in the interests of his own revived political career. De Witt brought his library, his scientific apparatus, his embryo collection of rocks and fossils and seeds along, and pigeon-holed them for his leisure. For the rest, his time and his devotion, plus his inestimable potentialities, were at the service of his State. The most significant characteristic he evinced at this the start of his political career was an interest in progress and also in national defense. And what was just as striking, this interest was wholly non-partisan. When the wave of warlike anger against France and her agents swept the country; and alike when revolutionary France clamored that free America should return a helping hand to a former ally; a corresponding wave of patriotic caution swept De Witt, and in spite of his party's traditional leaning toward France, he managed to convey his personal sentiments to the Assembly.

He was a polished, but not a showy, debater—an orator who, from the richness of his mental background, made his classical allusions and his careful deductions into a judicious mixture. He had a quick, alert mind allied to a slow and careful tongue, so that his speeches shone more brightly, perhaps, in the reading than in the hearing. There were those who found him somewhat monotonous as an orator, but contemporaries agree that he never wasted his oratory. He had swift and perfect judgment, so that he knew unfailingly when he had made his point, when he was not going to make it, and consequently when to stop. Dignity and knowledge hand in hand made him, even thus early, a conspicuous figure. According to Hosack, his style and deliberation closely resembled Pitt's. He never "ranted," was always calm and dignified in speaking, and could reason and illustrate well.

His public début completely successful, his private existence was no less so. The centrepoint was Walter, the apple of his father's eye through radiant childhood and into radiant memory. Clinton was at his best, and at his happiest, always as a father and as a husband (that seems to have been the order that his happinesses took).

When Walter was one year old, Mr. Clinton left the Assembly for a seat in the New York State Senate, representing the southern district. Here he shone particularly in the current debates on the gradual abolition of slavery within the State. He had himself been reared with the compulsory aid of slaves, but the men and women whom he personally employed were free, colored or no, and drew weekly wages.

There was a second birth in the year 1798—of a second son, named Charles Alexander. And as Walter and Charles grew to walking dimensions, their country began drifting a little more inevitably towards a war—against France. President Adams, straining all his powers to avoid it, was also preparing to prosecute it. His powers were great—his mental powers just a little greater than his party. He was a statesman. Had he been a whit more amenable, a little more of a politician, a degree less vain, a trifle more temperate in speech and more versed in popularity, he might have saved that party. But then had he been any one of these things, he would not have been John Adams. And had he saved his party, it might well have been at the expense of his country, which he saved instead. In pursuit of peace he met with the X Y Z *débâcle,* which placed him under fire from all quarters, and in particular from Alexander Hamilton, the guiding hand of the Federalists, to whom he had never been willing to bend the knee. In pursuit of preparedness, he gave the nation guns and ships—and peace. In defiance of Hamilton, he gave it, ultimately, Thomas Jefferson.

To young De Witt Clinton in New York, however, the word defense, and also the word preparedness, which after all had been handed down by Washington himself, as a watchword for those who wished to insure against war, had a very particular meaning. He had seen New York taken by force within his own lifetime. He did not wish to see it again—especially for lack of fortification. So with his telling voice he refused to go with his party in its attempt to repeal President Adams' scheme of war taxes, which the Republicans called another Stamp Act. Likewise he pledged the support of his State for the administration's measures against French aggression. More, with his strong arms he actually helped to dig and build fortifications after they were voted for. And he drilled with his artillerymen when his duties allowed him to travel down to New York City, practicing on the guns upon the Battery wall. His father, his uncle, had done such things before him. His grandfather had been forced to make a fortress of his house itself. It was in the blood.

In 1798 the Republicans in New York ran Robert R. Livingston for Governor against John Jay. It was a blow to Jay, thus to be opposed by one related to him by marriage and bound to him by the recollections of years of public and private companionship. It appears to have taken away the savor of the office, never very great, for him. There would be no more candidacies for Jay. He won this fight against Livingston, however, by a wide majority; but the vote was increasingly for him and not for his party. Details as to the measures of a Federalist administration at Philadelphia were slowly seeping through to the populace—and the populace did not find them to their liking. The Sedition Law, aimed at those who spread ill words regarding the executive, savored of kings; the Alien Law, intended to curb the voice of the foreigner too zealous for his own land, was dubbed an arbitrary check-rein on freedom of speech.

In the year 1800, Alexander Hamilton committed his supreme mistake by attacking the character of the Federalist President John Adams in a pamphlet supposedly intended for private circulation only. After that not all his arts could avail him against the Republicans. From then on it was for Aaron Burr, into whose hands a supply of the pamphlets fell, to seize upon them as Republican campaign material; to show his peculiar skill at political finesse; and ultimately almost to wrest the scepter of office from the waiting hand of Jefferson. Burr began his operations in New York, and with Jay expressing his firm intention of retiring to private life in 1801, the field there was clear. The result of the State elections of the year 1800 was a clean sweep for the Republicans. Triumphant, Burr turned his abilities to bear on the coming fight for the Presidency. He accepted a nomination in company with Thomas Jefferson, the understanding being implicit in the arrangement, though not at that time a necessity under the law, that the name of Jefferson was linked with the Presidency, that of Burr with the second place. The choice went by numbers in those days. The man who received a plurality became President; he who was given the second greatest number of electoral votes was Vice-President. The New York Republicans believed that the order of precedence was assured. So, by the grace of a little private effort, did Burr....

De Witt Clinton's views on the occasion, as expressed in a letter to Solomon Southwick of the *Albany Register,* were as follows:

> I thank you for your favor of the 12th instant. It contains information of some of the Northern Counties of which I was not before hopeful and which compared with the result of our elections elsewhere, places it beyond doubt that Jefferson will have the voice of this State for President. The consequence has been dismay and despair to our adversaries. Some others talk of abandoning the Country and all of them seem to give up their cause as lost; like most other companions in misfortune, they endeavor to shift the blame off from themselves upon others and their distress and dissatisfaction encrease. It has given an electrical shock to the Cabinet at Philadelphia. McHenry has re-

> signed upon a broad hint—Pickering would not take it and has been removed. The additional standing army is to be disbanded on the 15th of next month. These measures have been taken it is supposed with a view to softening if not of conciliating the republican party. Our prospects in most of the States South are almost equally good—they brighten even in Connecticut; all the calculating men—trimmers—office seekers—worshippers of power—who compose not an inconsiderable part of the community will now come over to us. In a word, the failure of aristocracy which has been erecting with so much care . . . for nearly twelve years. . . .

So it came about. Jefferson won the battle, though in the end rather in spite of Burr than because of him. Burr took the second place. George Clinton, whose name had inevitably been placed in nomination by a considerable group of his friends, was beaten largely by the forces that had almost beaten Jefferson, and though his hopes had not risen beyond the Vice-Presidential chair as yet, they were none the less crushed and dismayed by the triumph of Burr. But the State needed former Governor Clinton, and in 1801 he was once more a candidate for the office he had held so long and so honorably. His adversary, Jay, having retired from the field, was Stephen Van Rensselaer,—the "Patroon," owner by inheritance from Dutch forebears of vast estates along the Hudson in the region of Albany.

Meanwhile George Clinton's nephew was riding the Republican wave. In the year 1801, De Witt found himself not only still a Senator, but one of three Republican members of the Council of Appointment. . . . And by the time that Council of Appointment set to work, De Witt Clinton was the acknowledged leader of his party in New York State.

If such advancement seems, at a glance, amazing, let us consider first the personnel of the new Council, and then the current line-up and problems of the New York Republicans. De Witt Clinton's colleagues were Ambrose Spencer, Robert Roseboom and the choice of the doggedly Federalist eastern district, John Sanders.

Now Ambrose Spencer, related by marriage to the Livingston family, had been a Federalist himself until 1798, and a worker heart and soul with and for that party. In 1798, indeed, he had closed a year's office as a Federalist member of a Council of Appointment which was predominantly of that political color.

It was at this juncture that he had changed over to the side of the Republicans—some said because of the familiar disappointment at not receiving office (in his case that of Comptroller, which had gone to Samuel Jones). He himself staunchly denied the insinuation, declaring that his honest change of sentiment had become known long before Jones' appointment. In any event, whether it was love for Republicanism or no, it is certain that he conceived an abiding personal admiration for the youthful De Witt Clinton, and willingly fell into the rôle of his disciple. With Roseboom, who represented the western district, such a rôle was a foregone conclusion. Clintonian and not outstanding, he had been something of a political pawn in the race to secure a Republican majority in the Council. Add to this Clinton's abounding intellectual achievement, his family prestige, his already preeminent and dominant personality and his uncompromising straightforwardness, and the matter becomes more easily understandable.

Professor McBain, in his defense of Clinton's political principles and practices,[1] has this to say of him as he advances so abruptly into the spotlight:

> Young, energetic, dominating, it is not far to seek why such a revolution of politics should have swept him to the front, and it is even more easily understood why he should have left upon that revolution the imprint of his forceful personality. Both in his public and his private life his morals were good, but he had none of the sentimentalism that halted before the shattering of a precedent which he conceived to be ill-founded. He seldom broke forth into explanation of his plans or theories, but he had little to hide and was never unscrupulous. His mind was big, but his sympathies could not be played upon. He was ambitious of leadership but most of his ambitions were justified by his superior ability. He lacked perhaps the theoretic constructiveness of mind necessary to a great statesman, but he certainly was far above the intrigue and cunning of the mere politician....

As for the party line-up, Aaron Burr, that increasingly great factor, who had selected with the utmost care and skill a State Republican ticket composed of all the component parts of State strength, was about to assume the Vice-President's chair at the newly-ready city of Washington. The Republicans in New York

[1] "De Witt Clinton and the Origin of the Spoils System in New York," by Howard Lee McBain. Columbia University Press, New York; 1907.

were left in need of a vigorous leader as never before, to set their new and somewhat overwhelming powers in adequate motion. A Senate majority had not as yet been achieved. A strong majority in the Assembly, achieved largely by a judicious use of the still potent Clinton name, reposed its faith in the holders of that name.

Governor Jay's term of office, under the existing constitution, did not expire until July 1st, 1801. On February 11th, 1801, the new Council of Appointment met, with John Jay in the chair.

It must be recalled that since 1795 the Federalists had held uninterrupted sway in New York, and their system of appointments and removals had been such that when the Republicans came into power, all important State offices, and a great majority of the minor ones, were in the hands of members of the defeated party; for the wide sweep of the Council's power of patronage embraced a multitude of appointments, extending from that of Secretary of State to those of County Clerks and Sheriffs and even Notaries Public. And to John Jay's Councils, if not to John Jay himself, patronage had been more than a word. It was now to be Governor Jay's misfortune to come into conflict with a Council of Appointment whose leading member was determined to bring about a more equitable array of office-holders.

It so happened that Jay, when he first took office, had asked for an "explanatory enactment" as to the meaning of that clause in the State Constitution of 1777 which referred to the appointive power. The terms of the clause were somewhat vague, merely vesting that power in the Governor "with the advice and concurrence" of the Council, and giving to the Governor a casting vote, but no other. It was Jay's opinion that the Governor had the sole right of nomination, and throughout his consecutive terms of office as such he unfailingly assumed that right. But he wanted the point ruled on for the good of future government. His party, however, shied away, embarrassed, from the proposal. A Federalist Council had lately claimed the concurrent right of nomination with George Clinton. The party could not very well declare themselves for Jay on the same point now, even to make its own future safer. The Federalists in the Legislature therefore declined, being in the majority, and the question remained unsettled.

The possibilities of the powers of the patronage, broad as it was, remained unbounded. Governor Jay, despite his failure to obtain an enactment defining his right to the sole nominating power, had continued to exercise that right by virtue of successive Federalist majorities in the Council of Appointment. He intended to go on exercising it for as long as his final term of office endured.... But in this he had reckoned without his host.

De Witt Clinton, as the mouthpiece of the majority in the new Council, immediately put himself and his colleagues on record as disputing this right which the Governor claimed. Forthwith, the Governor put the matter to the test by placing in nomination one Jesse Thompson for the office of Sheriff of Dutchess County. The Republicans in the Council as promptly refused their consent to the appointment. They repeated their action each time Mr. Jay placed some one in nomination for the office.

There followed a number of minor agreements; but a crisis was inevitable, and it came. The Governor attempted to have his nominations entered upon the minutes of the Council. The majority of the Council immediately refused his request, on the ground that the right of nomination did not, under the Constitution, rest exclusively with him. Thenceforward—but the period was not to be long—the Council consistently negatived the names offered by the Governor; and the Governor as persistently vetoed those put before him by them, accusing them eventually of thus wishing to exclude him even from a concurrent right.

On February 24th De Witt Clinton came out with an express motion for the appointment of John Blake, Jr., a Republican, to the office of Sheriff of Orange County, thus formally registering his theory and his claim. Jay, confronted with this situation, delayed the putting of the question, and asked time to consider his course. The Council was adjourned. Jay never reconvened it. A great number of offices remained without incumbents until after his term had expired. The quarrel had had reference only to the filling of existing vacancies under the law prescribing the duration of the various periods of office. No removals of Federalists had been attempted so far. Jay and Clinton had fought over a principle, and achieved a deadlock.

On February 26th, Governor Jay sent a message to both houses of the Legislature, the gist of which was that owing to the late proceedings of the Council of Appointment, it had become indispensable that the question of the right of nomination and the express point as to the power of exercising it be settled forthwith in a manner conformable to the Constitution. He promised to guide himself by any enactment or judgment that should thus be passed.

This time the Federalists, who six years before had refused a declaratory act, were in favor of the request; and it was a Republican resolution in the negative that was successfully pushed through the Legislature. Jay thereupon addressed the judiciary upon the question, and asked them for advice. But Chancellor Livingston and Chief Justice Lansing pleaded the right of their department to stay out of questions affecting the executive, which might oblige them similarly to enter into those connected with the Legislature and ultimately into purely political controversies.

The deadlock thus continuing, the Council decided that its own side of the question needed airing. It proceeded to air it in a lengthy statement of the history, nature and merits of its claim, which was now expressly stated to be that a concurrent right of nomination had been tendered by the Council in courtesy to the Governor, but that in reality the *exclusive* right, by the terms of the Constitution, was vested in the Council....

The Governor tried again to have the matter settled by the Legislature, or brought before the Supreme Court, but all his efforts failed. The Federalist majority in the Senate continued to support him, and there were some acrimonious debates. The same majority moved, and passed, a resolution calling for a settlement of the question, and expressing the view that it would be proper for the Council to waive the controversy and proceed to business.

De Witt Clinton, in his capacity as a member of the Senate, sprang to arms. He moved a counter-resolution, hot and impassioned, reviling the suggestion that so weighty a question of law could be so "wantonly" and prematurely and unconstitutionally decided. Under persuasion he moderated his tone, but the Federalist resolution was handed to the Assembly, which, by the voice of Erastus Root, radical lawyer-legislator, repeated a former Assembly's resolution of non-interference.

There followed violent and prolonged recrimination between Senate and Assembly, and in the very greatest heat of the encounter the session ended. Then it was the newspapers' turn to take up the fight, and the current gubernatorial election, in which George Clinton was the victor, duly became the center of it.

Governor Clinton took the oath of office in Albany on July 1st, 1801, as the existing Constitution of the State required him to do. At the first subsequent meeting of the Council of Appointment, on August 8th (according to the then Secretary of the Council, Daniel Hale, a Federalist but still Secretary of State),[1] De Witt Clinton raised his voice, and

> ... expressed a wish to make some observations to the council. ... He observed, that for some years past, the administration of this State had been in hands which had made all the appointments in one way, to the entire exclusion of a large proportion of its citizens—that the people of this State as well as of the United States, had expressed their disapprobation of that administration, and of the principles by which it was governed, in the late elections for President of the United States, and the Chief Magistrate and Representatives for this State—that pursuant to the public opinion so expressed, he should feel it his duty to remove all the officers appointed under that administration—that he should concur in the removal of ... the ... Heads of Departments in the State, but did not suppose it would be proper to do more than equalize the officers in the respective counties.

In other words, the major offices were to be filled with Republicans, and the minor offices were to be divided equally between the party in power and the defeated party. There are further writings in Clinton's hand which show him desirous of giving the defeated party offices in proportion to their new representation. This is the policy which the Council now adopted, and in the perspective of political time and political evolution it appears a fairly magnanimous one. Had it been pursued throughout the years as closely as Clinton pursued it in 1801, many abuses and many enmities might never have been. At the moment, however, it was, put into plain words, revolutionary. Moreover, it meant, in effect, the turning of familiar tables on the Federalist party. And finally, and perhaps most significantly, it indicated that the young spokesman of the Council of Appointment was going to pursue a similar course with respect to the new Governor, allowing for the bonds of kinship and political sympathies and affection, as he had taken with the old....

He began, as a matter of course, with New York City, the traditional stronghold of Federalism in the State. He gave Richard Varick's place as Mayor to Edward Livingston; John Stagg

[1] As reported by the Albany *Gazette*, August 13th, 1801.

was appointed Sheriff; Sylvanus Miller (who was to be a lifelong personal friend of De Witt Clinton) was made Surrogate; and he filled as many of the remaining offices with Republicans as lay within his immediate power. But there were still no removals of officers whose terms were fixed under the law. Only those whose terms had expired were replaced according to the plan expressed by De Witt Clinton. It was only in the offices held at the pleasure of the Council that removals were made. These were of course the more important State offices, and some of the major city posts. The sole major officer who was in fact not removed was Josiah Ogden Hoffman—a Federalist and a former friend of the apostate Ambrose Spencer. That he continued a friend of Spencer's seems to have been the case. That Spencer eventually succeeded him in the office of Attorney-General, which he then held, gave rise subsequently to the rumor of a "deal" between these gentlemen to account for the singling out of Hoffman in the aforementioned manner.

And so it went on, the policy announced by Clinton being fairly literally pursued, even in the highly Federalist eastern district. There were, as a matter of fact, protests against such scrupulous good faith. Where the party needed strengthening, said the Republican press, without leaving much doubt as to its meaning, it was to be hoped that it would be strengthened. A portion of that press went so far as to voice the opinion that the "violent opposition" was being treated considerably better than it deserved.

Meanwhile it is to be noted that George Clinton, the Governor, was exhibiting considerable reluctance to remove any man because of his political opinions. The embryo statesmen who had officiated at the birth of the nation, himself among them, had certainly had their differences, but each man's opinion had at least been respected by his neighbors, and the thought of punishing any one for the way he thought was still abhorrent to this particular New York gentleman, who with all his arts was no politician. He was well used, however, to bowing before the pressure of a recalcitrant Council. He was keenly alive at all times to the necessity for smooth functioning of the government. And his faith and pride in his nephew were still unbounded. Nevertheless he withheld his signature, or registered his protest, on several occasions upon the minutes of the Council.

But that Council now functioned only through De Witt Clinton. When, in October of 1801, the latter was taken ill in New York City, its functioning came to a virtual standstill, and there is in existence a letter in the Governor's hand, urging his nephew to return speedily, as the other members refused to act without him.

In the Federalist press De Witt Clinton was now stigmatized as an "unprincipled tyrant," along with his friend Spencer. The two were accused of desiring judicial plums for themselves. The Governor was dubbed a weakling, for not preventing the numerous removals. And so on. But the question of Governor vs. Council was in process of being settled at last. In the height of the controversies of the previous spring, a bill had passed recommending the calling of a convention to limit the membership of the twin branches of the Legislature, the increase in population having made the earlier provisions for the purpose disproportionate. At the end of March there had been added to this an amendment extending the powers of the convention to that of deciding "whether any and what alterations should be made in the Twenty-third Article of the Constitution" (which was, of course, the article dealing with the Council of Appointment). This became law in April, and in October, 1801, the convention met, with James Clinton and George Clinton, Jr., his youngest son, among the delegates. De Witt Clinton was prevented from being present by the illness already referred to, and was still confined to his home at Newtown on October 24th, when the convention was in session.

Aaron Burr came to New York to act as president throughout the proceedings of the convention. Daniel D. Tompkins, as a fledgling politician, was there, voting with the minority. The vote itself seems to have been non-partisan, which is understandable, and the result was:

> that by the construction of the twenty-third article of the Constitution of this State, the right to nominate all officers, other than those who by the Constitution are directed to be otherwise appointed, is vested concurrently in the person administering the government of this State for the time being, and in each of the Members of the Council of Appointment.

Which meant not only that Republicans still shied away from vesting individual power in the executive, but that De Witt

Clinton, whether he was present or not, had scored another political victory, as his kinsmen and friends did not fail to inform him forthwith. He was, nevertheless, to live to rue the day....

Meanwhile there remained in New York the Clintons and the Livingstons; and also, even in *absentia,* Aaron Burr. The Schuylers and their Hamilton were fairly in the descendant. The last phase of the American Revolution, as Claude G. Bowers remarks in his "Jefferson and Hamilton," was over. With Jefferson's victory, democracy ruled. Hamilton's greater work was done. He still was hailed as the financial giant, the patriotic benefactor. His colleagues still numbered among their ranks the greatest statesmen of the day; but his party, the erstwhile mighty Federalist group—"perhaps the most brilliant and certainly the most attractive in American history," as Bowers says—was defeated completely enough to render it nationally a mild menace thereafter, and ultimately to divide it until a dozen factions would absorb it.

Of the ruling party in New York, the Clintons had sprung into the power of local patronage; and because the Livingstons, by force of numbers and prestige, in deserting the Federalist standard to embrace Clintonianism had contributed enormously to the ultimate result, De Witt, in his handing out of offices, did not forget them or any of their pro-Republican kin. The Clinton-Livingston accord was for the moment complete.

There was also Aaron Burr, who felt he had done even more than the Livingstons to place the Clintons where they were. When Burr, emerging from the hysterical and nationwide fracas which had been brought about by a tie between himself and Jefferson in the Presidential election, had ultimately been given the second place, his party in New York had almost deafened him with acclaim. Jefferson first and Burr second was what they wished (with the few but potent exceptions of Burr's rather silently-working lieutenants). A little later, however, some doubts as to Burr's good faith in the recent contest crept in. Evidences were forthcoming that Mr. Burr had desired the first, not the second, seat for himself, and soon correspondence and verbal testimony gave force to the suspicion that he had secretly worked to that end. New York's electoral voice was mighty in the nation, Burr's almost as mighty in the State.... And Presidential electors were still chosen by legislative caucus in New York....

The Clinton-Livingston faction, very strong for the President, weighed the evidence against Mr. Burr and promptly disowned him. It is probable that this was a step that they took with considerable relief. The tremendous triumph which Burr in person had won over George Clinton in the late Presidential campaign could not but still have rankled in the mind of the Governor. The thought that a dangerous rival for ultimate State leadership was thus being more or less eliminated could not have been absent either from the mind of the Governor's nephew or from those of the heads of the house of Livingston. For Burr was by no means wholly engrossed in his Vice-Presidential job. He had, however, never been wholly trusted, even by the leading lights of his own party; and the evidence of his secret influence in the late Presidential voting had confirmed a great many earlier suspicions. Also as Vice-President he had been working sedulously to influence the Federal appointments in New York in favor of some of his personal henchmen, though without conspicuous success.

As for his opponents, the most prominent, as he was to be the most tragic, Alexander Hamilton, had come right out with an expression of preference for his greater rival, Thomas Jefferson, if it came to a choice between him and Aaron Burr. "His (Burr's) elevation can only promote the purposes of the desperate and the profligate," wrote Hamilton to his colleague, Gouverneur Morris, from "an intimate and accurate knowledge of his character." "If there be a man in the world I ought to hate, it is Jefferson. With Burr I have always been personally well. But the public good must be paramount to every private consideration."

Those were now definitely the sentiments of the leaders of Burr's own party in New York. They were, beyond question, upright men; politicians always, perhaps, some of them; politicians never, others. And among the latter the Clintons must be numbered, if the word "politician" is to be taken in its less flattering modern sense.... But out of their new policy of exclusion—in vehement protest against it—there sprang up the group first known as the Burrites. The friends of that somewhat complex, somewhat fascinating personality were staunch and able and not too few; and their subsequent ramifications and additions were to come from outside in proportion as disaffection toward the Clintons waxed or waned. Thus, in brief, came the first division in the New York Republican party.

On January 29th, 1802, the existing Council of Appointment, being by the Constitution limited to a consecutive term of office of twelve months, gave place to another group; and it was at this precise juncture that Dr. Mitchill, then a member of the House of Representatives of the United States, wrote to Governor Clinton that a successor would have to be found forthwith for General John Armstrong of New York, who was about retiring from the United States Senate on account of ill-health. The matter of the replacement was urgent, said he, because the Republicans in Congress were desirous of collecting their full strength to put through the repeal of President Adams' Judiciary Bill....

The New York Legislature complied with the utmost speed; but it was six days after the repeal bill had passed that De Witt Clinton, having marked the close of his term as State Senator by moving a resolution for that change in the mode of choosing President and Vice-President which was shortly afterwards to be embodied as an amendment in the Constitution of the United States, found himself elected United States Senator, and bundled off to the Capital in some haste.

He came there at a somewhat thrilling moment. Jefferson, by his victory at the polls, had gained the right to lead, to show the way to—what? A nation, as it turned out, drunk, momentarily at least, with the triumph of the common man. Debt was rampant, and lawlessness was too. Men of the faith, strong men to help Jefferson in this dismaying state of affairs, were so few as to be lost in the cheaper crowd. Indeed, had the new President himself been a little less great, a little less of a personality and of a genius at coördination, Hamiltonianism might well have triumphed yet again, and democratic government waited long.

As it was, President Jefferson was proving equal to his colossal task, and it was a new United States that was in the building.

A thrilling moment indeed for a tyro to be entering the Capitol as Senator; with Gouverneur Morris, the Federalist veteran, as his colleague from New York....

De Witt Clinton was not quite thirty-three years old.

7

U. S. SENATOR

1802-1803

My nephew, Mr. De Witt Clinton, will have the honor of delivering you this letter. Permit me to recommend him to your friendly notice.... It is reasonable to conclude that I feel partiality for him, as well from the consanguinity that exists between us, as from his having, at an early period of life, been of my family, in the confidential capacity of my private secretary. But I can with great truth, assure you that these considerations have no influence upon me in giving you his character. His present appointment (which was from a large majority) as well as different elective advantages he had previously filled, afford good evidence of his possessing the confidence of his fellow-citizens. His political principles are pure, and he has too much dignity ever to deviate from them; nor will you find him destitute of talents and information.

THUS GOVERNOR GEORGE CLINTON to President Thomas Jefferson on February 9th, 1802. The letter is of uncommon interest, not only for its affectionate expression of opinion, but also in view of the fact that Henry Adams, in his "History of the United States during the Administrations of Jefferson and Madison," charges collusion between President Jefferson and De Witt Clinton in the matter of driving out Burr at the beginning of Jefferson's first administration—namely, in 1801. No proof is adduced. No fragment of evidence exists, or at least has come to light, that Clinton ever communicated with Jefferson until he carried his uncle's letter to that dignitary in 1802. On the contrary, the letter seems itself proof positive that he did not, and there is evidence that he had refused to approach the President in behalf of an aspirant for a Federal office, though his uncle's

Courtesy of Justice Phoenix Ingraham

DE WITT CLINTON

Probably by John Wesley Jarvis

influence by virtue of his position and history was both recognized and utilized in Washington. Henry Adams seems to have been led astray by the similarity between Jefferson's early practices in the matter of patronage and Clinton's, and of Jefferson's subsequent appointive course to the more local one of Clinton. He appears to class the reduction of Federalist power on the one hand and the destruction of Burr on the other as twin parts of a concerted plan. But Burr destroyed himself; and the new President's theories along the line of patronage were matters of public record. Above all, De Witt Clinton was established as his disciple and admirer. They possessed a great deal in common; and one further mutual viewpoint was to be made manifest before Mr. Clinton's service in the United States Senate came to an end.

That first session he appears to have played the rôle of listener and of initiate mainly. In the summer he retraced his steps, for a brief but vital period, to New York. His family was young and was increasing. His wife and babies were remaining in New York while he entered the Washingtonian fray. Therefore he hastened home to join them at Newtown on Long Island, to fill his soul with that which was always to be its greatest joy, the affection of his lady and of his children.

But there was war in the air of New York that summer—political war, and personal combat too.... Three years before, Aaron Burr, by a masterpiece of characteristic political maneuvering, had managed to put through the New York Legislature an act "for supplying the city of New York with pure and wholesome water." Now, a water supply was something New York had needed for many a year. Just before the Revolution, Christopher Colles, an Irish-born engineer, had advanced a scheme for transforming the Collect Pond into a reservoir and for piping the city, and had been authorized and subsidized to proceed. But war intervening, nothing further had been done, and New Yorkers continued to go to the pump to replenish their buckets, and to patronize the men with the barrels for water a little less brackish to drink.

Burr's bill, therefore, fell on grateful enough ears, even in a still largely Federalist legislature. The yellow fever had been playing havoc in the city. Pure water, if it could be obtained, would be a blessing literally unadulterated. But what the aforementioned ears failed to take in were the implications of that clause in the bill which authorized the Manhattan Company, formed for the business of supplying water, to utilize the surplus of its funds for "any constitutional purposes."

The result—almost the net result—was the organization and opening of the Manhattan Bank. The Federalists so far had controlled the only institution of the kind in New York City—the Bank of New York. They had also controlled in the nation Mr. Hamilton's bitterly-fought Bank of the United States. In 1799, Burr, as the god of the Republican machine, had felt, with considerable justification, that financial power was being wielded by the "Feds" both nationally and locally to their own advantage. He decided that the Republican party, by hook or by crook, should contrive to place itself in a similar position of influence. By hook or by crook Burr contrived it. Unsuspicious Federalists, who would never in the world have granted him his real desire, voted "aye" to his bill, and when the truth came out a political pandemonium broke loose. Unenlightened Republicans gave it both party and financial support, and were hardly less shocked by the subterfuge; for political subterfuge was still rather novel in these legislative halls. The more enlightened Republicans—Burr's personal following—were delighted; and Burr had his bank—till 1802.

In 1802, the Clintons and the Livingstons, following their aforementioned proscription of that gentleman, turned Aaron Burr and his closest friend, John Swartwout, out of the directorate of the Manhattan Company. Recriminations, denunciations, insults, poured from both sides. Swartwout openly accused De Witt Clinton of wishing to destroy Mr. Burr in order to further his own ambitions. De Witt Clinton (one of the Manhattan Company stockholders), exhibiting his first and perhaps his most serious lack of control over a hasty and frequently bitter tongue, called Mr. Swartwout "a liar, a scoundrel and a villain." Swartout promptly wrote a letter challenging Clinton to retract or to make redress, and sent it to Clinton by the hand of Colonel William Stephens Smith, the son-in-law of John Adams. Clinton replied that he had uttered the words complained of by Swartwout in the full belief that Mr. Swartwout had accused him of unworthy motives in proscribing Aaron Burr. If Mr. Swartwout would deny that he had made such an accusation, wrote Mr. Clinton, the words would be immediately retracted.

Mr. Swartwout made no denial, and on July 28th, 1802, Richard Riker, then acting Attorney-General of the State and a close friend of the Clintons, called on Colonel Smith at Mr. Clinton's request. Mr. Riker tried his very best to effect a compromise, embodying Clinton's former request for a mutual retraction in a paper which he offered for Smith's and his principal's approval. But Swartwout would have none of it. He demanded that Mr. Clinton should sign a certificate to the effect that he had made assertions with regard to Mr. Swartwout that were "intemperate and unfounded," and that he offered his apologies to Mr. Swartwout....

The result was a duel, which took place in a field on the Jersey shore in the late afternoon of July 31st, 1802. (The law already prohibited the fighting of duels in the State of New York.) The gentlemen rowed to the scene in barges, accompanied by Smith and Riker as their respective seconds, and by a surgeon and four "confidential" oarsmen apiece. Mr. Clinton had been on Long Island, and did not see the arrangements and rules made by the seconds for the encounter until a short time before he actually arrived upon the scene. When he had perused them, he asked that one clause be changed. Swartwout desired that he and his opponent should stand back to back; then turn, and, on the command, fire. Mr. Clinton said he wished to *face* his adversary; that he was not used to turning. But Mr. Swartwout, on being consulted, said it was too late to change, and the fight must go on according to the arrangements.

So the distance was measured, and Colonel Smith won the toss for the privilege of "giving the words." He gave them distinctly. The two men, standing back to back, with the measured-off greensward between them, whirled on the command; and fired. Neither fire found its mark, but Clinton, through his second, immediately asked Swartwout whether he was satisfied. He requested Mr. Riker to say that he bore Mr. Swartwout no personal resentment, and would be willing to meet him on the terms of their original friendship, which had been both equable and of long standing.

The message was relayed through Smith, and brought a curt refusal; whereupon the pistols were reloaded and the same scene was enacted again. On the third fire, Swartwout whirled a little before the time, and fired before Clinton. His bullet passed through Mr. Clinton's coat, but the latter steadily repeated his statement that this was no matter of personal enmity with him, and if honor was satisfied, he did not wish to go on shooting at a man whom he did not desire to injure. Mr. Swartwout disdained this advance like the others, demanding an apology or full satisfaction; and the duel went on, with Clinton a little angered at being presented again with the certificate that he had already refused to sign.

"I would sooner fire all night," he said, then, and he took his pistol from Riker's hand for the fourth time.

But this time both he and Swartwout took careful aim. And this time the fact that he was the better shot became immediately apparent. His bullet hit Swartwout in the leg, and the blood began to flow, so that Swartwout's physician, Dr. Douglass, was allowed to approach him and to inspect the wound.

By the seventh clause of the arrangements for the duel, if a surgeon extracted a bullet from the person of either of the combatants, the duel was to be deemed at an end. But Dr. Douglass, deftly and unobserved by Swartwout's opponent or his second, took out the ball that had passed almost through Swartwout's leg; and Swartwout rose and loudly demanded that the duel should go on.

It was Riker, this time, who was reluctant. The doctors both looked anxious, and Mr. Swartwout was exceedingly pale.

"Sir, Mr. Clinton bears you no resentment," said Riker, through the medium of Colonel Smith. "He is sorry for what has passed, and will meet you on the score of original friendship."

But Swartwout said no; he was not satisfied. He declared it useless to repeat the question; whereupon Clinton turned toward the doctors and the seconds:

"I beg you all to bear witness. I have no enmity to Mr. Swartwout, and I am compelled to shoot at a man whom I do not wish to hurt; but I will sign no paper—I will not dishonor myself."

And the fifth shot was fired; and once more Clinton's bullet hit Swartwout in the leg. Once more Swartwout, his boot now sodden with blood, demanded that the fight go on. But Mr. Clinton's doctor, Ledyard, at last protested.

"Mr. Clinton," he cried, from the bank, "don't fire again! Mr. Swartwout wants our assistance."

Clinton hesitated; took a step or two from his position. Satisfaction among gentlemen was so delicate a matter.... He asked the doctor whether it would be right for him to fire, and Ledyard again emphatically said no. He turned to Riker, and Riker, perplexed, looked at the doctors—at Smith—at Swartwout ... then made up his own mind, and Clinton's.

"Mr. Clinton shall not fire again," he said; and the doctors advanced on Swartwout as Clinton put his pistol aside. Riker himself ran to aid them, as they gave the wounded man brandy preparatory to pulling off his boot and performing the heroic and unalleviated ministrations of their calling. He helped get Swartwout into his barge, and then he went home and duly wrote out his view of the entire proceedings for the benefit of the New York *Spectator,* in which periodical his statement appeared on August 7th, five days after Smith had given his version in the *Gazette and Daily Advertiser.* Both are mentioned in a letter from De Witt's brother Charles to his father, which gives the family's view of the affair as follows:

> I send you papers giving both accounts of the duel between De Witt and Swartwout, which I received today. Col[l]. Smith tells the truth, but it appears by Mr. Riker's account, he does not tell the whole truth. You can judge by Mr. Riker's statement that the Burr party were determined to sacrifice De Witt, at the risk of one of the party—but they have failed, and should they not be yet satisfied, enough will be found to give them the same satisfaction.
>
> Yours affectionately,
>
> CHARLES CLINTON.

Now Colonel Smith's account, which he repeated and emphasized in the *Spectator* a few days later, showed merely that Clinton had quit the fight. The insinuation was that he had done so because he was a coward.... This was a point of view that it is perhaps understandable for the Burrite press to publish, but Colonel Smith, a Federalist and therefore with no sympathies save that of personal friendship for Swartwout, should have known better. Dr. Ledyard promptly made himself heard with a simple statement that Clinton had shown both bravery and humanity throughout; and more, that to have continued, in view of Swartwout's condition, would have placed Mr. Clinton in danger of committing an act which he would have regretted all his life. Riker in his turn pointed out that Mr. Clinton was quite obviously a far better shot than Mr. Swartwout, and inferred that, what was more, Mr. Clinton knew it. And he made public for the first time an incident that had taken place after the battle was over and Swartwout was reclining on the stone, bleeding profusely:

Mr. Clinton had advanced toward his adversary, who was half-sitting, half-lying upon a bowlder, and held out his hand.

"I am sorry I have hurt you so much," he said; then, turning to Smith and Riker: "I don't want to hurt him; but I wish I had the *principal* here. I will meet him when he pleases."

"Let us say no more about it," said Colonel Smith; and the affair was over.

As a matter of record, Clinton, whose personal bravery was to be proven on countless occasions, abhorred the practice of duelling. Like many of his contemporaries, he deplored the fact that a man might not refuse a challenge to mortal combat without being branded a coward. Like many, he chose the combat rather than the stigma; but he invariably gave compromise a chance, and on at least one later occasion he dared to refuse (which was bravery personified) because he did not consider his adversary worthy of the powder and shot.

The New York papers had by no means done with the late affair, however. The Burrite press said that the Clintonian faction regarded De Witt Clinton as their idol, and that they placed his name and his fame before all—Jefferson included. His friends (according to the same authority) were liars and parasites and sycophants to a man; not the least his late second, Mr. Riker. The rumor that Clinton's election to the United States Senate had been a prearranged affair between the Republican leaders and General Armstrong had its rise now, and died hard in spite of the known ill-health of the latter as well as his unimpeachable character, to say nothing of the irrefutable documentary evidence that the call for his successor and the choice of Clinton had occurred in consecutive order.

On the other hand, a recently established New York paper called the *American Citizen* was flinging the views and the news of Clinton at Aaron Burr every day, and bitterly attacking the political and private character of the latter. The editor was James Cheetham, a gentleman of nimble pen and sometimes equally nimble imagination—though in truth there was both force and substance behind the growing doubts as to Burr's good faith.

Burr's chief medium, the *Morning Chronicle,* replied by extending its condemnations to embrace both the Livingstons and the Clintons. It held Burr up to the public gaze as a tower of righteousness and light. A virulent pamphlet appeared, signed with the name "Aristides," and devoted to an attack on the public and private characters of De Witt Clinton and Ambrose Spencer. Its author was subsequently identified as William P. Van Ness.

But Burr's was a losing side. As time went on, more and more Republican journals began to follow the lead of the *Citizen* against him. It became increasingly plain that he was losing the good faith of the general run of his party by reason of his peculiar political methods, which seemed to favor himself fairly consistently as against that party. Before the next Presidential election took place, his political procedure had given rise to the amendment to the Constitution above referred to, requiring Presidential and Vice-Presidential candidates to be named and voted for as such.... As Burr receded from the forefront of the picture, a little active rivalry sprang up between the supremely ambitious Livingstons and the supremely popular and powerful Clintons. But in the midst of this development, De Witt Clinton went back to Washington and his duties as a member of the United States Senate as presided over by Vice-President Aaron Burr....

C. J. Ingersoll, in his "Recollections," refers to the United States Senate of the period as "a parody of the House of Lords." Its immediate prestige, however, was not even a parody of that of the august British body. With the voice of the common man triumphant, the more direct representatives of the common man were literally, as an entity, the popular branch of the Government. The Senate still lured men of ambition as a field for personal effort and as a stepping-stone to a greater future. But at the moment it was considerably handicapped by an almost equal division between Federalist and Republican members, so many Federalist senators being in process of completing their unexpired terms. Coördination in action therefore resided in the House of Representatives, where the Jefferson sweep was of course more universally manifest.

Nevertheless, vibrant moments were approaching in 1802, and an even division of the parties did not make the Senate debates less exciting from the point of view of the newspapers, lately admitted to witness and report the deliberations of that body for the first time in the brief history of the Union. The President's course of action with respect to a France now ruled by the all-conquering Napoleon and a Spain recently thrown into the complete power of that hero, enhanced the excitement to a breathless anticipation of crises yet to come. They came. Spain, colonizing in Louisiana, prohibited the use of the southern outlet of the Mississippi to the United States, impelled thereto most irresistibly by Bonaparte. Louisiana was a cherished dream of Bonaparte's. It was not yet even a dream to the United States; but the necessity for an outlet from the Mississippi was a stern reality, and the Spanish order was a direct breach of the treaty of 1795, which gave the United States the right to navigate the Mississippi from its source to the sea, and to deposit merchandise at New Orleans. On the instant, therefore, there arose, not a question of right, which all parties conceded, but a question, bitterly agitated, of the manner in which this indispensable end was to be brought about. President Jefferson called for an appropriation of two million dollars with which to negotiate for the purchase of New Orleans and the Floridas. He had, as Ingersoll expresses it, "an insuperáble aversion to war at almost any cost," and in view of the aspersions surrounding De Witt Clinton's subsequent bid for the seat at that moment occupied by Mr. Jefferson, the former's method of coöperating with the President at this juncture is perhaps of especial significance. Significant enough, however, that on the Mississippi question, which ultimately led to the Louisiana Purchase, De Witt Clinton, one of the youngest men ever to have taken a seat in that body, made himself signally heard in the Senate of the United States.

A motion had been advanced by the Federalist James Ross, of Pennsylvania, setting forth the absolute economic necessity for enforcing the right of the United States to utilize the southern outlet of the Mississippi. It voiced the aggressions of the Spanish rulers of Louisiana, and the crippling of United States commerce in that vicinity by the closing of the southern ports. It called for seizure of New Orleans, and the right of deposit there, vociferously claiming that if war should be the inevitable result of such seizure, war would have been inevitable in any case. This was the general stand of the Federalist members—this and a bitter antagonism to the views of Thomas Jefferson.

The bill for the appropriation of the funds requested had already passed the House of Representatives. It had yet to be officially presented to the Senate. Ross, a handsome but unpolished gentleman of Scotch-Irish descent, was considered by some the ablest man in Pennsylvania, and was a veteran Senator. He drew a grim picture of Bonaparte, whose rapacious clutch was already upon the Spaniards' Mississippi territory. He scoffed at the notion that Napoleon would sell the right to navigate the Mississippi to a nation that had no arms, no ships, no means of compelling him to let them through without. And he wanted the two million dollars, theretofore only discussed in secret by this branch of the Congress, to be expended on methods of compulsion and not in "bribery" or useless negotiation. He said this was what the settlers of the western frontier of the United States most urgently desired. He said they would revolt and go over to the enemy if they were not aided in this way....

Samuel White of Delaware followed, and read the order of the Spanish Governor of Baton Rouge, forbidding the inhabitants of Louisiana to purchase from or sell to the people of the United States.

John Breckinridge, Republican, of Kentucky, then offered a middle scheme—to prepare adequately for war, but to pursue the peaceable negotiation to its conclusion before taking armed means. He denied emphatically that there was danger of losing the settlers of the West....

> The next speaker (says Ingersoll) was De Witt Clinton, large, handsome, and grave young man, then in the flower of his age and rising eminence, grown up in opposition inherited to Jay, Hamilton and the whole Federal party of New York....

Mr. Clinton, unlike the majority of the Senators around him, had prepared his speech. It was thorough, it was well-organized, it was subdued. He would, he told his hearers, leave Mr. Ross and Mr. White to their "inflammatory appeals and their declamatory effusions." He went into the history of warfare and the history of diplomacy between nations, and pronounced Ross' resolutions a declaration of war. He cited precedent after precedent for peaceable negotiation in a situation such as that in which the United States at the moment found herself. He showed that international usage demanded that diplomatic demand for satisfaction should precede and if possible prevent an open break. He told what a war would cost—a hundred million dollars was his estimate; and he said the United States should rather deprecate a policy of aggression than pursue one. The United States, he declared, must not become a nation lusty for conquest. He said if Louisiana were to be seized, Florida would be the next goal, and then Cuba.... He said a spirit of greed for territory would serve his country ill, and that seizure by force of the territory of Louisiana, before any peaceable demands had been made, was not effecting a satisfactory solution of the Mississippi question, but was fostering such a spirit. He scorned the suggestion of disunion, and said that in the West

> such is the predominant love of union that all Western members of Congress latterly elected are avowed supporters of the present administration. And in Mr. Ross's State, following his total defeat, not a single member will there be in the next Congress of his party. With negotiation comes time for preparation; if the former fails, the latter may be effectual.

Jonathan Dayton, Federalist, of New Jersey, defended Mr. Ross, and William Cocke, Republican, of Tennessee, denounced him. During the continuance of the debate next day, which wound up with the adoption of the Breckinridge resolutions, Gouverneur Morris arose....

A commanding figure, Mr. Morris. Unimpeded by the loss of a leg in an act of civilian gallantry (as it is said), he sported a wooden member in its place, and managed to make it a not unsightly part of an imposing, even an elegant, appearance. Veteran of the Revolution and of French royal diplomatic excellences, he honored his period by continuing to powder his hair in the face of Thomas Jefferson and his "*citoyens*." The power of his tongue was still great, though he had no hope whatever of renewing his expiring Senatorial term. His message was: Contend with the Gallic Cæsar, or submit, as so many have done, to his lust for power, for territory.

With regard to his young companion from New York, he was pleased to be sarcastic:

> I will not pretend, like my honorable colleague, to describe to you the waste, the ravages and the horrors of war; I have not the same harmonious periods, nor the same musical tones; neither shall I boast of Christian charity, nor attempt to display that ingenuous glow of benevolence so decorous to the cheek of youth, which gave a vivid tint to every sentence he uttered, and was, if possible, as impressive even as his eloquence.

Morris' demeanor toward Clinton was not of the most benevolent. He was, as has been said, a man of some vanity, besides being a seasoned parliamentarian of the defeated opposition party. Youth stepping in at that juncture could be nothing to him but upstart youth—particularly a youth of such promise; particularly, moreover, one who had been anti-Federalist from his political birth. However, their extra-Congressional relations were harmonious. Indeed, there was only one untoward encounter in all of Senator Clinton's Washington experience. Jonathan Dayton, soldier, pioneer and also a personal friend of Aaron Burr, chose to pick a quarrel with Clinton on the floor of the Senate—a quarrel that would have ended bloodily outside the Senate, had mutual friends not stepped in and successfully averted a duel. It tainted, for Clinton, the latter part of a connection with the Capital that was otherwise filled with honors and satisfactions. An all too fleeting connection, it was to be. For when Jefferson, without relinquishing his pacific policy in the least degree, found himself with not only New Orleans, but the whole vast territory of Louisiana (on the subject of whose quite glorious potentialities he was yet to be advised), De Witt Clinton, who had lent his voice and his mentality to peaceable persuasion, was gone from Washington.

It happened that in August, 1803, Edward Livingston resigned as Mayor of New York. On September 3rd, George Clinton wrote to De Witt, then summering at his Newtown house, asking his "opinion on the delicate and interesting subject" of the choice of the next Mayor of New York. (The office was of course still an appointive one.) There was, it seemed, another Livingston in the running—or a member by marriage at least of the Livingston *coterie:* Morgan Lewis, then Chief Justice of the New York Supreme Court, who had gone over to the Republicans in company with his Livingston brother-in-law. Those who mentioned him wished to raise James Kent from his present associate judgeship to the head of that bench in Lewis' place. Ambrose Spencer was to be made a judge, and John Woodworth Attorney-General. Thus wrote George Clinton, who was not impressed by the arrangement....

His nephew, most emphatically, agreed with his point of view. He replied at length on September 11th, 1803. He thought that the Livingston family had been rewarded enough. He doubted the good faith of Morgan Lewis, whose "ruling passion," he opined, was "avarice and inordinate vanity." Nor had he much better to say of his former ally, Spencer. They were both too greedy for patronage, and he felt that Lewis at least would go to any lengths to obtain it. There was not a little justification for this conclusion; but the fear of placing Lewis in a position to form a Livingston "family junto," and of a possible alliance of such a faction with Burr for political aggrandizement, seems to have been the most potent. The prestige and power of the Mayor of New York at that day may be measured by the caution exercised in the matter of replacing one incumbent with another.

And meanwhile others had been communicating with both Clintons on this burning question. Their adherents in the State of New York were, as a matter of fact, besieging the Governor and the Council of Appointment with urgent requests that De Witt Clinton should be summoned home to assume the vacant mayoralty, and thus be restored to the bosom of his party in his State. Teunis Wortman even went so far as to say:

> They consider that appointment as essential to the preservation of Republican interest in this place.

When De Witt replied from Newtown, Long Island, to the Governor in Albany, he could similarly tell him of pleas to that effect.

> ...Various other candidates have been suggested (he wrote), the present Recorder, B. Livingston, J. Broome and Mr. Osgood. They have all waived their pretensions in my favor. I enclose you B. L.'s letter to me—and you will learn from other sources the opinions of others.
>
> You will of course be glad to know my views and sentiments

on the occasion. Delicacy would have forbid this communication, had it not been for your friendly and to me flattering enquiries. I shall speak to you with the sincerity and candor to which you are entitled from me.

I have a young and growing family to which I am tenderly attached and which require my constant attendance and care. An absence of six months is insupportable—I cannot therefore think of retaining my present situation beyond the next session. Add to this, that altho' my property is large, yet I have already sacrificed too much to public considerations—that the expence of three establishments, one here—one in Washington and one in New York is more than I can well afford. That my absence so long from the State is a serious injury to the Republican cause—that it has afforded and will afford busy and intriguing men an opportunity to further their pernicious projects and that my residence in N. Y. would give me an opportunity of detecting and controlling these conspiracies—in the confidence of friendship I may surely mention these circumstances without vanity—and also that in point of capacity and character there can be no solid objection. I am also a resident part of the year and am possessed of a large freehold there. To this I may add that so far as I can collect the general sentiment, it is the universal wish of the republicans of the Southern District.

Objections may however be exhibited to the measure and some of them of some force. It may be said that offices go into particular families. To this it may be replied that as it respects yours, the objection is of no weight—that not one of them holds an office in the State or Gen[l]. Gov[t]. *by appointment* or that is strictly speaking a lucrative one. To the observation that my political destination is already marked out by the gov[t]. and that I ought to serve out the allotted time, it may be answered, that the gov[t]. may when they please alter that destination.

To objections arising from delicacy on your account, it may be replied, that an appointment springing from the almost unanimous wish of the party in the City and whole District can never be charged with favoritism, but that the event would in all probability take place if you were not the chief Magistrate, and that your elevation ought not to injure your friends.

Youth can be no solid argument against the measure. A Senator of the U. S. is surely fit to be Mayor of N. Y. It may be added that the latter situation from its influence on the next Presidential Election is among the most important positions in the U. States.

Which last meant that the holders of the power and the patronage in the City of New York still showed, each four years, the way the electoral winds might be expected to blow. And power and patronage in New York City at that moment seemed unmistakably to spell Tammany. Lastly, Tammany, as will immediately be observed, was become anathema to Senator De Witt Clinton. . . .

Apart from all this, the office of Mayor, judicial in those days as well as executive, and also somewhat lucrative (the salary, plus emoluments arising from market and tavern license fees, et cetera, hovered around fifteen thousand dollars per annum), was not to be lightly set aside for a seat in the U. S. Senate as it existed and functioned at that date. And De Witt Clinton truly loved New York. He aspired to the greatest political position there, both because it was in his blood to do so and because he desired to be in the way of serving his country in his own fashion, from his own vantage-point, with all the powers he was so proud of possessing and with all the fondest dreams of his heart. His writings and his actions of the period show that the Federal Constitution had become for him something to defend and to improve.

It is impossible not to feel that he was misguided, nevertheless, in leaving Washington and the Washingtonian promise of his future as he did. His State's favorite son beyond the shadow of a doubt at that moment, despite the aspirations of his confessed and also his unconfessed competitors, there was, it would seem, no limit and no bar to his advancement in any direction his heart desired. Diplomatic honor or one of the nearby seats of the mighty must before long have offered, had he remained. And had he remained, the less pure, the dirtier, aspects of political existence might never have bruised him. Had he gained an ambassadorship, his course would have been, beyond the shadow of a doubt, brilliant and good alike for himself and for his country. His whole life is a demonstration of the correctness of such a deduction. Had he gained a Cabinet position either under Jefferson or Madison—but the possibilities with regard to what was currently known as "the succession" are too self-evident to require elucidation.

In the Fall of the year 1803, De Witt Clinton resigned his seat in the United States Senate, and became the Mayor of New York.

8

MAYOR

1803 - 1806

HE WAS a complete success as Mayor. How complete, only a work devoted entirely to this aspect of his career (a matter of some ten years in total of all his terms of office) could adequately convey. Suffice it to render some idea of the forces with which he had to contend, and the amazing multitude of good, both public and private, which he managed to do in spite of them.

It is time to tell Tammany's early story, briefly: As has been observed, Tammany was originally an outgrowth of the antagonism of the former "Liberty Boys" to the comeback of the Tories and the more "aristocratic" leanings of the patriotic Society of the Cincinnati. Tammany stood for democracy, but at the outset had no party affiliations and no aims save that the members were pledged to promote the welfare and the power of their State. It liked mock-Indian patriotic display, and had done some patriotic good as well, notably by its contribution to the making of peace with the Creek Indians in 1790. That was when De Witt Clinton had known it intimately, serving its variously-attended councils as Scribe, or secretary. His connection with it then, and with the museum which it set up in the old City Hall for the preservation of Indian relics, brought him into close contact and a community of interests with John Pintard, who ever after was to seek out Clinton when a museum or a society or an institute or an educational or religious project in which Pintard was interested needed founding or fostering. Pintard, scion of a French Huguenot line, was a merchant and auctioneer and sometime shipping magnate and newspaper owner, with a record of official and human contact with the unfortunate in the Revolutionary war. He was interested in all charitable, religious and educational work, and finding Clinton unfailingly sympathetic and interested no less, conceived for him a lifelong admiration and an abiding care for his welfare and success. As secretary of the aforementioned Mutual Fire Assurance Company, the first in the State, and later as a founder of the Bank for Savings, Pintard viewed both, and valued both, in proportion as they benefited the public. He was appointed City Inspector under Mayor Clinton's *régime,* and in that capacity was connected with many of that *régime's* notable city reforms and improvements. His political faith, from the moment when parties had become clearly defined, was that of the Federalists, though with one further exception he took no active part in political life. The opening of the nineteenth century marked the end of his friendly relations with the Society, and incidentally coincided with the abandonment into other hands of the interesting historical collection above referred to.

By this time Tammany's more purely patriotic days had already drawn to a close. The echoes of the French Revolution aroused in the breasts of the Sachems kindred democratic enthusiasms, or enthusiasms which they believed were akin. They embraced whole-heartedly the French and their cause. They drank toasts to the success of French arms and of French proletarian government, and the members paraded from "Tammanial Hall," as they dubbed their tavern meeting-place, in civilian dress, with a bucktail, the symbol of liberty, dangling from the cap of each. By 1796 the toasts had grown quite violently pro-French, and Federalist members were fast becoming conspicuous by their absence. "Citizen" Jefferson, the champion of French liberty as against the alleged champions of British aristocracy, was regularly given three times three. It was at this juncture that President Washington administered a blow to the pride and growth of Tammany by condemning "self-styled" patriotic groups "from an apprehension that their ultimate tendency would be hostile to the public tranquillity."

The rebuke acted like the hand of doom. The last Federalist member, and a great many of the anti-Federalist members also, those who had shouted the lustiest for France among them, promptly resigned from the Society. Party lines were not as yet so clearly drawn that a man could endure the imputation of false patriotism falling from the lips of a hero. At the 1797 anniversary celebration, there were only three members present, including William Mooney, the founder, a man in humble circumstances.... But Tammany survived.... From that date onward it continued to insist that it was a purely patriotic, non-partisan organization. But Tammany Hall gradually came to connote a supposedly separate entity, whose aims were soon seen to be political and partisan to the last degree. Mr. Jefferson was still, from afar, the prophet and the figurehead for this group.

In 1798, Abram Martling's Tavern, or rather his Long Room adjoining, became "Tammanial Hall." So far was this place of meeting from luxury or any pretension to handsomeness; so like was it to a mere whitewashed outhouse on some farm, that the Federalists familiarly referred to it as "the Pig-Pen." It gave the name of "Martling Men" to the followers of Aaron Burr, who although he was never an officer of the Society, was none the less its leader. They also enjoyed the recognizable cognomen "Bucktails."

The population of New York City numbered fifty-eight thousand that year, and amid this steadily-increasing number Tammany made its plans to smoke out Mr. Hamilton's long-established nest of city Federalists. It is necessary to emphasize the fact that Burr himself was not a familiar figure at Martling's Long Room. He worked through his friends and lieutenants, the chief and most influential of whom was Matthew L. Davis, who, as Burr's biographer, later acknowledged him to have been "our chief." Davis it was who carried out Tammany's first essays at shaping and directing the votes, originally by holding dummy meetings in the different wards, and publishing the strongest "resolutions" carried by those meetings; a little later by the registration, the rounding up, the persuasion of those enjoying the franchise, as well as by devious means of enabling the unenfranchised to vote. Officially, such campaign work was framed by the Republican leaders in the city, and all members of the party were invited to coöperate. But a growing number of the Republican local leaders were also Tammany officers, and the distinction between their political and their "patriotic" offices was not always quite apparent. Notices of party meetings frequently did not reach all their alleged destinations, and in De Witt Clinton's case the meetings were to be held with suspicious frequency at times when he was known to be unavoidably absent from the city.

Such was to be the Tammany machine throughout De Witt Clinton's lifetime. Its engineers were to use their best endeavors to make that lifetime, politically, a hell upon earth. And all too often they were to succeed.

Why? Because Burr had brought about the clean sweep of the New York Republicans in 1800, aided not a little by his *coup* in connection with the Manhattan Bank. The Presidential election had turned largely on the gratifying result. Yet when the battle royal in the House of Representatives had placed Jefferson first and Aaron Burr second, and the latter's friends had come forward with complete expectancy of Federal patronage within their State at least, Jefferson had disappointed them—notably Matthew L. Davis. In the first place, Jefferson, among so many others, distrusted Aaron Burr, and did not hide the fact. In the second, the Clintons were then in process of disowning the latter for his less public actions in the late campaign. And with the return of Republicanism, the Clintons were naturally once more supreme in New York State. That was what the return of Republicanism had meant to a great many New York voters when they cast their ballots. And if New York State was a power to be respected in the nation, it was Governor Clinton, not Vice-President Burr, who was the natural object of Thomas Jefferson's long-standing respect. The President had therefore requested the opinion of the Governor concerning Federal appointments in New York—which seems logical enough. The Governor had given his views and his suggestions as requested by the President. Burr's friends were not, in appreciable measure, rewarded. . . .

That was grievance number one. Then Burr and Swartwout had been neatly ousted from the directorate of the Manhattan Company. De Witt Clinton had expressed himself freely on the subject of Burr and his followers, and it was known that he held Burr a traitor and a conspirator against his party. The affair of honor with Swartwout had been a natural but hardly a conciliatory outcome; and the publication of the story that

Clinton had expressed regret that his adversary had not been "the principal" had added fuel to the Tammany fires.

On the other hand, De Witt had been more than ready to take up the gauntlet on behalf of his uncle and his electoral disappointments. Also he disliked Burr's political methods extremely and sincerely. Mr. Burr, through his Tammany agents, had begun in 1800 the practice of beating the existing franchise laws by forming groups of the poorer Republicans and arranging for them to club together and purchase each group a piece of property, each in a different ward, and each, beyond doubt, aided by the Bank. Only freeholders, and that in an established financial degree, might vote at that time. By the Tammany method many men became freeholders and also voters. . . . Burr secured his Republican majority for members of Assembly in 1800 by a majority of one vote—that of a butcher, Thomas Winship, so the story goes. Through it the election of Republican electors in the State of New York was assured. In 1801, following the same procedure, similar groups had bought houses in the Fourth and Fifth Wards. Some hundred or so were thus enabled to vote as freeholders. In 1802 the Tammany faction had accomplished so much by these and similar tactics that the Common Council was half Tammany, half Federalist, with Edward Livingston, the Republican Mayor, claiming a vote in the Council and throwing it Tammany's way. Since 1800 the great majority of elective offices in the City had been held by Tammanyites, and were so to be held till 1809.

All of which is why, when Edward Livingston resigned in 1803, the non-Burrite Republicans of the city had clamored for De Witt Clinton for Mayor—De Witt Clinton, who had prestige and ability and power galore, and who hated Burr and all his works.

It is necessary to keep the nature of this ever-present and potent opposition in mind while we consider his record as Mayor —not because it hampered him to the extent of rendering it acceptable as an excuse for any shortcomings on his part, but on the contrary because his remarkable and unsullied record shines the brighter for the fact that he had Tammany hanging constantly kicking on his coat-tails. And not only Tammany, but the old, the die-hard and sometimes startlingly resurgent remnant of the Federalist party in the State.

His appointment bore date October 11th, 1803, and was renewed each January for the next three years—meaning, such were the politics of the day, and such being appointive office, that Clintonianism was in the ascendant throughout that period. He lived, for a while, with his family, under his mother-in-law's roof in Cherry Street, but later moved them into independent quarters at No. 52 Broadway. Here callers flocked—the leaders of the worlds of medicine, of art, of culture and of public spirit, each one of whom found a kindred spirit in him. Here he was a husband and father of warmth and wisdom and tenderness. Outside—

Outside, he seems to have been a hundred persons in one, all of them completely and magnificently competent. The presiding justice, automatically, of what was then known as the Mayor's Court, he brought to that branch of his office all his long-dormant legal skill, all the fruits of that contact with men and affairs which his uncle had, so to speak, forced on him years ago; all the fine processes of his native mentality. Every variety of case, from petty theft to wilful murder, came within his jurisdiction, and all, from the gravest to the most trifling, received the full weight of his intelligent adjudication. His charges and his opinions earned praise from all quarters of the law profession, and were spoken of as pearls of legal expression and real contributions to legal practice. This picture is not spoiled by a perusal of them today. His mind, according to similar competent and contemporary judgment, was of rapier-like swiftness in grasping a whole cause, with its merits, although in speech he was always to evince such a measured and reasoning slowness. His decisions were fair and impartial always. He was a believer in the fullest penalty of the law, in capital punishment as the only antidote for murder. But that did not prevent him from giving the meanest murderer his chance; and his diary affords numerous evidences of his having helped a doomed man's family in a pecuniary way even while declining clemency through a conviction that full justice had been done.

Thus Mayor Clinton won the admiration of Bench and Bar for sheer intelligence, and of the public generally for uprightness. He could be radical in applying, or adapting, rather, the English common law to what was often peculiarly American crime or misdemeanor. Naturally there were jurists and lawyers, with feet long set in the ancient legal paths, who failed to follow him all the way along this new road; but even among these gentlemen, admiration of his knowledge, his ability, and of what might be termed his statesmanship, was rife. Washington Morton went so far as to assert that in any capital trial, Clinton was, in his estimation, superior to any judge he had ever known; that if ever he were to be put upon trial for his life, he would choose Clinton to judge him before any other man. Even his political opponents could find no fault with his judicial mien. He was called by Richard Riker, at a later day when friendly memories had been badly blurred by bitter antagonisms between Riker and Clinton, "cautious, attentive, of kind temper, patient of investigation, and discriminating with great care; and, in a word . . . the pure, impartial, patient and upright magistrate, one of the safest men that ever presided in a criminal court, and ever uniting mercy with justice, . . . master of all the great principles of criminal law." Hosack says his charges to the Grand Jury received the unanimous approbation of the Bar.

In the course of one of his earlier terms of office, there came before him a case involving as a witness a Catholic priest, whose testimony as to certain statements received in the confessional had been demanded. British law denied the sanctity of the confessional in like case. Clinton, presiding over his Mayor's Court, held that the tenets of a religious faith were inviolable by the forces of the law, and thus gave the initial glimpse of that broad non-sectarianism which, so far as his official duty was concerned, embraced all creeds.

Also outside the courts of law the Mayor was the busiest cog in the city machine. As head of the Common Council, he was a model to mayors for all time—not only a devoted public servant but an exceedingly dignified one. The Common Council was synonymous, in his mind, with the common good. He was tactful then, with his adverse councilors, as he had never been before with any one.

Moreover, he mostly won their support. His measures were invariably for the good of the public, and the public was at that moment making itself felt by a vigorous demand for a revision of the city charter. Until that year, a freeholder had a vote for every ward in which he held a freehold—a circumstance for which Tammany had often been grateful. Now, under pressure of public opinion, each citizen's franchise was restricted to the section of the city in which he actually resided. There had been agitation too for a choice of the Mayor by the people, instead of by appointment as hitherto, and for the salary of that official to be fixed.

A Mayoral election by popular vote, however, was to wait another thirty years; but the Common Council shared the view that something ought to be done about the Mayor's salary. Something was. De Witt Clinton's lavish fees as chief magistrate of New York City have been more than once commented upon, with a hint that he feathered his nest as more than one incumbent was said to have done before him. Nothing could be further from the truth. As Clerk of the Markets, all fees charged for licenses in that department were legally his, and they formed the bulk of his receipts. There were five thriving markets in the city at the time: the Exchange Market, at the foot of Broad Street; the Bear Market, at the riverside junction of Vesey and Fair (later Fulton) Streets; the Oswego Market, at the Broadway end of Maiden Lane; the old Fly Market, which now extended from Pearl Street to the East River on Maiden Lane; and Catharine Market, a sizable affair at the foot of Catharine Street. Renwick says (and a glance at the Minutes of the Common Council confirms the statement) that Clinton agreed with the Council that he would thenceforth divide his market fees in two, taking half for himself and placing the remainder back in the city treasury. This he did, and more, he felt that he owed it to his office to be both charitable and lavish. He was to retire from the Mayoralty a far poorer man than he had been when he assumed that office. He was consistently generous to young men who were starting out in public or business life, and he did not go outside his own pocket in coming to their financial aid, save for his consistent personal backing of notes taken up by the Manhattan Bank in behalf of some of those anxious to be started in business. It was not only his financial fortune that melted under this latter procedure. Youthful beneficiaries—and older hands too—are notoriously ungrateful. When a young fellow whose note Clinton had backed, or whose till Clinton had filled from his own pocket, failed in the business thus started, or even when he merely desired to rid himself of the annoyance of having to pay his debt, he frequently turned, true to human nature, against his benefactor and aligned himself with the opposite political party. Some of Clinton's most formidable opponents of later years were recruited from among his less successful *protégés* of the past. But then he never courted them; he does not appear to have expected anything more than the honor of a financial debtor from them; and he never upbraided them, though several of the more loyal of his friends and admirers did.

In the year 1804, Aaron Burr, seeing the hope of any national preëminence for himself fast fading, decided to seek the nomination for Governor of New York, a new election falling due. He did not obtain a regular party nomination. The Clintons and the Livingstons were still strong enough to bar the Republican path. Undaunted, he sought to be named by the Federalist party—and Alexander Hamilton, rising again, neatly foiled his hopes in that direction. But he ran, as a self-nominated independent, backed of course by Davis and Swartwout and the rank and file of the faithful. His Republican opponent was not George Clinton, however. George Clinton's name was currently up for Vice-President of the United States, completing Burr's more national disillusionment. . . .

The Clintons and the Livingstons, in the face of the new menace, came together over the choice of Morgan Lewis as the party nominee for Governor. The Federalists chose Gerrit G. Lansing, the Chancellor, as their candidate. But Lansing refused to run, and Burr's hopes of gaining the Federalist votes, plus a portion of those of the Republicans, revived. Vain hopes. There was still Alexander Hamilton, relentlessly opposed to Burr and all his political ways. The Federalists, not loving Lewis much more, nevertheless gave him their votes. And Lewis it was.

Burr, crushed, forthwith abandoned the subtler ways of revenge. He picked a quarrel with Hamilton which is amazingly similar in its details to that which Swartwout had previously picked with Clinton. The results were inestimably more tragic. In early July, 1804, Alexander Hamilton, who had retired from personal participation in administrative affairs some time before the enforced retirement of his party, and had returned to the lucrative practice of the law in New York City, set down the following words:

> My religious and moral principles are strongly opposed to the practice of duelling, and it would ever give me pain to be

> obliged to shed the blood of a fellow creature in a private combat forbidden by the laws.

On July 11th, 1804, Alexander Hamilton was fatally wounded in a duel with Aaron Burr. With his death, died also the practice of duelling between New Yorkers, to all intents and purposes. With him, Burr killed the remnant of his own chances for any political future at all. But Burr's faction survived, strong in sympathy for him and for his political tenets; even stronger in hatred of Mayor De Witt Clinton.

The Mayor went on, working unremittingly to improve his city and the lot of the people in it. And not even the most cursory reading of the history of New York during the period of his incumbency can fail to reveal that in these ends he more than succeeded. He familiarized himself with the region far and wide—as far, indeed (*vide* his diary for November 1st, 1804) as that enormous and beautiful tract of farmland beyond the creek called Spuyt den Duyvil, miles to the north, which honored a son of Holland and former owner by being called "The Bronx." The city, after all these years, was still in a surprising measure Dutch in its characteristics. The old Dutch Church in Garden Street had only recently abandoned its practice of conducting services exclusively in that language. The farmers and merchants who thronged the busy market places often drove hard bargains with the aid of shrewd asides made possible by a superior knowledge of that tongue. Street criers still used it, or mixed it with English with devastating effect; and Dutch houses, Dutch gardens, Dutch wharfs and Dutch gutters were by no means gone from the landscape. Dutch and English composed the elements of the remnants of the old landowning families. Dutch and English by race was the new Mayor; and completely New York in allegiance. His duties absorbed him. He was head *ex officio* of the local militia, and also of the watch, which took care of the policing of the town. He had given up his artillery commission with others of his company because promotion was more limited than they thought it should be; but as ranking militia officer, and actually as well as nominally the leader of what was then the New York police, he proved able to the *n*th degree. If roisterers disturbed the midnight peace, or if more sinister bands began rioting for this or that concession, in the manner of the day, as likely as not, when the forces of law and order arrived on the scene, Mayor

Clinton would be seen riding at their head. His uncle had done the same in the superior office of Governor. From such vantage-point Mr. Clinton personally quelled a number of incipient affrays. On one occasion there was a riot in a seamen's boarding-house in James Street. There had been a fight between the sailors and the watch, in which the latter had come off decidedly second-best. The Mayor was informed that the affair was rapidly growing to ugly proportions. He rode out with a small band of civilian volunteers, leaving instructions for the possible calling out of the soldiery.

In Chatham Street, however, the party met a number of militia officers returning from a parade, attended by a band. Mayor Clinton promptly requisitioned the officers, formed them into a street-wide line, placed their musicians behind them and himself before; ordered the second-named to play a charge—and led the charge. Arrived where the rioting was still in full swing, he succeeded in his brave show. The insurgents evidently thought that the whole of the local army was behind him. The ringleaders gave themselves up. The mob fled. An admirable exhibition of the merits of direct action on the part of a Mayor of New York!

He was more and more deeply interested in New York. Every scheme for its improvement and well-being found a willing listener—some of them a progenitor—in him. Perhaps now as much as at any period of his career he justified the estimate of him written down by his friend Joseph Delaplaine:[1]

> He has been called ambitious, it is true, but the whole course of his life serves to prove that he has devoted his talents to his country. He desires to excel only that he may benefit mankind.

In the matter of education, for instance: Moneyed men were sending their boys, and occasionally their girls, at some expense, to private schools, or having them tutored at home. Poor men had to teach theirs themselves, or let them go without an education, unless they were members of one or other of the religious denominations which had established charity classes. Of these last, the most active in the matter of free education was currently the Society of Friends. It was, indeed, the Quakers who came together with Mayor Clinton over this matter. His uncle as Governor had long since urged free and widespread instruction. He

[1] Delaplaine's Repository, Vol. I.

himself, as a power in the political world, had expended extensive speech and thought on the subject.

The Quaker gentlemen who came to him now were John Murray and Thomas Eddy, the latter a Federalist by political persuasion but never active in politics and never ruled by party considerations: a man who will be seen to have been a leading figure in all enlightened measures. They were trying to enlist the sympathies of all the leading lights of the city in the cause of free schooling. They had had a measure of success in doing so, but nothing practical had been achieved. They came to Clinton, and talked to him of the Lancasterian system of elementary education, then being used with great success in Mr. Lancaster's native country, Great Britain. Mr. Clinton studied the literature on the subject that his friends were able to show him, and, interested, got into communication with Lancaster himself, who later visited the United States and found a personal friend in Clinton. Mr. Clinton's enthusiasm mounting, not only for the system, but for the whole scheme of providing free education for the masses, he conferred personally with all those interested in the subject; and while he digested his information, Murray and Eddy set to work to call meetings and to organize their group.

Meanwhile a new Presidential election, saddened by the nation-wide regret for Hamilton, and envenomed by the universal condemnation of the man who had sent him to his death, had taken place. Thomas Jefferson entered upon a second term as President. George Clinton, successful, took his official leave of New York and went to Washington to assume the duties of Vice-President. Morgan Lewis succeeded him as Governor. The good feeling between Lewis and De Witt Clinton seems at that moment to have been complete, and this feeling of friendship toward the new Governor on the part of Clinton was not lessened when in January, 1805, that executive included the subject of common schools in his message to the Legislature, and recommended the scheme whole-heartedly as a State-wide measure.

The meetings organized by Messrs. Eddy and Murray took place in February. A committee was named, to report on the need for a system of public schools in the city, and to prepare a memorial to the Legislature. The committee reported promptly. Its memorial was signed by a large number of prominent men, and was duly dispatched to Albany. But it was De Witt Clinton who drew up a working plan for a Common School Society, and put his name at the head of the subscription list with a donation of two hundred dollars. It was De Witt Clinton who journeyed up to Albany in April and applied personally to the Legislature for a charter for the new Society.

The charter was granted, but without any financial support from the State.

Mr. Clinton, nothing daunted, returned to New York and began to spend his evenings, in company with a young friend named Frederick De Peyster, a public-spirited citizen and long a member of the Society, in calling on the householders of New York City and soliciting voluntary donations. The results were amazing: almost five thousand dollars in all collected by means of these personal visits and by personal appeals. But not easily, and not soon. It was not till May, 1806, that the first class was able to meet, in a house in Bancker (later Madison) Street.

Meanwhile Clinton had been chosen President of the Board of Trustees of the Society, with Leonard Bleecker Treasurer and Benjamin D. Perkins Secretary.

If only he had been able to permit himself to be public-spirited and nothing more! If only the filth of the slowly-advancing mud of politics had not gathered about the hem of the noble garment of his social, humane, scientific and utterly altruistic greatness! He wanted New York to be great, and he wanted it to be remembered. When John Pintard came to him in November, 1804, in the interests of a proposed historical society, De Witt Clinton responded with the eagerness of a man to whom the preservation of his State's records and antiquities and relics had long been a project most dear. So did a large and eminent group of others. But Clinton was now in a position to foster such ventures in a direct and practical way, and the first recorded minutes of the New York Historical Society show that he gave both official hospitality and personal coöperation to that Society from its inception. At that first meeting, which took place in the Picture Room of the City Hall, he attended in company with Egbert Benson, the Rev. William Linn, the Rev. Samuel Miller, the Rev. John N. Abeel, the Rev. John M. Mason, Dr. Hosack, Anthony Bleecker, Samuel Bayard, Peter Stuyvesant and John Pintard. From that moment he lent a zeal unflagging to the interests and aims of the group. Egbert Benson became its first

President. Pintard was the earliest Secretary. De Witt Clinton, at the start, might well be dubbed ambassador without portfolio to Albany....

At least he used his public office invariably for the good of the greatest number. In 1805 he agitated for better land traveling facilities between Albany and New York—a need which he had good personal reason to call pressing. In summer, travel to Albany was easy by the sloops that plied the Hudson. In winter, with the river frozen, and the roads frequently so badly mired that they were utterly impassable, communication between New York City and the Capital was often completely cut off. Mr. Clinton drew up a petition, and presented it on behalf of the citizens, to the Legislature that year, praying for the incorporation of the Highland Turnpike Company, which a group of substantial men wished to organize for the purpose of constructing a road from Poughkeepsie to Kingsbridge. The request was granted, and although the funds raised proved inadequate to the fulfillment of the project, the attention of the Legislature had been signally directed toward the need for such a road, and improvements in existing communications were shortly after effected, paving the way for the later provision of adequate facilities along that line. Incidentally an object-lesson had been provided for Clinton himself in the inadequacy of any private charter to the effecting of a great public improvement....

His days, however, as a mere commuting petitioner between New York and Albany were numbered. His was a name and a fame and a personal forcefulness too great to be left alone by the politicians, even had that been his desire, which it was not. The impression one gets is that he took it completely as a matter of course that politics were a necessary part of the life of a Clinton of New York; but none the less his views of public policy, however they were put to political use by his followers, remained completely detached from the exigencies of political existence.

In the matter of banks, for instance: opposition to financial power in the hands of the Federal government was of course inherent in his make-up. An almost unlimited power was enjoyed by the financial institutions of the day. They were banks of issue, circulating their own paper money and in a position to compete with any governmental financial body that sought to do the same; issuing loans unchecked or withholding them for whatever reasons they chose. Thus when the government had badly needed money, Hamilton's United States Bank had lent it. When opponents of the party in power needed funds, they mostly had to go elsewhere. A bank was a political implement, in short, and party groups sought it as such. Clinton's undeviating support of the Manhattan Company, of which he was a stockholder, was in the accepted political tradition of his day. His fear of a centralized money power was handed down to him from his Revolutionary forefathers. His distrust of all who would enter and support new banking ventures was a natural concomitant.

But his feeling went further than all this. He saw a real danger in the undue extension of banking privileges; in the chartering of bodies that could issue money without check and too frequently without value, with resulting unnatural fluctuations in local confidence. There was no general corporation law in his day. A company seeking a charter of any kind had to prove its right to one in its application to the Legislature, and even if successful, the period for which it obtained such charter was limited. But in the matter of banks, too often it was politics, and too often the offer of a share in the spoils and a sop to this or that charity ruled the day. As for the use of financial power by the Federal government, De Witt Clinton was at one with his uncle in deprecating it. As Vice-President, George Clinton used his casting vote in the Senate of the United States to defeat the application of the first United States Bank for a renewal of its charter. In a statement as to his motives for so doing, he voiced once more the ancient Republican protest against Hamilton's original assertion that the Constitution bestowed banking privileges on the Government with all the other rights. He expressed his fear of such a financial weapon in the hands of a body properly dependent on the will of the people for the extent of its powers and its duration in office. ... In New York State his nephew voiced a similar sentiment regarding those ambitious to return to power. And these two were not alone in their general fear and distrust of banking ventures. On April 11th, 1804, the New York Legislature, following the political tradition above outlined, had passed a bill forbidding unincorporated companies to conduct any banking business. De Witt Clinton opposed the consequent application of the Federalist-owned but unincorporated Merchants' Bank in New York City for a charter in 1805 with all his might. His medium was Ambrose Spencer, a member once more of the Council of Appointment. Of the Livingston faction, however, only Spencer now aligned himself with Clinton. Insidious practices were resorted to by the less high-minded of the Federalist party in the course of this fight, and when De Witt Clinton had finished with these worthies he had proved that bribery of members of both Assembly and Senate had been resorted to. He even managed to impeach the good faith of Gouverneur Morris, a member of the latter body, in this connection.

But the Merchants' Bank was chartered. No Clinton, it now appeared, was going to dictate to the Livingstons. Governor Lewis was going to act for himself, and give his loyalties where he thought they were due. . . . The net result was that those who felt with Clinton and Spencer that the charter should not have been granted, particularly in view of the circumstances surrounding the passing of the bill, sent De Witt Clinton to Albany again as Senator from the southern district in place of John Broome, who was currently stepping up to the Lieutenant-Governorship. This entailed no relinquishment of the office of Mayor of New York on the part of Mr. Clinton. Dual office was not yet frowned upon. James Fairlie and others variously deputized as Mayor when De Witt Clinton was called to Albany. And no later than the first session of the new Legislature in 1806, New York was rendered signally aware that Mr. Clinton was more than equal to his double duty.

DE WITT CLINTON

By Charles C. Ingham

9

CITY AND STATE

1806-1809

MR. CLINTON'S diary for January 9th, 1806, runs: "Attended Court from 11 o'clock to half after 4 next morning, on a trial for murder." Incidentally, and characteristically, the entry of two days later is simply: "Children attended a party." His home life was totally uncomplicated by the multiplying calls of his public existence—a fact which redounds to the credit of both his wife and himself. He was to be seen at a ball at John Watts' house on January 17th, and continuously and devotedly in the company of his brother George (who had duly married Maria's sister Hannah); of his sisters, Mary, wife of R. B. Norton; Elizabeth, wife of William Stuart; and Catherine, the widow of Mr. Norton's brother Samuel. He was on terms of great personal friendship with Henry Remsen, the President of the Manhattan Company. He had also as a frequent visitor in those years Thomas Paine, who valued the friendship and also the advice and aid of De Witt Clinton in these Paine's later and less fortunate years. He was intimate with Colonel John Trumbull, to whom he had recently sat for his portrait; and both he and his lady were solicitous and attentive to the widow of another hero of the Revolution, the aged General Gates, whose resplendent funeral had been the event of the past year.

In both Albany and New York there was always, for him, the cream of social encounter. Besides a fairly regular round of political dinners, his table, his talk, were the magnets for the great, the brilliant, the charitable, the heroic and the hardy. His visiting-list, indeed, sometimes reads like a list of the prominent men of the hour. Sometimes they were venturesome men; a great proportion of them were visionaries and idealists, sometimes combining those qualities with political acumen, but never practicing the two together at Mr. Clinton's table. Politics do not appear to have been welcome alongside his board. Intrigue was a fashionable art so manifestly foreign to his forthright nature, which attacked and condemned and fought, but despised artifice, that even when it was practiced in his behalf he invariably remained aloof and totally uninterested. When it was urged on him personally, to smooth his own path, he disdained it without equivocation.

But of course it was practiced in his behalf. He still had many friends—too many, politically speaking. Some of those who came into the latter category now conceived a plan to overthrow the Livingstons, or the Lewisites, as they were now termed. With Burr fallen from grace, there appeared to these gentlemen no reason why Burr's followers, if they were amenable, should not be received back into the bosom of their party—meaning, of course, the bosom of Clintonianism. Thus far, apparently, Clinton himself went with them; and his friends thereupon made overtures, which were kindly received for the simple reason that Mr. Davis, Mr. Swartwout and their companions were anxious to go a little further still. In brief, they hoped to reinstate Mr. Burr himself as a condition of any reunion.

The two factions had dinner together at Dyde's Hotel in New York City on February 20th, 1806. Mr. Burr's friends were frank. Mr. Clinton's friends were anxious—anxious to overcome the Lewisites at all costs, as it now appeared. In short, in Mr. Clinton's absence, his lieutenants agreed to recognize Burr and to give his friends a sizable slice of the patronage. There were toasts, and much mutual good fellowship.

But the coalition died in the very birth-throes. Those Tammanyites and other Republicans who had not been favored with an invitation came together at Martling's to revile their mates. The Federalist press followed with jeering quotations of Clinton's remarks regarding Burr and Swartwout in 1802. And Clinton himself? Clinton wrote to General Theodorus Bailey, the leader of the scheme in his behalf. He said that in his opinion the proceedings at Martling's were proper to a degree. He said that neither patronage for Burrites nor reinstatement for Burr should have been asked or promised as a condition of reunion between the factions. The enmity between the Burrites and Clinton forthwith flared up stronger than ever.

But it is to be noted that dissatisfaction with Tammany was not currently confined to Mr. Clinton. In 1805 the Society had applied for and obtained a charter from the Legislature as a "charitable body." In 1806 the powers that were in the political incarnation of that charitable body found it politic to abandon hypothetical "meetings" and "resolutions," and established a system of ward and nominating committees; but manifestly something even more than committees was still needed. Tammany continued prominent in Mayor Clinton's Common Council. But that did not enable it to prevent the removal of Benjamin Romaine, one of its guiding spirits, from the office of City Comptroller in 1806, for malfeasance in office; or the subsequent similar and summary action against four other public officials who were also Tammany men, for fraud and extortion, all charges proven. It had been the obvious weakening of the hold of Tammany on local public imagination that had encouraged Mr. Clinton's ambitious friends to hope that Tammany would prove submissive, and that out of union might come strength—for Mr. Clinton.

In any case Clinton's support in the State Legislature was tremendous. So tremendous that the Assembly was able to take it upon itself that year to choose a Council of Appointment by general caucus, instead of dividing the vote up into districts as had been the practice theretofore. The Lewisites were furious. The southern district, left to itself, would never have elected Clinton to the Council, they asserted. But Clinton it was, and Adam Comstock, and Henry Huntington, and Robert Johnson, and this Council proceeded to its now time-honored business of dismissing its rivals from office and appointing those of their own party. Governor Lewis, registering his protest without avail but with complete regularity, was no longer considered by that party as one of its members. His alliance with the Federalists was open and, for the moment, complete. His friendship for them, and his antagonism toward those who had nominated him for Governor, had lent color to a great many of De Witt Clinton's earlier doubts and vindication to his earlier actions.

In March, the matter of corruption in the Merchants' Bank legislation came up. It was Senator Clinton who moved a resolution for the expulsion of Senator Ebenezer Purdy for bribing and being bribed. Purdy resigned, his guilt unquestionable, before the charges were actually tried.

But Clinton, as usual, had lent himself to mere party politics only temporarily. Colonel Henry Rutgers had recently presented a plot of land on Henry Street in New York City to the Free School Society. But there was still no money with which to build a school on the plot, and while the first class was meeting temporarily in the house in Bancker Street, Mr. Clinton was in Albany, presenting to the Legislature a petition of the Society for financial assistance from the State. The petition was referred to a committee, of which he was named the chairman. His report on the educational needs of the State of New York, and the value of the Free School Society to the fulfillment of those needs, is one of his major efforts. It resulted in an enactment by which the immediate sum of $12,000 was granted to the Society, and further an annuity of $1,500 per annum, the whole to be raised by the revenue from lottery subscriptions in the manner of the day. Clinton was to raise his hand against this method of financing public measures a little later, but for the present he was well content. Back in New York City when the Legislature rose, he devoted himself untiringly to the proper launching of the project. His house at 52 Broadway was the frequent meeting-place of the Free School Society. His door-to-door calls with De Peyster did not cease.

His next outstanding Senatorial contribution probably preserved an extremely rich heritage for the State. This was in the matter of the will of Robert R. Randall, who had left his estate to a group of trustees for the purpose of establishing a home for poor men of the sea, to be called the "Sailors' Snug Harbor." Thus far, the only conclusion arrived at in the Legislature, to which the legal tangle arising from the will had been carried, was that a man could not by will vest his estate in a permanent official body, because by so doing he was creating, in effect, a corporation. It looked, from this and other angles, as though the will would be declared void, and the money and lands would go to next-of-kin yet to be found, but certainly not resident within the State. Mr. Clinton announced it as his opinion that corporate powers could be conferred by law on the trustees named by Mr. Randall, of whom he was one, and he drew up and presented the bill to that effect which was eventually passed.

He also drew up the bill for the removal of all political disabilities from those of the Roman Catholic faith, and personally pushed it through to victory. By the same token he won the friendship of many excellent men of that faith for all time. He framed "An Act to Prevent Frauds at Elections." . . . He won a charter for the Association for the Manumission of Slaves in the city of New York. He failed to win similar articles of incorporation for the Society of the Cincinnati, however, and even the mere attempt seems to prove his hardihood, such was the dislike on the part of his party for that unquestionably honorable and patriotic and would-be charitable body.

In short, those projects which came to his attention and caught his enthusiasm as Mayor, he constantly carried up to Albany, where his enthusiasm and also his political ascendancy were put to practical purposes. This was also the case with regard to the condition of the insane in the city of New York. His interest in all branches of medical practice, as in all branches of education, was unflagging. A member of the Board of Managers of the New York Hospital, he secured State grants insuring its permanent support, and he also presided over the preliminaries and ceremonies in connection with the opening of an institution in Chambers Street, known as the Almshouse, in 1807, where sick and insane alike were treated by voluntary visiting doctors. This somewhat crude beginning was to lead eventually to the banks of the East River and the great institution named for the ancient estate upon which it was built—Bellevue. But meanwhile one aspect of it at least seemed to require immediate consideration. So Clinton and his fellows on the Hospital board were discussing the fate of the insane. No provision had as yet been made for the harboring of those completely bereft of reason, and their condition was pitiable. The managers of the New York Hospital therefore petitioned the Legislature in 1807 in behalf of the insane of the City. Mr. Clinton, in his Senatorial capacity, was named, as usual, to the head of a committee assigned to report on this petition. The report, drawn by him, won a legislative grant sufficient to enable the New York Hospital to erect an asylum, and meanwhile a temporary shelter was provided in one of the existing buildings of the Hospital, near Broadway to the north of the Common.

He also aided the Society for the Education of the Deaf and

Dumb by winning for them a grant of $5,000, gaining with it their undying support and gratitude.

There were at this time almost nightly fires in the City of New York, doing damage to private property and extensively to trade, for wood was still the predominant medium of builders. To such proportions, indeed, had the fire hazard grown that the mutual assurance associations were no longer able to rise to every emergency. Policies were held by some householders in certain of the British companies, but there was considerable clamor for a legally chartered New York insurance corporation. The substantial representatives of this popular demand now veered quite naturally to Mayor Clinton. It was desired to form a corporation under the title of the Eagle Insurance Company, if he could win them a charter. He drew the charter up, presented it, and won it.

In the deliberations of the Common Council he was no less indefatigable, and his aims were no less high. He persuaded the Common Councilors to vote $2,000 of the city funds for the purposes of the new School System, and to sanction the use of an abandoned public building in Chatham Street, which duly became Public School No. 1.

He shone in a legal way in Albany at this time, too, for as a Senator of that day he was also a member of the bench of the Court of Errors. It was in this capacity that he gained a further juristic reputation which in its greatness is amply justified by a current reading of some of the judicial opinions he rendered. These reveal in him, it is true, a certain arrogance and more than a little impatience with regard to opposition; but they also show him learned and well informed to a degree. His colleagues were his fellow-members of the Senate, plus the Chancellor (Lansing), the Chief Justice of the Supreme Court (now James Kent), and the Associate Judges of that Court (Ambrose Spencer was among their number, with Brockholst Livingston and Daniel D. Tompkins, for a part of this period at least.) The outstanding characteristic evinced by a majority of these combined groups of gentlemen in their capacity as a court of last resort was a passionate adherence to the rigid and archaic forms of the English common law. This was what Clinton now fought wherever it attempted to exalt those forms above simple justice, or to bring monarchic privileges into conflict with republican liberties. When Kent and Lansing upheld the right of the Court of Chancery to imprison a man for an indefinite period for alleged contempt of court, without privilege of jury trial or of appeal,[1] Clinton wrote:

> Here is a case (excluding the favorable interposition of the executive or the legislature) where an unjust or tyrannical judge may, at pleasure, imprison an innocent man for life, and yet place punishment at defiance.... I trust we have nothing to apprehend from such practice in the times in which we live, yet we ought to keep our eyes fixed on futurity.... Why are we to expect exemption from the common lot of nations?...

Where an arrest of judgment after trial had been granted because of alleged technical defects in the pleadings,[2] he said:

> Though the system of pleading may be denominated a science... it originated in a Gothic age, when the light of genuine knowledge had shed but feeble rays upon mankind, when the jargon of schoolmen had infected every branch of science, and when the subtleties of a false logic had completely bewildered the human understanding. Though purified and refined by the extension of knowledge, yet it still partakes, in some degree, of its original character. Distinctions without a difference, subtleties which puzzle and perplex, without enlightening the mind, a minute, a servile observance of forms, and attention to words, without a due regard to ideas and matters of substance, are evils which ought to be banished from our courts of justice; they, at least, ought not to be countenanced in this court of *dernier resort.*

He wrote his opinions with the immeasurable future ever before his eye. When the valuation of certain spacious farmlands a mile or so to the north of New York City, on the banks of the East River, came up as the principal question in a case,[3] he said:

> A person called upon in May of 1804 to estimate the value ... ought to have calculated not its value in gross or in mass ... but he would have taken into consideration its favorable position, its propinquity to the city, the sales of neighboring lands... and the immense price which the place would bring when converted into town lots.... An immense mass of population was confined within a narrow strip of land surrounded by the waters of the Hudson and East Rivers. This mass was invigorated by industry, enriched by commerce, animated by enter-

[1] John V. N. Yates vs. the People of the State of New York; 6 Johnson's Reports 337.

[2] Bayard vs. Malcolm; 2 Johnson's Reports 550.

[3] Rogers vs. Cruger and others; 7 Johnson's Reports 558.

> prise, and was progressing with a rapid and unceasing step. It was breaking with irresistible force through the limits in which it had been confined, and was extending itself, with astonishing celerity, into all parts of the country. The rise of land in the vicinity of the city was then as certain as the extension of the city, and as its increase of inhabitants. This population was not only augmented by natural increase, but by crowds of strangers from France, from Great Britain, from Ireland and the West Indies, who took refuge in our peaceful clime from the ravages of war and the oppressions of despotism. The commercial and enterprising genius of New-England also perceived that New-York was destined by nature to command the commerce and to be the great store-house and emporium of two-thirds of the United States, and to that place her sons resorted from all quarters, and prospered.

In all these opinions, and in a great majority of others—some of them involving momentous questions of international law—, he prevailed, often against considerable odds. And if he did not invariably gain the complete concurrence of the men who adorned the Bench of the Supreme Court, at least he won and retained their profound respect.

In Albany meanwhile he became more and more of a social lion. Gorham A. Worth, sometime President of the Albany City Bank, recalls him as a light that shone amid a luminous circle that used to foregather at the Tontine Coffee House in East Street. Here, if the circle were small enough, he would relax and be extremely entertaining. He was always something of a dual personality quite apart from his dual rôle in public life. With strangers he was slow to unbend. Dignity, reserve, and a rather unfortunate habit of abstraction appear to have hedged him round on all his more formal occasions. Informally, the consensus of opinion, emanating from the most credible sources, is that he was the soul of geniality and even of a very gentle wit.

However, the fact that he had any time at all for social pursuits is a matter for wonder. Before he had been a Senator for more than a year, the specter of political animosity had raised its head again. The alliance of Lewis with the Federalists resulted, in the 1806 elections, in a majority in the Assembly for that coalition. The political color of the 1807 Council of Appointment was thus a foregone conclusion. So was the ousting of Clinton that year from the office of Mayor of New York, and of all the appointees of his own recent Council of Appointment from their various offices. The Revolutionary veteran, Marinus Willett, succeeded him as Mayor, leaving Clinton free to devote his energies and his powers of mind to Albany. Likewise his prowess for political recuperation....

He had been exceedingly busy in the interests of those who would render New York City more sanitary, more safe and more beautiful. He had lent his weight and his personal interest to the progress of the work on the new City Hall at the head of the Park. He had moved a resolution and won an appropriation for the improvement of Canal Street, and had organized a commission to study and report upon a plan for laying out the streets of a greater Manhattan. He had aided the Orphan Asylum by winning legislative sanction for the extension of its work, and a legislative grant of five hundred dollars annually out of the city auction duties. At the moment of his temporary but enforced retirement from the Mayoralty, his record in that office was (as indeed it was ever to be) unsullied and outstanding. His personal popularity among the populace was both merited and wide.

His family was now composed of a lively group of five boys. Walter and Charles, now schoolboys, had been followed by James Henry, born in 1802; De Witt, whose birth took place in 1805; and George, who arrived in this year 1807.

They had lived, in New York, and summers at Newtown, an uncomplicated existence. Books were still entertainment highlights for the head of the house, and the venturing forth to the public bath to give one's whole body a wash was still a matter to be recorded in one's journal. So was the homecoming of one's boys from school, and the jolly fishing-trips in the neighboring creeks that were a natural consequence. So was the weather, for upon the weather depended one's journeyings and one's health, to say nothing of one's farming, so essential in the matter of sale and sustenance. Mr. Clinton kept the family account-books and still, like his fellows, did the family marketing. He noted prices—prices he paid for bread and meat and occasionally for a succulent turtle; what it cost to send a horse into town for shoeing, a traveling chair for repairs. Expenses for pistols, powder and shot. Prices he got for potatoes and for pigs and for sapling trees and for hay. He was a good husbandman, and also a meticulous, if not a wordy, diarist. He recorded the buying of "a box of segars" and even of "a toothpick for Charles." Such details and the nice noting of them went to complete his daily life.

He liked a mild wager on occasion, though he frowned on public affairs of chance. "Bet a beaver hat with Ingraham that we fail in the Ninth Ward," says the diary for November 16th, 1807. But that "we" now signified a certain indifference to minor failures, and indicated a deep upheaval in party politics yet again. A new gubernatorial election had taken place, and Morgan Lewis had of course been patently out of the running for the regular party nomination. The Republican nominee, and also the victor, was Daniel D. Tompkins, youthful associate judge of the Supreme Court, a man of some Republican legislative experience, of unexcelled personal charm and also of a welcome freedom from major family ties, politically speaking. This last rendered him unexceptionable to the bulk of the faithful of the party. De Witt Clinton himself could not at that moment have swung a majority vote in person as nominee for Governor, such was the competition of the leaders of the various factions and the fear in some quarters of his power. He gave the great weight of his influence to Tompkins, and emerged once more, in the manner of the day, into the light of favor. Tompkins, upon securing the good offices of an entirely friendly Council of Appointment in January, 1808, promptly put Clinton back into the Mayoralty of New York City....

At that moment, international affairs were also something to bet over. As recently as November, Clinton had, *vide* his diary, been wagering one more beaver hat with editor Cheetham "that there would be no war with England." The bet never came to be lost or won, because Mr. Clinton and his hitherto ardent supporter of the fiery *American Citizen* were to split on this very question.

The United States at the moment was, academically speaking, in a position to reap a golden harvest by reason of the war between England and France. The produce of the fields of the agricultural American states was in increasing demand as the battles absorbed the attention of the man-power of both countries. But England would not let neutral ships carry wheat or anything else to France, and now issued her Orders in Council to that effect. Napoleon retaliated by means of his Berlin and Milan Decrees, proclaiming neutral laden ships bound for England liable to seizure. It was a blow to the roseate hopes of the American grain-growing states, and since both France and England increasingly needed some supplement to a diminished supply of vital commodities, President Jefferson, still averse to war measures where peace measures would do, protested first, and when repeated protests failed, decided to hold both countries to the letter of their orders, and placed an embargo on the trade from this to both countries.

And here, at first flush, we have De Witt Clinton disapproving of a Jeffersonian principle. To understand his attitude, it is necessary to realize that his uncle was writing to him from Washington with great regularity, describing the state of the country and the status of international affairs. George Clinton upheld the embargo because he had a wide view from a lofty national vantage-point, and felt that, strong measures being needed, this was the strongest that the peace-loving Jefferson could be persuaded to take.

De Witt Clinton, agreeing with his uncle that strong persuasive measures must be taken, opposed this particular measure at first. A narrower panorama than his uncle's was before his eye. The Embargo Act bore heavily on the grain-growing State of New York and the dreams of its would-be merchant princes. And the welfare of the New York merchant was always very close to Clinton's heart. While Mr. Willett was still Mayor of New York, therefore, Mr. Clinton had visited the city to preside over a public meeting to protest against the embargo. Cheetham's (or, as some said, Clinton's) *Citizen* vigorously supported him. He also had the surprised approval and even admiration of many of the Federalist party; but the mass of the Republican party of course supported Mr. Jefferson. Tammany in particular applauded the Act, and seized the opportunity for one more denunciation of Clinton. The Livingston-Lewisite faction now decided to abandon the Federalists and back Tammany to a man. Jefferson and his Cabinet also began looking at De Witt Clinton somewhat askance for taking such an extremely Federalistic stand. It was whispered that Clinton was openly courting the Federalists; but this point of view was somewhat refuted by immediate developments.

In the first place, he resumed his old dual rôle of Mayor of New York and Senator. And round about New York harbor, as elsewhere in American waters in 1808, Britain was impressing allegedly British seamen into her active service by seizing them by force from American ships. All Mr. Jefferson's much-debated efforts had failed to put an end to this practice.

As far as Clinton in his official capacity was concerned, he had this and other kinds of trouble with England and with France as well. As Mayor he was responsible for the safe-conduct of foreign ships in the harbor. But Britons liked to trap French vessels there, and Frenchmen relished nothing more than bedeviling men-of-war flying the British colors. Also neither side was any too careful of the lives and property of neutrals unfortunate enough to get in their path. One American sailor was actually killed by a flying shot from a British frigate in New York waters. Mayor Clinton dealt directly with the commanders of these vessels, and actually succeeded in insuring free passage for vessels conducting themselves according to the usages of belligerents in neutral territory. And this was no easy task, for all the forts that the harbor yet boasted numbered one—Fort Jay, on Governor's Island. And all the guns were the small battery at the foot of Manhattan. The eastern shore of Staten Island and the quarantine station that lay there were totally unguarded. There were quarantine regulations, but no way of stopping the French when they systematically defied them. The waters approaching the Narrows were similarly unprotected. There were ceaseless complaints of impressments in those waters, but nothing to prevent the British from continuing the practice....

In the year 1808, De Witt Clinton asked and won from the State legislature an appropriation of $100,000 for the fortification of New York harbor. He thought the Narrows should be fortified to command the quarantine station, and he drew up and presented a report to this effect. He also presented a bill for the support of the quarantine station itself. Financial advocate, he was also the President of the actual Board of Commissioners of Fortifications, and the works on Staten Island now grew to fruition literally under his eye. In March he wrote to Dr. Samuel Mitchill, then a member of the United States Senate, regarding a bill in debate for obtaining title to land at Sands Point and erecting a lighthouse there. In April he personally agitated for the removal from the mud of Wallabout Bay of the hulk of a British prison ship which had lain there since the war, and successfully petitioned the Legislature for a grant for the decent burial of the bones of American patriots which had lain rotting with her. Tammany, always anxious to prove its purely patriotic purposes, was the originator of this petition; Clinton the head of the legislative committee to which it was referred. The Society came out in grand display, and further petitioned for a grant of land to build a monument to these forgotten men. This petition, too, was successful. Private persons contributed cash. Eighteen years later, the public was still inquiring as to what had become of the land, the cash, and a further grant of one thousand dollars which was subsequently made by legislative action.

Clinton was likewise busy, and completely successfully so, in behalf of his friend the merchant John Jacob Astor. In January Astor had written to him a series of letters defining the fur trade as it affected Americans anxious to engage extensively in it, and also as it might affect the trade prospects of the United States. At the moment, Mr. Astor was traveling to Montreal once or twice a year, to purchase furs for sale in the United States. He was also acting as agent in the United States for several Montreal fur-dealers. He was not the first to complain that the rich trade in skins trapped largely in American territory was exclusively in other hands than his countrymen's. Almost a century earlier, Cadwallader Colden had written extensively and persuasively to an English Governor on this very subject. The fur trade of America was then in the hands of the French, who governed Canada. The change that later came about in the possession of that vast territory had briefly made Canada and its southern neighbor one. Now they were two again, and fur-bearing animals were once more trapped in the territory of the former British colonies, and taken to that which was still a part of Britain, to be sold. Mr. Astor set down on paper for the benefit of Mr. Clinton the fact that three-fourths of what he called "Am. furrs for haum consumption" had to be obtained from Canada. Frequently, between trapping and selling, they had been carried overseas to London peltries, and those who desired them at Montreal had to pay for the privilege of importing that which had gone out from American soil.

It was still, of course, largely a matter of the Indians, who did the trapping. The United States had established friendly relations, for the most part, with the Indians, and maintained posts at strategic points for the express purpose of furthering those friendly relations. But the fur trade had remained in the north. Now, Mr. Astor was willing to relieve the United States from the financial obligation of keeping up the Indian posts. He was anxious to take over those stations and through them develop a direct trade in furs with the Indians. His personal reputation, the fact that he was willing to give up all other commercial interests and to invest fifty or a hundred thousand dollars of his own in the venture if he could obtain the right authorization, and the obvious anxiety of the several gentlemen who were desirous of joining with him to make that venture a success, were cited as guarantees that nothing would be done by the new company to lessen the friendly relations for which the Indian posts were maintained. Mr. Astor's western limit for the territory he wished to cover was the Pacific Ocean, the vague limit of unknown thousands of miles of equally unknown lands.... He had a definite plan for trading posts in direct line from the fur country to the sea at New Orleans and New York. His aim was world trade—but he wanted a legislative charter for himself and some dozen or so other responsible fur-merchants. His claim was that his company would provide increased employment for Americans, improvement in transportation facilities, and a new prosperity for the country. But he wanted a monopoly because, as he claimed, his pledge with regard to the maintenance of good understanding with the Indians could not well be kept if all comers, however irresponsible and however fleetingly ambitious, were allowed to compete.

His language was crude, for he had had little time for schooling or penmanship; but his meaning was brilliantly clear. As far as Mr. Clinton was concerned, he wanted to know whether that influential member of the Senate was sufficiently interested and sympathetic to recommend to the State Legislature the granting of a charter. If so, Mr. Astor was going to Washington to tell Mr. Jefferson what he proposed to do. He wanted not only his charter from the State, but the blessing of the Federal Government upon it; for though New York would be the center of his operations, other States must be penetrated in pursuit of them.

Mr. Clinton replied to Mr. Astor with enthusiasm. He was

greatly interested, and he was more than ready to lend his legislative influence to the furtherance of a scheme so vastly progressive. Mr. Astor duly approached Mr. Jefferson, who in turn asked General Dearborn, his Secretary of War, to make inquiries of the Vice-President concerning Mr. Astor's reputation. Vice-President George Clinton forthwith replied that Mr. Astor was "a man of large property and fair character, and well acquainted with the fur and peltry business." Thereupon, Mr. Jefferson, expressing his approval of the active entry of America into the fur trade in words that implied that he had not been apprised of Mr. Astor's desire for a monopoly, gave the latter gentleman the official encouragement he desired.

It was now De Witt Clinton's turn to act. He went before the Senate with a complete and carefully-framed bill for the incorporation of the American Fur Company. He termed it a patriotic movement that had both the welfare and the commercial future of the country at heart, but that could not be carried to fruition by individuals or unincorporated groups. His petition treated of the Western wilds and the Indians dwelling in them—country yet to be explored; red men, trappers, to be approached and conciliated. It went widely into the possibilities of a vital trade yet virtually uncompeted for by the United States, and the reasons why the United States should compete.

The American Fur Company was chartered on April 6th, 1808, for a term of twenty-five years, with a capital of one million dollars. At the end of two years the company was authorized to increase its capital to two million.

And that was not the only charter in which Mr. Clinton was actively interested that year. In Albany in 1808, the watchword still was banking. The charter of the Manhattan Company was before the Senate committees for renewal, and Clinton was in regular correspondence with Henry Remsen on the chances for success. He was, incidentally, equally interested in Mr. Remsen's personal affairs, and when that gentleman currently went courting he wrote:

> I am rejoiced to hear of your brilliant prospects at the north-east end of the town. Go on, my friend, in this praiseworthy course. Settle yourself down in the arms of an affectionate wife—and depend upon it, after all our toils and struggles in making money and gratifying ambition, that true happiness is not to be found beyond our firesides.

He himself never ceased to be a family man, and of all his sons, now at varying schools, Walter, the first-born, an affectionate child, was the dearest to his heart. There are innumerable occasions upon which his brief journal entries of weightier moment give place to mention of the boys; of going to the play with Walter, walking and particularly talking with Walter, attending the circus with De Witt, attending Church with both. On the 10th of January, 1809, the entry is "Went to the Theatre Picturesque with J. Pintard and three boys." And always there were visitors, morning, noon and night. "No visitors" was news; to be carefully recorded in its place. And always there were duties—duties voluntarily assumed, and the important duties of his various offices. The laying of the cornerstone for a new State Arsenal in New York City, which ceremony he performed in June, 1808, was symbolic not only of the more nationally threatening aspects of those duties but of one more "preparedness" bill successfully presented by him at Albany. The echoes of war were growing louder in men's ears. The appropriation which he won in behalf of the College of Physicians and Surgeons that year represented interests more peaceful and just as close to his heart. He had recently become a member of the Board of Regents, in which capacity he helped organize the aforementioned medical college.

The Bank of Manhattan Bill duly passed into law that spring, thanks in great measure to Clinton's tireless efforts. The Bank had naturally many powerful enemies, and many rather more insidious competitors. But Clinton knew and had faith in the Manhattan Company, and he distrusted "fly-by-nights"; and that spring the Company was, as Clinton wrote to Remsen, "established beyond reach of its enemies."

> ... Let me now tell you and the Board, that nothing but a single concurrence of circumstances and, let me add, not a little good management could have carried us through triumphantly. The bank is now placed on ground from which she may look down upon her enemies and put them to defiance. The thirty years limitation attaches only when the *sale takes place,* and it is in all conscience long enough....
>
> We work like slaves at the oar. In the morning we assemble in our legislative and in the afternoon in our judicial capacity....
>
> Give my best compliments to the gentlemen of the Board, and when you see your dulcinea, tell her that I hope the intended

and happy change in her estate will . . . be the cause of introducing me to the honor of her acquaintance in the respectable character of wife of my friend.

He was interested in the matter of establishing branches of the Bank, and investigating, in his thoroughgoing fashion, the location and value and desirability and price of sites at Poughkeepsie, Utica and elsewhere that were petitioned for and offered.

Also that year this man of many parts took up the cause of the Academy of Arts. Founded in 1801, it had acquired a wealth of display material and treasure, but had never yet obtained either a home or a charter. Mr. Clinton obtained both. He persuaded the legislature to grant the Academy a suite of rooms in the disused Government House at the foot of Manhattan, which, built for George Washington, briefly occupied by George Clinton, had finally fallen into varying tenants' hands and more or less into decay. Simultaneously, he became a director of the Academy, whose president was the aged Robert R. Livingston, and a constant attendant at its meetings. For he liked to discourse on art as on most other æsthetics and sciences. He could and did, moreover, do as much to encourage and promote the love of art in his native State as any one member of the Academy.

And all this time he was keeping a sensitive and fearless finger on the pulse of national affairs. Four days after he took his seat in the January, 1809, session of the Senate, he arose and addressed that body with considerable vigor. He had become convinced, and he did not fear to say so, that the embargo was a measure of protest better than no active protest at all, and that a determined stand seemed to be increasingly indicated. He preached preparedness and the vulnerable state of the country. He damned the Federalists for not seeing the light for themselves, and incidentally earned the eternal enmity of several of the leaders of that party by quoting from Milton at their expense, presenting as the Federalist watchword, "Better to reign in Hell, than serve in Heaven." He then introduced resolutions pledging the support of the State to the Executive of the nation.

The "Feds" now roundly denounced him, together, anew, with the embargo. So did his quondam friend Cheetham, who charged him with bad faith. This was the net personal result, plus an abiding distrust of him on the part of the so-called "Virginia Dynasty" thenceforward for his temporary lapse. The last is the most significant.... The winter had brought again the burning question, Who is to be the next President? With all his might, De Witt Clinton had worked to make George Clinton the successor of Thomas Jefferson. Many Republicans, his followers in the State, assisted him; but in the nation, and also in the Tammany stronghold of New York City, the party placed the name of James Madison, the Secretary of State, first, and George Clinton second—which is the order of the ultimate result of the election.

George Clinton was not pleased. In fact he was once more exceedingly disappointed, and wrote in that vein to his nephew. This time he had not at all desired or felt that his nomination should be for the second place....

His nephew, however, was soon to have disappointments enough of his own with reference to President Madison.

10

ASPIRATIONS

1809 - 1810

THERE HAD not been absent, even from this campaign, a desire to see the younger Clinton elevated to the first place in the nation. The plaint from the South, that George Clinton was too old to take on the cares of the Presidency, had sufficient plausibility. George Clinton was seventy. But there was a younger and perhaps a stronger Clinton available, and his followers did not fail to say so.

The name was received with so little warmth in certain vital quarters, however, that Solomon Southwick, editor of the *Albany Register* and a devoted Clintonian, adverted in his paper to the fact that it seemed the Virginia Dynasty did not believe that any New Yorker was worthy of the first place in the nation.... The *Richmond Enquirer,* of Virginia, retaliated with a list of the public appointments and the enormous power of the Vice-President's nephew in New York, as though those were pretensions better confined to New York alone. The Lewisite-Burrite combination now managed locally to disseminate the feeling that De Witt Clinton, after changing his stand regarding the embargo, had not really renounced his opposition at all; that he and his party and even his uncle were working against Mr. Madison. They now rounded up those whom De Witt Clinton as a Councilor had disappointed in the matter of patronage, and also some of those who owed him substantial sums of money. They assured many of those who had been rewarded that their appointments were due to the personal intercession of Governor Tompkins, and not to Mr. Clinton. Mangle Minthorne, Governor Tompkins' father-in-law, was a prime mover in this, the "Bucktails'" new campaign against De Witt Clinton. Tompkins personally avowed himself Clinton's friend, and indeed he had reason to be; but the quality of that friendship even at that moment seems to have been problematical.

Mr. Clinton remained outwardly unperturbed. He continued both a tireless and a fearless servant of his city and his State. The yellow fever stalked the city of New York again that year, as it had done more than once during his tenure of the Chief Magistracy. He was always at his post. More than one city official sought a country retreat, and Greenwich village had an influx each time which invariably left it with a substantial increase in its permanent population. Mr. Clinton was never absent from his seat on the bench, from his chair at the head of the Common Council, from his vital and newest office as head of the City's Board of Health, save when his duties carried him to Albany.

He moved his family out of town, however. On February 8th, 1809, he wrote in his diary, "Mrs. Clinton brought to bed of a daughter this morning at 3 o'clock;" and babes in arms—this one was Mary—were no fit citizens in a time of epidemic. He was once more constantly in communication and frequently in the company of his friend Doctor Hosack, and through that hardworked medical man he kept himself aware of conditions and of possible alleviations.

Before public sickness was well over, there was considerable public joy. The trouble with England was apparently brought to an end. April 24th, 1809, was a public holiday in New York because President Madison and Mr. Erskine, the British minister, had signed a pact which entailed the raising of the Orders in Council as they affected American commerce, and the rescission by the United States of the Embargo Law against Great Britain. The United States immediately carried out the preliminaries to its part of this bargain by partially raising the barrier to trade.

It was now for the Republicans of New York to indulge in a little rejoicing. Defections in their party, fostered by the enduring hardships which the restrictions had put upon mercantile prosperity, had contributed, in the April State elections, toward the first Federalist victory at the polls since 1799. Indeed the news of the so-called treaty had come too late to do any good that year. Even in New York City the Republican majority was small, but this was due in part to the continued investigations into the affairs of Tammany officeholders, including those of Tammany's founder, Mooney, and involving startling disclosures of extensive defalcations. It was at this juncture that Teunis Wortman, a former friend and *protégé* and incidentally the substantial debtor of Mr. Clinton, emerged as the voice of Tammany and undertook to show the Republican voters which public men were their friends and which their enemies. And he left no doubt that he would include in the latter category the Mayor of New York, currently playing his part in the removal of the Tammany defaulters.

But all this faded momentarily in the rejoicing of Republicans throughout the State. Republican measures had succeeded, and the party felt a rising wave of confidence in the immediate future. Once again, with Tammany prestige declining, the Clintonians made an effort to consolidate the party, and there actually took place a meeting between the leaders of all the factions for the purpose of taking measures to counteract the new power which the Federalists had gained with the achievement of a majority in the Assembly. But once again there arose the cry of "bargain and corruption"; and once again a proposed coalition came to nought.

As a matter of fact, the general joy was without a great deal of foundation. Great Britain repudiated the arrangement which had been entered into by her minister, denying his authority to act in any such way. But the unpopular Embargo Law had been modified and was ultimately abandoned; and if continued need there were for preparedness, as far as New York was concerned she was playing her part. There were brand-new fortifications on Staten Island, which Mr. Clinton's boys examined under their father's auspices in July. Their father had helped to build them. He knew that, if they should be needed, they were wholly inadequate unless extended. Unremittingly versed in the general state of the country by his letters from his uncle at the seat of the Government, he had become firm for adequate preparations for war. His subsequent history, disastrous in this aspect, shows him unyielding on that score, and uncompromisingly against trusting to any half-measures.

However, national danger, and also the personal danger of epidemics, was over for the moment. The Mayor was to be seen with his friends of the New York Historical Society at its regular meetings, and also familiarly and actively engaged in its behalf. That year the Society celebrated in style the two hundredth anniversary of "the discovery of this part of North America by Henry Hudson," and many gratified New Yorkers—some who, possessing valuable letters and papers, had expressed hesitation about intrusting them to the custody of an "ephemeral society"—began looking upon the history-collecting group with a new seriousness and a new interest. Encouraged, the members were moved to apply to the Legislature for a charter and a grant. Mr. Clinton, in the Senate, moved both. The charter was granted. The request for a grant went through the Senate but came to grief in the Federalist Assembly, on the ground that "too many lottery jobs had been authorized already."

Meanwhile the winter had been a full one and rather a sad one for Mr. Clinton. His brother George was dead—the brother with whom he had enjoyed for so long the closest affection and harmony. It was well that the winter was indeed so crowded with action, with interest, and even with excitement. "Dined on board the Constitution," says the diary for September 28th, 1809. "Dined at the Navy Yard with Captain Chauncey," is the entry for November 2nd; and on November 30th Captain Chauncey dined with him, in company with a group of men whose names in a list together read like the roster of some Hall of Fame. "At dinner:" says the diary, tersely, on that date, "Commodore Rodgers, Captain Chauncey, Robert Fulton, Judge Livingston, Captain Hall, Dr. Hosack, Dr. Mitchill."

It will be gathered that around New York at least the waters brimmed with preparedness. If new ships were tardy in the building, famous old ones were not lacking then in this vulnerable spot, where already there had occurred many outrages; and where there was every expectation that the outrages would increase. For England had repudiated the so-called treaty; and France, annoyed at any parleying with England at all on the part of the United States, was directing considerable war-feeling in the direction of the last-named.

As for the appearance of Robert Fulton's name on Mr. Clinton's visiting-list, it marks the beginning of active effort on the part of Clinton to further the aims of the steamboat inventor. A rather minor member of the Legislature when Livingston had first applied to that body for the exclusive right to navigate steamboats within the State of New York, he had not joined in the general howl of ridicule with which the whole notion that boats could be motivated by such means was received, even while the request was somewhat laughingly granted. A supremely influential member when Fulton and Livingston had asked for a renewal of that right in 1807, he had given his support to the assent which was given. By that time the *Clermont* had successfully navigated the Hudson, and men had ceased their taunts and their laughter. Now Mr. Fulton and his wealthy partner and patron were interested in ferries and extensive steamboat lines, and Mr. Clinton was asked and was willing to do his best to further that interest. Fulton looked upon him as a valued friend, and not alone because of his great influence. Nor was this esteem in any way lessened by reason of the fact that Clinton systematically negatived all suggestions of personal participation for gain even in those projects of Fulton's which lay outside the State.

In friendship, in learning, life was smooth sailing for this man. With scholars he was completely at home. With dreamers, pioneers, pathfinders likewise. With politicians, though he had such ample opportunity and indeed tried all his life to make himself at home, he never quite succeeded. He was unable to surrender his personality, his principles, completely enough to party, though in theory he was a party man heart and soul. Thus the rifts within the party itself, and the pendulum that swung first one, then another faction into power, carrying with it the spoils.

All through December, 1809, Mr. Clinton was occupied with Masonic duties. A Freemason from his youth, he was to rise to the office of Grand Master, and was much in evidence at the general post-Christmas reunions, and at all lodge ceremonials and routine proceedings. He also found time to put his son De Witt to school that month, which meant that a quartette of his boys were pleasingly launched on their education. He was happy, that winter, over his boys. . . .

At the end of January, 1810, the Federalists, with a majority in the Assembly, proceeded to try for a Federalist Council of

Appointment. Their success in this attempt did not make itself immediately apparent. Daniel Parris and Amos Hall, Federalists, were chosen, but there were no Federalist Senators from either the southern or the middle districts. Those districts, as currently represented in the Assembly, chose Israel Carr and Robert Williams, both avowed Republicans, respectively—and when the Republicans of the middle district began to realize what had happened, some of them were already numbered among the ejected in the ranks of the office-holders.

For Williams, successively a Burrite, a Lewisite and a Clintonian, had decided that he needed the only other change in politics that was open to him. He entered into a secret affiliation with the Federalists in power, and when he took his seat in the Council of Appointment, the secret was a secret no longer.

> ...The Federalists (wrote Clinton to Remsen), by securing a Senator from the middle district, have the Council of Appointment in their hands. The Senator is Robert Williams, who has damned himself to eternal infamy. No man here entertains any doubts as to the impurity of his motives. The consequence will be a *general sweep* of the Republicans from office, but certain success at the ensuing election. The infamy of the defection will attach to the Federal Party with a grasp that cannot be shaken off. You can already perceive consternation and conscious turpitude on the countenances of the leaders, and Williams looks like the idea we have of Judas Iscariot when he was about hanging himself.
>
> I can assure you with confidence that the Republican Party will triumph in the election of Governor. The western district is extremely favorable, and a spirit is rising which nothing can resist.

He proved a good prophet. The year 1810 saw him once more ousted as Mayor through a Federalist edict from Albany, and Jacob Radcliffe at the head of city affairs in his place. It saw Governor Tompkins, not unaided by Mr. Clinton, victorious over the Federalist nominee, Jonas Platt. The result of the general spring elections was a complete overthrow of the previous year's Federalist victory at the polls—save in the city of New York.

And De Witt Clinton was busy as he never had been before. The financial side of his public life had developed into something exciting. In constant communication with the Manhattan

Company board, he could inform the members of that board that their business had taken on the aspects of a party battle.

> ... Mr. Tibbits ... a director of the Farmers' Bank, told a friend of mine in the Senate that an attempt would be made in the legislature to restrain the M Company from establishing branches, and that the provision is to be retroactive. I have no doubt but that a serious attack will be made.

He got ready for it, as was his wont. At the worst he would fight to keep the Utica and Poughkeepsie branches, already successfully established. He begged Mr. Remsen to send him the petitions of the people of those villages for the establishment of branch banks there.

> The attack will be a party one, and will be whetted by all the rancor of pecuniary and political hostility.

He was right. There were would-be Federalist bankers out for the scalps of established Republican financial magnates. As Burr had once feared Hamilton and his New York Bank, so Federalists now were afraid of Clinton and the power of the Manhattan Company.

Their attacks by way of a sympathetic press were personal and violent.

> If I were disposed to cherish a spirit of vanity, (he wrote in March, 1810,) I should certainly overrate my consequence, when I consider the pains that are taken to kill me before my time. In 1807 I was shot in a duel. Last session I fell a victim to a pleurisy; and this season I have been again killed in single combat. My last murderer is a character with whom I cannot possibly come in collision, and who has never, that I know of, given me cause of offense. These rumors are calculated, and perhaps intended, to distress the feelings of one's family, and they would very much mortify me did I not know that Mrs. C. is a woman of great fortitude.

The fight on the branches continued, and Clinton, terming it "an abominable violation of our charter," played his part. He was fighting the multiplication of banks generally, and he was at the same time struggling to multiply the branches of the bank in which he was a stockholder. If such political procedure seems strange, let it still be remembered that banking and politics were even more closely associated then than at a later day of banking (and also political) crisis.

But the proceedings of the Federalist forces in the Assembly did indeed give weight to Clinton's accusations against them. They harried him personally at every turn, till the stormy session closed and De Witt Clinton went back to New York City, where he was that year a comparatively free man. He gathered his family and carried them gladly across to Long Island, to fish and to ride once more with his wife and children, and forget political animosities and official aggravations, and bask in the secure affections of his home. It was the last time he was to feel that security quite complete—the last time his love for his children was to go unaccompanied by fear. He was happy that spring. His boys strove to please him. Walter in particular, his best-loved and first-born child, always the most demonstrative of the group, clung to him with greater affection than ever.

But there came a night in May when Walter, embracing him, would not let him go. He must kiss the child again and again; must repeat his goodnights and his caresses for as long as the boy could possibly contrive to cajole him. Mr. Clinton remembered a great many years afterwards how it warmed his heart. It buoyed him with an assurance, a confidence, a hope of something beyond the mutations of political and public fortune—a hope that really had no promise whatever, save of doom. For that same night—May 2nd, 1810—the beloved Walter died, quite suddenly; too suddenly for Dr. Hosack and his colleague Dr. Post, who were frantically summoned, to be of avail. The details of this purely personal occurrence are essential to a study of the life of De Witt Clinton. The loss of this young son Walter colored—shadowed—the remainder of his existence. He never forgot it—or Walter. He was for this once, but never again (and this is significant) completely a prey to the shafts of adversity. Many shattering blows were to be aimed at him during his lifetime and even beyond it, but young Walter bequeathed to him an armor against calamity; and the aliveness of the memory that once, months later, made Clinton cry "Walter!" in the street because he saw a boy that resembled his lost lad; that let him, ten years later, write of that tragedy in detail; is the measure of the strength of the armor in which it forever encased him, letting his affections out but keeping his sufferings in.

He did suffer then, however. Even his wife, by tradition and custom the weaker vessel, laid her own grief aside to comfort him. For the moment, he carried his heart on his sleeve—but only for the moment. Then Walter took his place forever inside his father's heart, and that father resumed to all intents and purposes, save an occasional revealing involuntary act, the equable place in his family and the somewhat less equable public position which he had uniformly enjoyed. His brother Charles still survived, and they foregathered often. His father, remarried, still dwelt in the Little Britain homestead, which he had sustained and spasmodically occupied since the last of his elders had died.

And there was always occupation. There were books, there was art, there was history, there was science; the winds and the waters and the birds and beasts gave this man delight. Also there was duty, still, within the city of New York. Sometimes his diary reveals him as performing the dual rôle of banker by day and beggar by night. "Called on F. de Peyster," says the diary for May 21st of that year, "and went with him to collect for Free School. Collected $590." And there was sociability—a never-ceasing demand for that. He mentions seeing Cooke in "King Richard III" in company with Governor Tompkins, Judge Spencer, General Armstrong and Mr. Macomb. He dined out frequently, and entertained more frequently still. At the moment the name of Martin Van Buren, whom Clinton and his Council of 1806 had given the office of Surrogate, was a recurrent one on his lists of visitors; lists of a weight and a magnitude increasingly appalling. But that description also applies to his engagements and obligations in the line of friendship and of culture. On November 30th he was a pall-bearer at the funeral of General Gates' widow. On December 6th he dined with his fellow-members of the Historical Society at the Washington Hotel. On the 15th he went with his friend John Jacob Astor to look at the house called Richmond Hill. Here Aaron Burr had gone into residence after Vice-President John Adams had departed. Hence Burr had gone from the scenes of his major mistakes, not soon to return. He had bought the place, and eventually he sold it to Mr. Astor, who now offered it on a lease to De Witt Clinton, for whom a spacious residence not too far from the city was indicated clearly enough. So the year closed with an engagement to take over for a short term this extremely historic mansion.

However, that year 1810 had held far more than merely this constant social and political round. It had, as no other year of his life, perhaps, marked an epoch; certainly an important step toward that which was to be his life-work. For it was in the year 1810 that an amazing group of men in public life eschewed for the moment the petty spoils and artifices and hatreds of politics and, because De Witt Clinton, with all his power in the State, had never failed to use it in the interests of that State's improvement, came to him with the word "canal" on their lips.

11

THE CANAL

1810

THE MERE fact of a man's being able and willing to put his party prejudices aside in the public interest was not, of course, a novel one. The day was almost upon New York when political jealousies would in the name of political sophistication drive out disinterested coöperation. But in 1810 it was not quite here. Hence Thomas Eddy the Quaker, who was staunchly a Federalist at heart though he did not practice politics, went to the then leader of the Federalist party in the State, Jonas Platt, with a suggestion that represented the culmination of many years of more or less abortive effort on the part of a great number of public-minded men. And Jonas Platt, kindled with the possibilities latent in Mr. Eddy's somewhat modest plea, pondered on the paucity of actual results in the past, upon the desirability of irresistible action in the future—and forthwith sought out De Witt Clinton, the leader of the Republican party in the State and also the one man in the State who had the will, the ability and the driving force to push an improvement project unremittingly until it became a fact.

Now Mr. Clinton had recently referred to Mr. Platt in his richest vein of sarcasm as "the would-be Governor," and they had by no means seen eye to eye on the subject of the banks; but that was a matter of Federalism versus Republicanism, and it did not prevent the Republican leader from lending an ear to a non-political suggestion. Mr. Platt well knew that as the mouthpiece of a group bent on a public improvement, he would find courtesy at Mr. Clinton's hands. He hoped (and indeed had considerable grounds for hoping) that he would also find sympathy.

Nowadays, that which he had to suggest would appear as a straightforward if controversial project enough. In those days, however, there was rather more to the word "canal," as applied to New York State, than the prospect of increased commerce and an opening of ways. Since 1724, and a great deal earlier, "the West" had possessed a particular significance, first for British America and, after the transformation, for the United States. Nor was it purely a matter of greed for land, since pioneers were still few and those who knew what lay beyond the Mississippi even fewer.

It was, in its elementary stage, a matter of national survival, and it is in the light of this fundamental cause that De Witt Clinton's canal contribution is to be considered, as well as for the blessings, the benefits and the prosperity that he brought upon the State. Thus Hosack and other memorialists of Clinton have found it necessary to delve at some length into the early history of the canal project, in order to present an adequate picture of Mr. Clinton's part in it. The necessity, it appears to the present writer, still remains. Clinton brought order out of chaos, success out of decades of abortive attempts, shining reality out of dreams. The chaos, the timid measures, the dreams, are all a part of the picture, a background for the clear-cut quality of his fame.

In the year 1724, then, Cadwallader Colden, as Surveyor-General of the Province of New York, had sallied westward to the Mississippi, to find out what he could about the French, the fur trade and the Indians. He reported the results to the then royal Governor of the Colony, Burnett. They were significant. The fur trade, as has been mentioned, and also, it might almost be added, the Indians, were exclusively in the hands of the French, then in possession of Canada, or "New France." What this actually meant was that the unknown but apparently limitless West, if British America did not speedily do something about it, would drop into the hands of Gallic Louis likewise. Trading with the Indians along the Mississippi, friendly and studiedly protective toward them, the Frenchmen could, and did, boast that New France was wide and long and deep. The southern and eastern bounds of New France, said the royal French geographer, and made a map to prove it, extended from the mouth of the St. Lawrence river to the mouth of the Mississippi, and he blandly

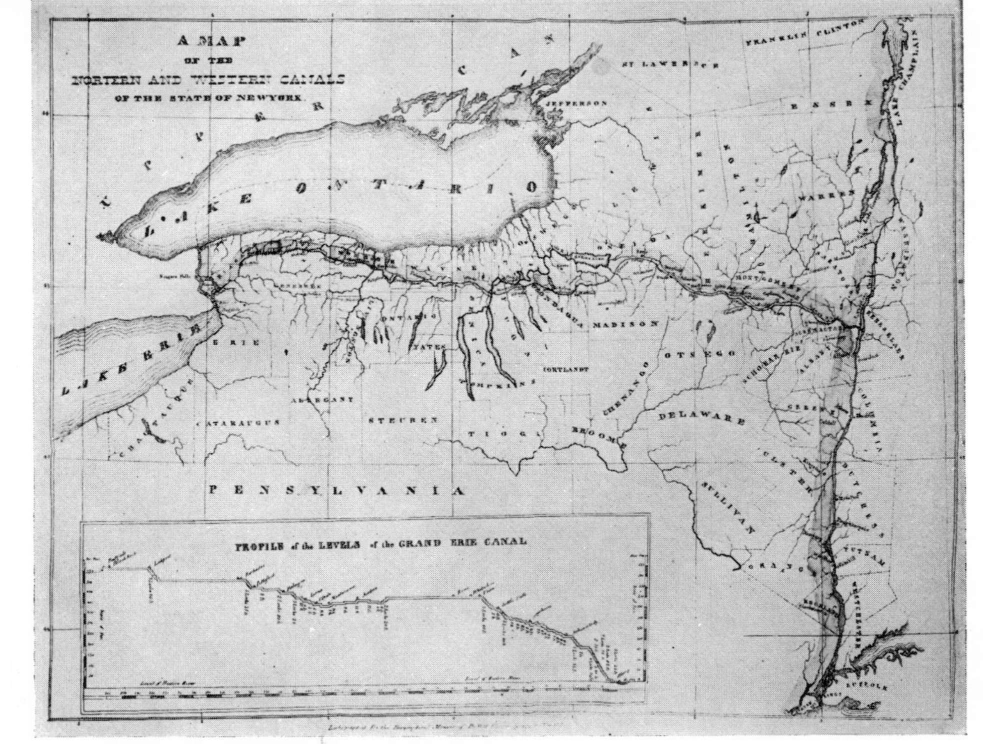

MAP OF THE ERIE AND CHAMPLAIN CANALS

took in certain strategic sections of South Carolina and of New York. Colden came home with a story of that map, and asked, if that were so, what of the foregathering British colonies along the Atlantic seaboard? Were they to be pushed, when the West grew too confining for the French, into the Atlantic Sea?

He suggested a remedy. Britain, he said, could easily compete with the subsidized royal French fur company, whose prices were restricted by law and levied upon by the King. Navigation, moreover, of the St. Lawrence was vastly more difficult than navigation of the Hudson. Commerce between Albany and England was appreciably easier of accomplishment than traffic between France and Montreal; and Albany could serve the West. ... Also, England and her possessions produced a great many articles that the Indians coveted. France produced but a few, and had to buy the rest. So that what with the expense of the trading articles and the difficulties and restrictions incident upon contact with the homeland, France ultimately paid more for the skins she bought from the Indians, and got less for them, than need be paid or received at Albany. Sometimes, indeed, enterprising Frenchmen, and enterprising Indians too, traveled down to Albany to buy articles to sell to the French which the latter could trade again to the Indians for furs, and made a handsome profit.

Why, then, asked Colden, could the trading articles not be carried direct from Albany to Lake Ontario and the adjacent Indian territory, without trespassing on the country of the French? Why should the French continue to monopolize the fur business and with it all the implied good will of the red men? Why should goods and confidence too, and the possible profits from at least a portion of a rich trade, be actually taken from New York to render the French the shining hope of the tribesmen? Some of the Albany merchants, selling their goods so freely, did not see it in quite that light, and showed no signs of patriotically sacrificing such a golden opportunity. But one who ran, knowing the history of the British versus the French, learning much about French methods of winning or coercing the necessary friendship of the Indians, could read a future that held untold danger unless England competed once more, and effectually, with France in North America. Peaceably if possible. There had been almost incessant war. It was time for good British subjects to do something before it was too late. Colden in 1724 therefore advocated extending British trade in the Great Lakes region to traffic in furs and other profitable articles. He had seen the rich soil that bordered the Mohawk River, and envisioned a golden harvest of hemp to make rope for British shipping. He had seen the great pines of western New York and, even thus early, dreamed of masts piled high and borne eastward. Did not England have incessant need for naval stores of the kind? And was not this England?

He described the Indian method of portage from river to river, and through one natural waterway into another, whereever possible. The American colonists had picked up and amplified this method of carrying by water as far as they could, and of making their Indian barks frail enough to be borne on men's shoulders overland. The drawback was, of course, that their freight, their merchandise, must likewise be in quantity light enough to be similarly transported. The method did not lend itself to piled-up tree-trunks or even to piled-up hemp.

Colden had stood on the banks of the broad Mississippi. He had realized the potentialities of such a mighty center of inland navigation. He had pondered on how to render it easier for the frail craft of far-venturing traders from the east to find this mighty stream. The difficulties of navigating any vessel in the shallows and against the rapids and tides of some of the smaller rivers through which they must make their way were always disheartening and often insurmountable. How to make the way clear, the journey unaffected by the vagaries of the seasons?

He did not solve the problem he had thus set himself, or help to solve it, save in one important particular. He wanted the royal Governor to think at least of the possibility of extending New York's frontier, then barred by the nearer settlements of the Indians of the Five Nations, to the Lakes. Between Lake Ontario and Lake Erie, he said, dwelt the Senecas, friendly toward the British and strong enough to have prevented the French from setting up stockades there such as they had erected in the passes between the other Great Lakes, to enable themselves to trade in peace with far tribes of Indians of whom the British had never even heard.... Here in the Seneca country, British America might establish a frontier and set up a competition for the riches that lay in furs and the potentialities that lay beyond them. Rivers and streams could be made to join and thus to serve men's purposes, and Colden believed that if men merely dug the connecting links, natural gravity would do the rest. His ignorance of the formation of the western country was to be shared by some who came after him.

The only concrete results that appear to have come from his suggestions were the posts that the British authorities erected along the Mohawk, the Oneida outlet and the Onondaga River, and the fort which they erected and garrisoned at Oswego, unless one counts the fact that in 1766 the denizens of Fort Stanwix,[1] at the head of the Mohawk, installed a system of sluices between that river on the one hand and Wood Creek—a deep but sluggish stream, emptying itself into Oneida Lake—on the other, to save the portage between. It was a foretaste of that which was to be flattered by the name of New York's canal policy for a great many years—until, in fact, De Witt Clinton arrived upon the scene. "The Mohawk to Wood Creek" is a phrase that will be seen to be ever-recurrent in New York's early canal history, and understandably so. As Christopher Colles later remarked in surveying that territory, "the ground between the upper part of this (the Mohawk) River and Wood Creek is perfectly level, as if designedly to permit us to pass through this channel into this extensive country." It was to be a great many years before men would be persuaded that the hill country east and west could be conquered likewise, and the rise of that greater vision is as completely contemporaneous with De Witt Clinton's introduction to the cause of the canals as his full maturity is glorified by his work in giving that vision a concrete and practical maturity likewise.

In 1768 Governor Sir Henry Moore recommended the removal of obstructions in the Mohawk River by a system of sluices similar to the aforementioned, for purposes of trade; but nothing was then done. Britain, however, did the "something" necessary to remove the peril of a West ruled by France. But that did not help when the East, in the shape of thirteen British colonies, ultimately became an independent republic. Rather, it transformed one peril into another, and possibly a worse; for here was England possessed of Canada and all the St. Lawrence; friendly with

[1] Later Lynchburg, and, still later, Rome, N. Y.

the Indians along the Mississippi; and undoubtedly not averse, both for politics and for trade, to encircling the victorious rebels.

Meanwhile Gouverneur Morris, whose name is to be linked with the ultimate glory of the Canal, had already begun talking of linking the Hudson river with the Lakes. He also, however, was of what may be called the school of natural gravity, of whose theory's practicability as applied to the topography of New York State much is to be deduced by his own subsequent experience. He, too, bowed to natural levels and distrusted lockage, but his is the name of canal pioneer for all that. Morris, as early as the 1770's, had vision in relation to the West and the riches that he realized lay waiting there. His scheme embraced Lake Ontario, with a harbor at Oswego and a possible artificial waterway out of the extremity of the Lake and around Niagara Falls to Lake Erie. And he believed it could be accomplished by digging on an inclined plane "from the head of the Onondaga River . . . if practicable, into the Mohawk River," with a "branch" from the Onondaga to Oswego on Lake Ontario.

Morgan Lewis, then an officer of the Continentals, recalled later a romantic visit of Morris' to General Schuyler, in camp after the evacuation of Ticonderoga. Mr. Morris was representing the Committee of Safety, investigating the state of the American forces in a period of defeat. Off duty, Lewis has him cheering the officers with a vision of the West and of the future of their soon-to-be-freed country, and outlining his canal scheme with zest to General Schuyler.

Morris' services certainly cannot be assayed too highly. He pushed the project of the Canal with a zeal excelled only by that of De Witt Clinton. When he became the colleague of Clinton in the interests of this cherished plan, he had nursed it so carefully, and used, besides, his connections and influence abroad to such effect that a European loan of five million dollars was his for the asking in financing it. His scientific knowledge, however, was somewhat lacking. What may be called his engineering instinct, as will be observed, was not so keen as Clinton's. But he loved New York. He knew it well. He talked and wrote of its beauties, its potentialities, with a poet's and a lover's zest. And within the limits of his own capacities, wide enough as a statesman, a philosopher, a diplomat and a student of affairs, he aided more than most men in its future.

Nor must the unofficial contribution of De Witt Clinton's own father to New York canal history, as represented by his ingenious triumph over the forces of nature at Lake Otsego during the Sullivan expedition, be forgotten. There is evidence[1] that his father's experience there, and his intimate knowledge of the land about, contributed toward De Witt Clinton's canal education.

One whose vision of a mighty West is too well known to need further particularization is, of course, George Washington. He had seen existing rivers and streams used with devastating effect in war. He knew why transit by water ought to be extensively developed in peace time.... When the Revolutionary War was over, Washington had begun a series of purposeful journeys into the interior of the United States; among them a surveyor's tour of the State of New York, which he took in company with New York's first Governor, the uncle of De Witt Clinton. George Washington and George Clinton both were ambitious for that inland wilderness. The former, while the States had been still British colonies, had been responsible for the passage of a bill to open the Potomac so as to increase its navigable extent to one hundred and fifty miles. He had plans which included the River James, and they were in process of execution when the Revolution broke out. In 1784, Washington and others returned to the subject of internal navigation with added zest and incentive. Among these others was Thomas Jefferson, who would place Washington in command of the Potomac project "to prevent the public money from being squandered to no purpose." Washington's heart was in Virginia, but his thoughts and his loyalty embraced the country in its explored and unexplored entirety, as his written sentiments show. His hopes of linking the Potomac and the James to the Ohio and the Lakes, often expressed, show the way his mind was tending. His careful exploration of the portage between the Mohawk and the head of the Susquehanna River when in New York evinced his desire to link the Chesapeake with the future of United States trade. Indeed he told his fellow Virginians, and also the people of Maryland, whose coöperation he sought for his James-Potomac plan, that if they did not act, and quickly, New York and Pennsylvania would assuredly combine to acquire a monopoly of the western commerce, which it would be hard to wrest from them later.

[1] Diary of De Witt Clinton, New York Historical Society.

> I am not for discouraging the exertion of any State to draw the commerce of the Western country to its seaports (he wrote). The more communication we open to it, the closer we bind that rising world—for indeed it may be so called—to our interests, and the greater strength we shall acquire by it. Those to whom nature affords the best communication will, if they are wise, enjoy the greatest share of the trade. All I would be understood to mean is that the gifts of providence may not be neglected.

Washington knew the political significance, the international significance, of the West. But Washington's voice, while winning a measure of success along the Potomac and the James, was merely to be one of the many, crying in the wilderness, as far as the broader vision was concerned. A younger man—a mere stripling then—was destined to coördinate the cries into a vital, irresistible plea in behalf of his own native State, and to turn abortive effort into success.

In 1784, Christopher Colles, the Irish-born mathematician and mechanic aforementioned, who had settled in upper New York State and was interested in adequate water transport as well as in adequate water supply, asked for permission and aid from the State to open the waste-land from the navigable end of the Mohawk River to Wood Creek by removing the obstacles in the river so as to make it negotiable by boats of burden; and he and those associated with him were granted permission to undertake the work, with a grant of one hundred and twenty-five dollars to help them. With this they were to make their survey and begin the work, and the ultimate profits from transportation through their improvements were to go to them, subject to regulations and restrictions, in return for their defraying the remainder of the expense. In 1785 Colles published a pamphlet entitled "Proposals for the Speedy Settlement of the Waste and Unappropriated Lands on the Western Frontier of the State of New York, and for the Improvement of the Inland Navigation Between Albany and Oswego." In it he, too, exhibits a Washingtonian vision of extended internal trade and population, and safe communication in time of war. He describes the land, and includes the Lakes. He refers to England and the glories of her recent canal policy. By 1786 he had won enough of his cause to enable his friends in the Legislature to bring in and put through a bill bestowing on him and his associates further funds with which to pursue his measures. But ultimate lack of coöperation and support prevented him from carrying the project further. Added legislation along the same lines, however, was debated without concrete result through 1786, and it is the name of Jeffrey Smith that is linked with the first official mention of Lake Erie in a roundabout connection with the canal. He was a member of the committee to whom Colles' proposals had been referred. He presented a bill "for improving the navigation of the Mohawk River, Wood Creek and the Onondaga River, with a view of opening an inland navigation to Oswego, and for extending the same, if possible, to Lake Erie."

Elkanah Watson also had claims to the title of canal pioneer. In his youth he had traveled extensively in Flanders, Holland and England, in all of which countries he had made the utmost of golden opportunities to study the construction of canals. To General Washington at Mount Vernon in the later seventeen-eighties Watson talked of internal improvements—notably of uniting the Potomac with the "Western waters." In 1788 he journeyed from Albany to Fort Stanwix, where State commissioners were presently treating with the local Indians for the purchase of their Western lands. Watson was of the "natural" and also of the national school. That is, he favored the inclined plane theory, and even more the theory that America ought to divert trade from British and Spanish possessions. In 1791 he was westward bound again, from Schenectady to Geneva with a party of friends. They went, wherever they could, by water. They wished to discover whether a communication between the Lakes and the Hudson was feasible. Watson returned with the conviction that it was not only feasible but highly essential to the future policy of the State. He wrote a journal of his expedition and delivered it to General Schuyler, then a leading member of the New York State Senate, with whom he was intimate as a fellow-resident in Albany. It embraced the probable route of a practicable canal, the description of obstructions and how to remove them, an estimate of the likely expense, and a hint of the possible return. His terminus was Oswego (which incidentally was then still in the hands of the British because of non-execution of the treaty of peace). Not for Watson, then, the vision of an Erie Canal. He would merely and modestly join existing rivers and existing lakes by smaller artificial waterways; and if he was as anxious as any one to win the West, at least he was honest as to his limitations.

> We never entertained the most distant conception of a canal from Lake Erie to the Hudson. We should not have considered it much more extravagant to have suggested the possibility of a canal to the moon.

There were those of the same school who were to be rather less honest than Watson.

As for George Clinton, he had since his days as a boyish subaltern in the expedition against Fort Frontenac known and loved the country of western New York, and the waters thereof. In his message as Governor in 1791, while his nephew De Witt was acting as his secretary, he adverted to the theme of binding the West to the eastern States by a system of waterway improvements, and as a direct outcome of his speech, legislation had commenced which ultimately led to the formation of the Western and Northern Inland Lock Navigation Companies. General Schuyler in the Senate now exhibited the fruits of his contact with Watson and others. He was a prime mover in the founding and chartering of the companies, and he was placed at the head of the dual organization. Watson continued to be his friend and aide. Surveys were authorized and made to the west and also to the north (for Lake Champlain was already a second objective), and the various bills presented on the subject made all-embracing mention of Lake Ontario to the west and the Hudson to the east, with possible lockage around Niagara Falls into Lake Erie, for which purpose a corporate charter was actually obtained.

But the question of expense still ruled the day. The legislature could always be induced to vote sufficient funds for digging in flat lands and clearing rivers and checking the force of rapids, but further funds were urgently needed elsewhere. So "Mohawk to Wood Creek" continued to be the watchword, though in 1796 we have Thomas Eddy, traveling in his capacity as a member of the Western Inland Lock Navigation Company, with an English engineer of note named Weston, surveying the possibilities of a canal to connect the Mohawk River with the Seneca River, and so avoid Wood Creek, Oneida Lake and their dangers altogether. But their report was shelved.

What the navigation companies actually effected was the harnessing of rapids here and there, the clearing of rivers and the construction of a real canal—a useful canal but an extremely local one—between the two familiar points: the Mohawk and Wood Creek. And there the whole thing rested. Schuyler eventually went to Washington and a seat in the United States Senate, and Elkanah Watson was left complaining without effect that the General had been the only influential person whose imagination reached beyond Fort Stanwix—that "stopping at Fort Stanwix was only half doing the business." But the companies had actually accomplished a great deal, in comparison with past efforts.

Meanwhile men of pioneer spirit were buying or renting western lands from soldiers who had received them as pay and wished to turn them into cash. These hardy spirits, still traveling Indian fashion, began to settle the wilderness west of Lake Seneca, the end of the existing water communications in that direction. But the settlement was sparse because the transit was so difficult, and many who set out became discouraged and turned back. How would they live? They could raise crops, but how transport them? The cost of carrying them to a market was higher than the price they would fetch when arrived. There were big tolls on the little canal. There were losses from delays caused by swollen or dried-up rivers. There was the long, hard portage between Schenectady and Albany after one had struggled out of the West, and through the so-called improvements. The building of the State road from Utica to Buffalo arose out of all these difficulties. It joined the turnpike through the Mohawk valley, and it had the effect of killing the last usefulness of the Mohawk-Wood Creek canal by rendering land transportation cheaper than transportation by water. The price was, nevertheless, prohibitive, and the settlements in the West remained few and far between.

In 1803, Gouverneur Morris came home from Washington and began talking canal once more—to Simeon De Witt, the Surveyor-General, this time, and to Charles Brodhead, a land surveyor, of whom he requested data as to heights, levels, etc., of the country between the Great Lakes and the Hudson, amazing them both, apparently, by the magnitude of his schemes. Since his early interchanges with Schuyler, he had traveled by land and water to Montreal and through the St. Lawrence to Lake Ontario and across that lake to Niagara, whence he had gone by land to Lake Erie. Hence, it is probable, his later leanings as to the best canal route. On seeing nine great ships in Lake Erie in 1799, he had dreamed of forests of masts, of processions of laden boats, of wealth flowing out to the sea and in again, multiplied, from far countries. His letter to John Parrish of December, 1800, envisions it:

> Shall I lead your astonishment to the verge of incredulity? I will: Know, then, that one-tenth of the expense borne by Britain in the last campaign would enable ships to sail from London through Hudson's River into Lake Erie. As yet, my friend, we only crawl along the outer shell of our country. The interior excels the part we inhabit in soil, in climate, in every thing. The proudest empire in Europe is but a bauble compared to what America *will* be, *must* be, in the course of two centuries —perhaps of one.

Surveyor-General De Witt later asserted that Morris mentioned "tapping Lake Erie and leading its waters in an artificial river directly across the country to the Hudson River," which De Witt said he repeated to James Geddes in 1804. Geddes amplified this by recalling having mentioned the suggestion to Jesse Hawley, who plays his own part in canal history. But Hawley in his turn emphatically denied that such was the source of his inspiration, or that he ever knew of any such scheme of Morris' prior to entering the field himself. It is interesting to note that the only source ever acknowledged by Hawley as the inspiration for his subsequent essays—and that only after he had nursed the idea for years—was President Jefferson's message to Congress on Internal Improvements in the year 1807, which included a suggestion as to "the propriety of devoting so much of the national revenue as the exigencies of the government do not require to making roads and canals." Incidentally the surveyor Brodhead always asserted that Morris never mentioned anything to him but a canal from Lake Ontario to the Hudson, and the engineer Benjamin Wright, subsequently his colleague, shared his opinion that Morris never contemplated reaching Lake Erie save by lockage around the Falls.

For when triumph had been wrought, this was to be the vexed question of the hour—honor to whom honor was due for the inception of the Erie Canal idea. James Geddes remarked:

> Canals between the Hudson and northern Wood Creek, and between the Mohawk and Western Wood Creek, must have been contemplated by the first navigators of these waters. Things so obvious must have early struck everyone, but the idea of the Erie Canal is of a very modern origin.

Be that as it may, the western country, in spite of all the efforts and all the legislation, remained a wilderness, and swamp and quagmire and primeval forest continued undisturbed. Jesse Hawley it is who probably correctly stands first in advocating direct canal communication between Lake Erie and the Hudson.

His was a highly significant contribution in any event. Canada then was still hostile and fiercely competitive; which was why the link with Lake Ontario and around the Falls was impolitic and, to many, unpatriotic. Not yet was the day of unguarded frontiers and hands across the sea, when trade competition would be keen but no longer warlike, and men would bring Lake Ontario into the scheme of the State canal system actually to further and facilitate the contest. The suggestion of digging through directly to Lake Erie was therefore of very special import. It was, in effect, steering clear of dangerous waters. It was striking out for the right to growth and survival. Above all, it was penetrating to the limitless undeveloped wilderness of the West indeed. It was pointing a finger in the general direction of a practically unbounded future—straight in that direction, instead of by devious and partly international routes.

De Witt Clinton, under the pseudonym "Tacitus," later wrote the story of the Canal Policy of the State of New York. He there remarks:

> To an intelligent and observing mind, the physiognomy of the country west of Rome to Lake Erie must present great facilities for artificial navigation. The abundant supply of water from the intermediate lakes, rivers, springs and creeks—the general and gradual ascent to the west—the great extent of champaign country—and the wide valleys through which canals might pass, are too obvious not to strike the observation of any traveler.

Mr. Clinton, who never laid any claim to the original inception of the idea, gave Hawley the credit for first introducing the subject to him. Writing to Hawley in 1822, he remarked:

> I have no hesitation in stating that the first suggestion of a Canal from Lake Erie to the Hudson River which came to my knowledge was communicated in essays under the signature of "Hercules," on internal navigation, published in the Ontario Messenger at Canandaigua. The first number appeared on the 27th October, 1807, and the series of numbers amounted, I believe, to fourteen.

Jesse Hawley was the author of the essays of "Hercules," but his scheme was still for conducting the waters eastward by means of an inclined plane, and his canal plan stretched no farther than from Buffalo to Utica, where it was to join the Mohawk River, suitably improved, to Schenectady and the long-used portage thence, for the time being, to Albany. Hawley had from his early days as a flour merchant at Geneva, New York, seen the need for improving on the primitive Mohawk-Wood Creek Canal, and in 1805 he had begun talking of that need and of the practicability of this greater waterway. He was laughed at for his pains. His friends of the Genesee valley had long joined with him in "wishing that an arm of the North River had been extended into the Genesee country by the Author of nature." But to assume the Almighty's functions, and build a canal—! Hawley, however, continued to study the subject by taking in the story of the European canals. He journeyed to Lake Erie, and made due obeisance to God for forming Niagara and giving to Erie power to spare for men and ships and inland waterways. Then he went home and wrote his "Hercules" essays, outlining the mighty project of an artificial canal from Lake Erie to and into the Mohawk. Pretending to no scientific knowledge of canal construction, he attempted to disseminate none, but the probable results—what such a canal would mean to the villages and the undeveloped lands along the way, and in particular to Buffalo at the beginning, Utica at what would be the junction, Schenectady at the head of the navigable waters—he realized and could describe. He knew but imperfectly the topography of his scene of action, and had accepted blindly an earlier mistaken notion that a workable level existed along the ridge to the south of Lake Ontario. Hence his inclined plane theory, to which Mr. Morris was later to adhere with such disastrous results. But the general geography he knew; and history he would make. He foresaw the mercantile end of it. He, too, saw forests of trees converted into thickets of masts and spars. He saw salt and potash transformed into golden wealth, and all by virtue of a system of transportation that must cut the prohibitive price of portage of heavy commodities, the impracticable length of time which it took to convey them down, to proportions within the working reach of man. He, too, saw extension to the west—indeed, his ultimate scheme verbally embraced Chicago and also the entire route of the Mississippi—and possible trade from a competitive north. He wished the national government to underwrite the project, rather than any company of individuals. That the State might be equal to the occasion was beyond the bounds of his fertile imagination. He saw success so clear as eventually to wrest from Schenectady the ostensible river-head and carry the navigable waters by lockage past the Cohoes Falls to Albany and the Hudson. And last but not least he gave an estimate of six million dollars as the probable cost of construction of such a canal, which was to prove, in the result, strikingly near the mark.

These essays were looked upon in many quarters as the emanations of a lunatic. But De Witt Clinton, in acknowledging them as the first suggestion that caught his attention of a canal directly connecting the western Lake Erie with the Hudson, as distinguished from the discussions that had gone on since his boyhood days of a waterway linking the Hudson to the northern Lake Ontario, honored them for all time.

In the year 1808, Joshua Forman, Federalist member of the Assembly from Onondaga County, referred to Jefferson's message of the year before, and proposed a resolution "to direct a survey to be made of the most eligible and direct route of a canal to open a communication between the tide water of Hudson's River and Lake Erie." This was the first reference on record in the Legislature to any direct canal between those two points. It also marks the earliest coöperation between Republicans and Federalists in regard to the canal, for Forman enlisted the aid of the interested in the opposition ranks, and secured a fusion "Canal ticket" for presenting his resolution. Forman in his turn was a student of canal navigation, and an opponent of the time-honored theory that improvements in existing river communications constituted all that was needful. He was enthusiastic on the subject of cutting through to Lake Erie, and he broached the subject to Wright and also to General McNeil of Oneida. Wright remarked that it seemed folly to make a canal for one hundred and fifty miles "abreast of a good sloop navigation to Lake Ontario." Forman explained that the canal would pay for itself by reason of the towns that would spring up along its route, which towns would ordinarily develop along the Lake shore if the waterway were to be taken to Lake Ontario and up around the Falls. Wright then concurring, Forman drew up the resolution aforementioned, and presented it to the Assembly on February 4th, 1808. It was aimed at the Federal Government, but without much hope, even though it referred to President Jefferson's expressed views. Nor did it meet with so much as a kind reception, even in its native State. The epithets "wild" and "foolish" were freely hurled at it, and though Forman addressed the House strongly and somewhat angrily in its support, not for him were those epithets to be retracted.

However, all he had asked was a survey, and he did finally obtain that. In 1808 Simeon De Witt was directed to have such a survey made. He duly complied by commissioning James Geddes to make a technical study of the possibilities of the Ontario route, as proposed by Gouverneur Morris.

But Geddes' surveying tour convinced him not only of the shortcomings of Mr. Morris as a practical canal projector, but of the complete feasibility and utter desirability of leading an artificial waterway over the more equable and therefore less expensive levels to the southward, directly to Lake Erie. And no sooner had he presented his report, in January, 1809, than Joshua Forman journeyed to Washington to lay the project before Mr. Jefferson as a desirable Federal measure. He described how it would develop the resources of the land and benefit the country. Mr. Jefferson said the idea was a worthy one, and opined that the times might be ripe for such a scheme about a hundred years thence.... He pointed to Washington's pet Potomac plan, which still was incomplete, and said,

> Why, sir, here is a canal of a few miles, projected by General Washington, which if completed would render this a fine commercial city, which has languished for many years because the small sum of two hundred thousand dollars necessary to complete it cannot be obtained from the General Government, the State Government, or from individuals, and you talk of making a canal three hundred and fifty miles through the wilderness! It is little short of madness to think of it at this day.[1]

None the less, Thomas Jefferson was to live to see that wilderness conquered by the canal, and to comment on it too.

It was on the strength of Geddes' report, then, that Thomas Eddy, a director of the Western Inland Lock Navigation Company and a tireless worker in its behalf, approached the party

[1] "Memoir of De Witt Clinton," by David Hosack, G. Seymour, New York; 1829.

leader Platt with a modest request that the existing companies should be further subsidized for the purposes for which they had been organized—namely, the clearing of rivers and streams, the building of connecting canals where practicable, and the harnessing of rapids. He wanted a new survey made for a canal between Oneida Lake and the Seneca River.

Mr. Platt, who dwelt in the western portion of the State and knew the history of the collective canal efforts from the point of view of a very personal interest in that West, came back with a suggestion that the companies had not contributed any action of outstanding note in the past, and, voicing a growing but very doubting hope, proposed that Eddy and his *confrères* lend their support to a movement to build a single canal from the Hudson to Lake Erie. He finally persuaded the badly startled Eddy to agree.

The next step was to secure sufficiently powerful support to make ultimate success a probability. Eddy, like his new colleague, knew only too well the history of the canals. Both men, by the same token, appear to have jumped simultaneously to the same conclusion—De Witt Clinton, successful advocate of the seemingly unattainable and the visionary since 1800. It seems fair to conclude that political considerations did not enter greatly, if at all, into this choice. He and his party were coming back into power, and indeed had never wholly lost it; but Federalists had desired a canal before, and Clinton had been powerful from the beginning of the century. No man had yet sunk party differences for the sake of Clinton's influence and his aid in this connection. To Platt and Eddy, then, the credit for a momentous choice. They went to Mr. Clinton with their plan, together with Geddes' report and other facts. They suggested that if the movement appealed to Mr. Clinton, Mr. Platt should offer resolutions calling for a canal commission to examine the subject in its entirety; to make their own survey; and to report in due course direct to the Legislature; the commission to be composed in equal proportions of members of both parties. Mr. Clinton, who had a family history in the surveying field and a personal one in the scientific and naturalistic, was asked by Platt if he would consent to be included in the Republican portion of the membership.

> Mr. Clinton listened with intense interest and deep agitation of mind (wrote Platt later). He... said that he was in a great

> measure a stranger to the western interior of our State; that he had given but little attention to the subject of canal navigation, but that the exposition of our plan struck his mind with great force; that he was then prepared to say that it was an object worthy of thorough examination....

Mr. Clinton thereupon promised that if Mr. Platt would move the resolution without suggesting the names of the possible personnel of the commission, he would feel free to second it and support it.

> From this period (adds Platt) Mr. Clinton devoted the best powers of his vigorous and capacious mind to this subject, and he appeared to grasp and realize it as an object of the highest public utility, and worthy of his noblest ambition.

This was the picture that then appears to have burst upon De Witt Clinton's view: internal improvements—that rallying cry whose echoes were to swell and resound in the years to come—was still only a phrase; a rather frightening pair of words. The citizenry had with great regularity envisioned ruin as the result of the stupendous cost of developing the country's resources before the country had amassed sufficient wealth. They did not see that wealth would come when resources were developed to carry it. It was left to the older countries to prosper by the most modern means of transit. True, Virginia, Pennsylvania, Maryland and Massachusetts had their brief internal systems of canals; but where in all this illimitable land was a waterway in proportion to itself? Where was the method of intercommunication big enough to bestow on the States that occupied a fragment of the continent an outlet through each other? Wealth, commodities were hopelessly tied up, imprisoned within their insufficient territories because of the cost of carrying them far on wagons, on animals' backs or on men's.

And still there beckoned the West—the undigested and still collective West; a territory not of neatly parceled states of a close-bound Union, but of adventurous pioneer settlement, of Indian land and of forest. Also of a Future, which might, by the grace of the Indians, the settlers and the natural trends of economic growth, go to the English, the Spanish or even, still, the French, while the United States waited for moral courage and financial vision to push along that way. Such a twist of that glorious future would mean shrinkage, bloodshed, pressure, war, instead of growth and fulfillment. Oblivion perhaps. The United States had increasing need to remember that in its natural development, it must push that way, or be finally pushed into the sea. War threatened. War might change the face of the American continent.

In 1810, Robert Fulton's steamships were already regularly plying the Hudson River, but sailing-vessels, when the ice permitted, still carried the bulk of the merchandise and passengers bound from Albany to New York and back again. Such freight, as to the inanimate part, still depended on long portages and short river rides to bring it from the interior, while humans traveling in those same parts were only removed from the same classification by grace of the infrequent stagecoaches. Hence commodities came high, and journeys little less so.

Visions, however, dwell in impossible regions, as far as everyday mankind is concerned, and no one, from 1724 to 1810, had proved equal to the task of proving to New York that the project of an artificial waterway to carry freight and passengers from the Great Lakes to the Hudson was anything—could be anything—but visionary. It needed a man with the power to grasp all the complexities of the subject as it concerned New York, and to present it to the people themselves with the voice to put it through. In 1809 General Brooks, a member of the Assembly from Ontario County, had brought the letters of Jesse Hawley to Albany and eventually left them with Simeon De Witt for investigation. Simeon's young but powerful cousin had read and digested them. So had others who for decades had been fervent for the plan. And because, in the last resort, they had reached the hour and needed the man, in 1810 the advocates and some at least of the progenitors of the Lake Erie to the Hudson Canal turned to De Witt Clinton because of what he was and also because of his undeniable power in the State. As for him, he listened to them because grandfather, uncle, father, teachers, even the first President of the United States, had shown him the desirability of expansion to the west and of commerce by inland waterways instead of by portage.

Now he went into the matter, thoroughly, as was his wont. He sought out surveyors and engineers and merchants, and absorbed all the data they could give him. He read. And when he had read his fill, and listened to good purpose, and written to some purpose, too, he began to talk. To the Legislature, of course.

The net result must be judged in the light of the efforts that had gone before—and indeed it is the only excuse for having enlarged upon them. On the 13th of March in the year 1810, Mr. Platt presented his resolution. Mr. Clinton seconded it, and proved in word and deed what he had meant when he had pledged himself to support it. On the 15th, it passed both houses by a unanimous vote. And on the 16th, the names of seven men were presented and duly inserted in the blanks left at the request of Clinton, that he might be unembarrassed in lending it his legislative support. Platt himself insisted on being left out of the final choice, for similar reasons of delicacy—which was a pity. There seems little doubt that he would have graced the commission at least as well as one or two of its major members, and perhaps to better and speedier effect.

The names were: Gouverneur Morris, Stephen Van Rensselaer, Simeon De Witt, William North, Thomas Eddy, Peter B. Porter and De Witt Clinton.

12

PROGRESS

1810 - 1812

FROM THE first, Mr. Clinton refused to accept any compensation whatsoever for his labors in connection with the canal. He did so in order to remain unhampered by imputations of ulterior motives in any of his canal activities. He emerged in the sight of the people of the State of New York with his head above the muddy waters of politics, and though politicians subsequently tried their hardest to blur that view of him, the vision never faded quite completely.

The Commission met at the Surveyor-General's office in Albany on July 2nd, 1810. A steamboat had carried Mr. Clinton and Mr. Eddy in thirty hours from New York City. In itself a symbol of an entire new era in water transportation, it thus helped a pair of pioneers in that field to keep an appointment with the future.

The Commission was an unusual one, and its members were all rather remarkable men. Simeon De Witt, first cousin to Mr. Clinton, was to fill his high office as Surveyor-General with honor for a total of fifty years, through all the sudden upheavals of party and overthrow of office-holders. He took the essays of Hawley along with him on the journey, subsequently returning them with the compliments of the Commissioners on their usefulness. Clinton also wrote later to Hawley:

> The Board of Canal Commissioners which made the first tour of observation and survey in 1810 were possessed of the writings of "Hercules," which were duly appreciated as the work of a sagacious, inventive and elevated mind, and you were at that time and since considered the author.

Gouverneur Morris, Minister to France at the outbreak of the French Revolution, statesman, scholar, soldier, scion of two distinguished lines, colleague of Clinton in various capacities, and one of the many who claimed the inception of the canal idea for their own, was speedily named the senior member of the Commission.

Stephen Van Rensselaer, who had the distinction of being the last of a line of great Dutch landowners, or "patroons," having inherited the Hudson Valley domains and the privileges of his ancestors before the Revolution, was widely loved, even apart from his tenantry and his Federalist constituents. Which speaks well for his modernized point of view in a day of triumphant democracy. Still called by all "the Patroon," he patronized every public improvement, and was to be actively connected with more than this one great development in transportation. He was at this time a member of the State Assembly.

Thomas Eddy, possessing no practical party affiliations, brought his years of experience and untiring effort in connection with the existing companies to his new task.

General North was a veteran of the Revolution, a Federalist and a man of considerable political and social weight and mental ability.

Peter B. Porter represented the region at the extreme west of the State, and his intimacy with that region and his jealousy for its local interests were to have their own part to play. A Congressman at the moment, he had already distinguished himself at Washington in the cause of internal improvements.

Mr. Geddes was engaged as an expert to attend the Commission on its journey of investigation, and to exhibit the possible route he had found. A corps of assistant surveyors accompanied him.

The course lay primarily along the line of the Mohawk River. Morris and Van Rensselaer elected to travel by land as far as Utica, where Geddes and his staff were to meet the party. The rest, with the exception of Porter, who awaited in his Western fastness at Black Rock, proceeded to Schenectady by stage and there embarked in a pair of river boats. No floating palaces these. The day of marine luxury was very much in the future. The Commissioners, or their servants, who occupied the second boat together with a ton and a half of miscellaneous domestic and personal equipment, might catch fish and shoot fowl along the way, if they were lovers of either as a table delicacy. But they must land on a convenient bank if they wanted to cook the catch. Or they might buy food and wine ashore, and eat it cold. Or they might take the "ordinaries" in the taverns along the way. There were no facilities aboard. They stopped each night in the shelter of the near shore, and the handiest inn was their sleeping place. Their boats' decks boasted awnings of canvas as protection from sun and rain, but for shelter no more. Their mode of travel depended upon the elements. They rode under sail when the wind blew fair. Men poled them along when the breeze was less helpful or was absent. In a storm they had no recourse but to heave to and lie as close as possible to the shore. Thus their roofs varied from night to night. Their tables ranged from a grassy knoll about a fire of sticks to a tavern board or, on rare occasions, the shining mahogany of some hospitable and well-met acquaintance.

As far as De Witt Clinton was concerned, he was one to enjoy the novel experience of such a water voyage. The scientist came out from his hiding. River, land and air were fields of wonder; fossil and stone and formation; bird and beast and fish; flora and fauna as well as humans a source of unending information. His diary is full of the pleasure he extracted from those days. Hardships there were, and sometimes repulsive ones, for from fleas to mosquitoes the insect world ran riot, and even if an inn could boast freedom more or less from the former, it was harder to drive the latter out. There was adventure, too. Rapids through which few boats penetrated were negotiated by these. Mr. Clinton put up with the annoyance and the hazard. He noticed them, indeed, more as a phase of the education that was always a part of his life, than as anything to fret over. Conditions of existence in all their gradations he noted along the route of the proposed waterway. He collected stones and plants as he gathered anecdote and history, and ever he wrote in his commonplace-book his theories of how the world about him had developed. It was all grist to the mill of his many-faceted intellect.

And meanwhile he closely attended his companions and their joint errand. All made notes of the lay of the land along the Mohawk River. Not all saw the future written in that land, as Clinton did, or noted that, as did he. It was on the fifth evening that they came to Utica, to find Morris and Van Rensselaer arrived by the single daily stage, and in full occupation of the best inn in that quite unimportant outpost of three hundred houses and sixteen hundred and fifty inhabitants. From this point west the stages ran thrice a week as far as Geneva. Further, no public transit at all was available. Eastward, both river and land freight came high.

The Board met briefly, and the entire party then took to the boats again. On the 12th of July they held a meeting at Rome, to lay their final plans. Here Lake Ontario versus Lake Erie was once more discussed, for the *whole* of the canal suggestions lay within the Commission's province, and it was at Rome that the two proposed routes branched away from each other.

Clinton still reserved decision as to the practicability of the direct route to Lake Erie. He wanted to see for himself, with the expert aid of Geddes' findings and Hawley's theories. But on the subject of the desirability of that route he did not hesitate to express himself freely. He had weighed the patent possibilities of the Ontario route, following the almost continuous river and lake communication familiar to traders and their canoes from the days of the Dutch. But at the head of the Mohawk he looked out toward the western land, almost undeveloped from here as far as Buffalo and the Lake and who knew just how far beyond? He saw the settlers who would flock to the line of a waterway from the Hudson, saw the canal-boats plying to the westernmost end and receiving rich cargoes from ships and forests and fields. He saw, with the direct westward trend of the canal, a commerce unshared with those who had so lately been, and would in the probable course of events so soon be again, the enemies of his people. He did not want a waterway into Lake Ontario then, in the direction and perhaps some day at the disposal of the Canadian north. He wanted a waterway into Lake Erie and the western United States of the future. That is, if feasible he desired it.

Morris agreed with him on the main point—but Mr. Morris was by no means in agreement that it was necessary for *him* to wait and see. At Rome:

> The senior commissioner talked wildly (writes Clinton). He was for breaking down the mound of Lake Erie, and letting out the waters to follow the level of the country, so as to form a

sloop navigation with the Hudson, and without any aid from any other water.

The absurdity of such a suggestion was to be revealed to Mr. Morris' colleagues at least, all along the way. But it was not till the final meeting of this investigatory tour, at Chippewa, that Clinton committed himself. He had then seen for himself, and having seen, he knew that the clearing and joining of rivers along the way, which had also been suggested, would be as impracticable as a means of effecting a water passage across-country as Mr. Morris' plan of letting the Erie waters rush out and along and down a simple continuous bed. He had learned, as had others before him, that rivers were far too dependent on the elements, rising and falling as they did with the rains and the droughts, to provide a reliable means of heavy trade communication. He also knew (and Geddes and most of his colleagues now agreed with him) that the Hudson-Erie route would allow of the construction of an artificial canal to conduct the waters of the Lake by means of a minimum of lockage into the Hudson. He had seen the old brief scrap of a canal between the Mohawk and Wood Creek. It was the basis of their calculations and the natural center of their interest. He knew that a canal by the Ontario route, by the nature of the land, would be cheaper to construct. He also knew why the Erie route was nevertheless primarily the desirable route—because trade and growth and progress lay that way....

Their journey took them all the way from Albany to Buffalo, with a deviation on the part of the water-going portion of the Commission for the purposes of inspecting the Ontario route. From Rome they had followed the old canal to and into Wood Creek. They had sailed the length of the Creek and out into Oneida Lake. Here the voluntary detour began. They crossed, and passed the outlet to Three River Point and into the Oswego River. By July 16th they had negotiated the rapids of that river to its mouth at the village of Oswego. This was the downward route from Three River Point which the canal would take if it ended at Lake Ontario. They came and they saw, and when they had seen, they walked back along the banks of the Oswego for five miles, so that the boats would be light enough to make the return journey up the rapids. They came again to Three River Point, whence they followed the shallows of the Seneca River to its junction with Cayuga and into Seneca Lake. On the 24th they came to Geneva, disposed of their boats, and took to hired carriages. They rode to the Canandaigua outlet, and explored the site of Geddes' proposed embankment across the Irondequoit Creek from the Genesee River. They stood on the banks of the Genesee, at a spot where men who followed the canal would one day build a town and call it Rochester. Thence they rode all the way to the Niagara River, which they crossed to view Niagara Falls, and finally went by the new ridge road through the woods to Lewiston on August 2nd, when Morris and Van Rensselaer and Porter duly joined them.

On August 3rd the final meeting of the tour took place at Chippewa. On August 3rd, in the year 1810, De Witt Clinton first gave voice to the things he had seen, the conclusions he had drawn, the hopes he entertained, and the decision at which he had arrived with regard to the Erie Canal. The land across which Mr. Morris would guide a natural stream, across whose indentations and ridges he would make embankments to carry that stream on an inclined plane, they had all seen for themselves. All except Morris appeared to have grasped the indubitable fact that there were valleys in this westward part of the State which were certainly not to be overcome by mounds of earth as Mr. Morris suggested; that there were heights and levels and swamps that were matters for practical engineering and frequently, of necessity, of lockage. A portion of the Commission still clung to the outworn theory of clearing rivers and streams and joining them. Clinton now felt able to tell them how futile such schemes would be from the point of view of heavy freight navigation. Mr. Porter alone, but unofficially supported by local interests both British and American, still clung to the Ontario route, but on this point was in such a minority that his capitulation was a matter of time. Clinton argued with Porter that the land west of Rome as far as Lake Erie in direct line had potentialities which, if realized, would in themselves support the finances of the project. He pointed out that canal cargoes would have to be regularly shifted from barges to lake boats if Oswego and Lake Ontario were used.

As for Mr. Morris—Mr. Morris was the official head of the Commission, and he had insisted that Providence would provide the means whereby the canal could flow naturally down to the Hudson.... It will be seen that the Erie Canal was Mr. Clinton's canal from that moment. He took up the burden, and never, of his own volition, let it go.

Already signs were not wanting that it was to be no easy task. All along the route they had been objects of interest and speculation, if not invariably of admiration. There were politics, even along the line of the projected canal, where all might have been expected to look for profit and improvement from the scheme. Indeed, one of the objects of the tour was to overcome, by the presence of these able and prominent men, the more local ignorance and doubts and fears. At home, there was already arising the faction that would never cease to dub the canal "Clinton's Ditch." It did take vision to realize the potentialities of the plan. It did take foresight to picture sparse villages, weedy settlements, as roaring busy townships because a waterway ran through them. Some men, a few, shared this foresight with De Witt Clinton, and in them the excited current of anticipation ran high. They were the coöperators, the smoothers of the path where only they could smooth it. With others, cupidity ruled. With not a few, stupidity.

From the moment of their leaving Gregory's Tavern at Albany, however, to the day they reached Buffalo and the end of their journey, no detail of the present and the possible future escaped Mr. Clinton's mind. The countryside was almost incredibly static. The village of Schenectady was dead, says Clinton, even on the Fourth of July. And who knew better, in that year 1810, than a Canal Commissioner who perforce spent the holiday there! Schenectady was still a village indeed, and it dwelt almost exclusively in the past. Its inhabitants still intoned long stories of the massacre, which they had first heard, some of them, from survivors at first hand. They gossiped in the friendly shade of Powell's Hotel, which constituted the mainstay of the village. They farmed; they ruminated; they liked to see strangers, but they had heard of canals before, and they still viewed no waters but those of the Mohawk.

Utica seemed a more flourishing village to De Witt Clinton, according to his private canal journal. It is an extremely human and highly interesting journal—one of those very few portions of his diary in which he had leisure to reveal himself. He is here the complete Clinton; scientist and scholar; man and boy; and, fairly large in the background, politician. He picks up stones and sees them with the eye of a geologist; he catches strange fish and describes them with the pen of a naturalist. He joins in a practical joke with zest, but is circumspect withal. He meets with flattery, but adds a grain of salt. He meets with slander, and a little vinegar is forthcoming. He loves the white gleam of a sail on a blue expanse of river; the color and the nature of a flower in a field. He likes to meditate in a solitary pew in some plain Presbyterian church. And he is, above all, thoughtful about this quiet and beautiful but rather stagnating countryside. Utica, he remarks, had consisted of one house only twenty-two years before; and now it had its three hundred, with "two newspapers, a bank, a post-office, and several churches." It was destined to grow a little faster than that as an outcome of the canal men's visit.

It was near this point, incidentally, that Clinton's canal wanderings were to bring him a find of rare significance. He discovered there a species of wheat growing wild, and proved himself equipped to analyze it and differentiate it positively from any offshoot of a cultivated crop. This discovery of his was the cause of a mild sensation, not widespread in his own country, but markedly so among European scientific bodies, among whom he also distributed specimens of the grain. The whole theory of the origin of the human race came into the limelight because of it, for wheat growing wild on the shores of the Caspian Sea had made men identify Asia as the cradle of the human race, whence man had gone with his wild-grown sustenance to make his home and raise his crops elsewhere. A flutter of honorary diplomas and memberships descended on Clinton as a result.

But let us return to him as he makes his somewhat difficult way along the line of a problematical canal. There was, for instance, Three River Point, that junction of natural waterways along the outlet of Oneida Lake. This place they christened "Bug Bay," for obvious reasons. One room at the inn seemed to have more than its quota of fleas, and it was decided that the unsuspecting Mr. Morris should be enticed into occupying it—for it was a spacious chamber. But the glee of Mr. Clinton, at least, was short-lived. In his loftier and more modest ærie, he was not undisturbed himself that night....

There were anti-Clinton pamphlets at Smith's Tavern in Oswego; but at the moment the Commissioners were as much concerned about their health as about their political reputations.

There was a threat of fever, for swamps prevailed in these wilds where sanitation was unknown. Incidentally Mr. Clinton's efforts to solve the mystery of the connection between swampland and fever were to be unremitting throughout his life. He was to suffer for having lived before his friends of the medical profession pinned the mosquito down to its fever-carrying iniquities.

Meanwhile one of the gentlemen had brought his flute along, and "a song and a jest," says Clinton, "more than our most powerful medicines, were the best antidotes to sickness." But existing antidotes to sickness interested him endlessly. Medicine as a study attracted him as did all the other sciences, and his diary is full of notes of experiments with remedies for this ailment and that.

The meeting at Chippewa adjourned with a resolution for renewal of its deliberations in New York. The party then proceeded to Buffalo. And Buffalo, when they came to it, seemed to realize the potential future to the full. The hope of becoming the gateway to an apparently limitless West had taken hold of little, insignificant Buffalo—a city in name only, though already a port of call for the intrepid; a gathering-place for sightseers from Ohio and the Mississippi territory, and for travelers there. Mr. Clinton's description of Buffalo in 1810 reveals a village of "thirty to forty houses . . . five lawyers, and no church." But local society there was, and what there was turned out, both from the American side of Niagara Falls and from the British. So did the neighboring point, Peter Porter's home village of Black Rock, already evincing hope of ousting Buffalo as the ultimate westerly outlet of the canal. That hope was to live a valiant life, and to die hard.

But such struggles were still in the future. Mr. Clinton was looking over the waters, upon the white sails of the merchantmen of Lake Erie. Here lay the thrill of the whole expedition. Here was the rainbow at the end of the trail—the gateway, indeed, to the West. He seems to have torn himself away from the tangible West with quite an effort. Mr. Geddes remained behind, to continue his surveys—to find levels and grades in the Tonawanda Valley, and so forth. Mr. Clinton went back by way of Geneva and a detour to Ithaca; thence to Auburn and so by road to Schenectady, to Albany and by steamboat to New York.

On March 2nd, 1811, the Commissioners duly presented their

report. It was drawn by their senior member, Mr. Morris, still clinging to his theories and his faith. Honor had been paid to Mr. Morris' years and prestige and standing by naming him the head. Tact had been subsequently used on him. Clinton had argued with him, and a majority of the Commission was apparently convinced that he had been more or less won over to Clinton's views. But the report was a curious mixture of his own views plus the influence that had been not quite able to move him. Its safety-valve was Geddes' reports, to which it referred the gentlemen of the Legislature. These showed the practicability of the direct Erie route. Also (and here the hand of Clinton is apparent), the report recommended the debarring of private individual or corporate ownership, as prejudicial to economy in transportation. It described the western part of the State—and it presented Mr. Morris' plan for a continuous waterway on an inclined plane, with an average descent of six inches per mile. Calmly Morris advocated bridging the Genesee, the Seneca and the Cayuga valleys with embankments, to conduct his gentle, if wide and deep enough, stream across their chasms. His estimate was five million dollars, which in view of the state of invention and the development of resources in his day, might have taken care of a single one of his valleys. He had, however, been willing to add that better ways than his might conceivably be found by practical men in the future; and that the question not only of sloops versus barges, but of inclined plane versus "a line ascending and descending," must be a question of "expense and utility."

Some of the Commissioners had evinced considerable reluctance to sign this document, and even a desire to present individual reports. It was Clinton who urged unanimity; who said that the important thing was to get the whole question, and not a conflict of opinions as to routes and ways and systems, fairly before the public, by the best means available. As James Renwick, who knew him well, remarks, "Clinton was a believer in the final triumph of good sense in all questions fairly submitted to the people."

There was a cry of horror at the magnitude of the scheme; a chortle of incredulity from those with even a smattering of engineering knowledge; and also a certain degree of patriotic pride that it could even be suggested that a young nation (the Federal government was still the goal) could undertake such a project. There was not a little disappointment on the part of those most ardent in the cause that such a patently amateur hand had been permitted to draw the report. But at any rate there was a world of discussion, and a continuation of legislation. In April Clinton introduced a bill in the Senate, empowering the Commissioners to continue their investigations and to ask aid from the Federal government or the individual States in behalf of the canal. It duly became law, and the Board appointed Clinton and Morris to proceed to Washington to solicit Federal support. On May 8th, Robert Fulton, who had a canal history of his own, and Robert R. Livingston were added to the Commission, and further surveys were ordered, with a grant of fifteen thousand dollars from the State. The Board as newly constituted proceeded to circularize the various State governments, but without any more result than a series of expressions of fervent interest in the project. In November Benjamin Wright, who was a native of Rome and one of the engineers of the old Navigation Companies, surveyed the land along the north of the Mohawk, and proved that no inclined plane canal such as Morris had advocated could successfully be constructed there. Copies of Geddes' reports and maps were sent to the engineer Weston in England, who gave them his unqualified approval. All this as preparation for the journey of Clinton and Morris, so that they should go well armed.

It was therefore not mere impracticability that stifled the canal proposals altogether for the time being. It so happened that in the year 1811 the United States had other things to think about than internal improvements. External affairs were at their most critical. England's aggressions at sea were, designedly or not, stifling American trade. And England's attitude was the reverse of conciliatory.

Mr. Clinton himself had other things to think about, too. The sweeping victory of his party in the State elections of the previous year had put him back into the Mayoralty of New York City. It was in this capacity that he presided, that summer, at the trial of those who had participated in a serious riot that had recently taken place in Trinity Church, during the proceedings of the 1811 Commencement of Columbia College.... One of the graduating students had been requested by the College faculty to change the language of his oration prepared for the occasion, which did not appear suitable. He had refused, and his diploma had been withheld. At the Commencement exercises, he had made an appeal to the audience, with the result that the exercises had been speedily transformed into a mêlée. The ringleaders included Gulian C. Verplanck, Columbia graduate and later prominent legislator, litterateur and philanthropist. They were rounded up and brought into the Mayor's Court; and New York City sat back to see whether the Mayor would dare offend the old families of the State, some of whose sons thus came before him.

The Mayor was severe. He addressed the miscreants in no uncertain terms, in the presence of their families. He refrained, in view of their youth, from imprisoning them for their dangerous and hot-headed conduct in the Church; but he condemned them and fined them heavily. It was from this date that Gulian C. Verplanck, to whom politics as well as literature were then only beckoning, was to be counted among the most inveterate political enemies of De Witt Clinton.

But he had enemies enough, and his party's resurgence had lent new zest to the efforts against his continuing power on the part of the opposing factions of that party. It is all the more surprising, viewed in this light alone, therefore, that that same summer Mr. Clinton voluntarily placed himself in a position of more or less complete political impotence, as far as direct participation in State politics was concerned. Lieutenant-Governor Broome had died in August, 1810. On March 14th, 1811, De Witt Clinton was nominated by a party caucus to fill his place.

On the instant, a Tammany storm burst forth. In Martling's Long Room, Teunis Wortman, Mangle Minthorne and the rest stood up to declare that Mr. Clinton was no Republican; that he was "determined to establish in his person a pernicious family aristocracy; that devotion to his person had been, in a great measure, made the exclusive test of merit, and the only passport to promotion." They said he had opposed the election of Mr. Madison, and they metaphorically drummed him out of the Republican Party. They nominated and largely supported Marinus Willett for the Lieutenant-Governorship. Those who did not support Willett voted for Nicholas Fish, the nominee of the Federalists—although alleged pro-Federalism was one of their chief complaints against Clinton!

Clinton won, by a small majority. But the split in the Republican ranks had once more lent strength to the Federalist party. Clintonians voted in part for Federalists because they hated Tammany nominees. Tammanyites did likewise, for the reasons already mentioned. The new Assembly had a Federalist majority; but De Witt Clinton remained Mayor of New York City as well as Lieutenant-Governor of New York State. There was no longer universal hatred of him in Federalist ranks.

It would appear plausible (many different theories have been advanced) that Mr. Clinton removed himself from the more active of Albany politics because of the canal—because in the office of Lieutenant-Governor he would be in contact but not in collision with Albany politicians. There is no doubt whatever that the canal from that moment was the supreme interest of his life. Hammond, the political historian, however, who was later to be condemned by Clinton's loyal widow for his view of that gentleman's political motives, takes the stand that Clinton knew that the southern district would not return him again as Senator, and thus insured his own presence in Albany and his contact and continued power in the State and in the party at all costs.

He went back now to Albany to finish his term as a Senator, and found "a mania in favor of banks, to an alarming extent." The war-clouds had brought a country-wide depression, and the Federalists were blaming it on the closing of the United States Bank. De Witt Clinton's views continued to stand against the undue extension of the banking privilege. Other people's views were still largely a matter of politics.

> The City Bank is represented in Albany as the only means of uniting the Republican Party in New York, and is supported by our city representation, except Captain Farmer, who is a wise and virtuous man. The Bank of Manhattan is again assailed.

But the champion of the Bank of Manhattan, the sincere enemy, notwithstanding his affiliations, of extension and of the existing curse of widespread unofficial inflation, once more proved his mettle. On March 22nd he reported to Henry Remsen that the City Bank had been rejected "this minute," 59 to 26. Also the Long Island and the Western District banks,

> ...so that you see the Banking Mania is effectually at an end....
>
> I have encountered much ill-will, and expect to encounter more, for my conduct on this occasion, but I have acted from

> the most mature consideration, and from the purest motives, and with a single view to the best interests of our country, and so acting, I feel the approbation of my conscience.

By the end of the month he had grown very weary of constant bank legislation and bank propaganda. There was trouble with the Columbia Bank which was making an attempt to monopolize the salt industry in the State. There was bitterness against the agents of the would-be Bank of America, who were "whispering like Satan into the ear of Eve." On the 30th, "a spirit of high resentment is rising up in all parts of the country against the multiplication of banks." April brought more rejections, and a fervent but vain hope from Clinton that all the legislation on the subject could be cleared away before the 9th, when the Legislature adjourned. It all brought a bitter taste in the mouth, a cloud to the mind, of a man constituted as was Clinton. In the words of Philip Hone:

> ... he was ... deficient in that quality of a politician, which is unfortunately too often considered as essential. His was not that cold, calculating policy, which, congealing the natural currents of the heart, would check its godlike impulse, and prevent him from loving those who loved him, lest it might interfere with his political plans: he was not of that class of politicians, who fearing to do something wrong, are content to do nothing right. By professional politicians he was condemned for this, but this it was that endeared him to his friends; and few public men have ever possessed in so great a degree the affections of ... personal friends.

The Clintons moved into the Richmond Hill mansion that year, with its lawns and statues that Abigail Adams had once described so beautifully, its spacious rooms and imposing aspect, its view of the Jersey wheatfields across the river. It was nearer to the city now than it had been in Mrs. Adams' day. That is, the city was creeping up on Greenwich village. And that great project with which De Witt Clinton was predominantly and increasingly identified was to bring to the section, logical outgrowth of New York City, a sensational wave of land prosperity that would ultimately sweep the city of New York right over Greenwich and far beyond.

Meanwhile Richmond Hill remained a country seat, and the Clintons' seventh child—a girl named Juliana, was born there in

August of 1811. The gracious Maria did not suffer herself, however, to be long removed from her duty of rendering her house, as ever, a center of hospitality for the distinguished statesmen, doctors, philosophers, soldiers, navy men and scholars who were her husband's friends. The men who came to dine at her board were increasingly from happier hunting-grounds than that of politics. John Pintard, with multiplying interests in religious, social, educational and charitable spheres, turned unfailingly toward Clinton whenever he needed support or aid. Unfailingly aided, he appears, from his correspondence with members of his own family, to have looked on Mr. Clinton as a kind of demigod. They saw each other whenever the exigencies of their various affairs permitted them to be within the bounds of the same city. With John Jacob Astor, Clinton was increasingly intimate, and in the summer of 1811 was frequently dining and often breakfasting with that gentleman. With De Peysters and Van Cortlandts and Van Wycks he was on terms of mutual affection. With cultural groups he was more and more at home. In December, as second Vice-President of the Historical Society, he delivered the anniversary oration—a discourse on the Iroquois nation of Indians. It remains one of his major essays. It is romance wrought from reality. It is knowledge and understanding. It was when he spoke it, and has been since, a model of historic narrative.

On August 1st, 1811, he "laid the cornerstone of the new Alms House at Bellevue, where dined with the Corporation." In September he writes, "Went with Mr. Delaney to view the sewing-machine." On the following day he is recording with interest a great eclipse of the sun. And all through that year 1811 he was lending his aid to Fulton and Livingston in the interest of their projected Ohio Steam Boat Company, protecting patents, furthering plans, even helping to raise funds. But Fulton was only one of many who called him benefactor. All improvements, inventions, betterments were grist to his mill. He was interested in everything—machines, the developments in natural science, celestial phenomena, and earth's more everyday problems. Certainly no Mayor of New York ever had greater zest for the potentialities, the wonders and the promise of his day.

The new building that was to house him and his subordinate city officials—the City Hall at the north of the Park—was in process of completion that year. Of Stockbridge marble front and brownstone rear, it was a creation in architecture perhaps the most ambitious, probably the most handsome, of any erected in the United States up to that date. On November 25th in the year 1811, this building was near enough to completion for Mr. Clinton to be receiving visitors there, and for such intensely interested New Yorkers as John Pintard to be gazing with pride upon the city's most beautiful edifice, and consciously describing its wonders for posterity. (That same edifice is still, of course, one of the city's major beauties.)

Yet all improvements, all interests, as far as De Witt Clinton was concerned, now boiled down to the one great project that he had adopted for his own—the western Canal. In January, 1812, he and Gouverneur Morris journeyed to Washington to lay the plan before a select committee of the House of Representatives, consisting of one member from each State. Mr. Morris, as President of the Canal Commission, did the talking and presented his report. Indeed it is significant that every report on the canal scheme was written by Morris save one—the final and only successful report, that of 1817, which Mr. Clinton wrote. Not that Morris' speech, or even his several reports, lacked, or could lack, ability. But on the practical side he still had the old shortcomings. His inclined plane theory, to which he in part still adhered despite the opposition among his colleagues, and which of course was the theory of a widespread school that had put it to practical uses in more appropriate regions, sounded wrong as applied to the land which Geddes had surveyed. So did Mr. Morris' estimate of the probable cost. And then there is little doubt that some ground existed for the complaint which grew stronger as the years progressed—that considerable coldness existed on the part of Mr. Madison and his personal adherents toward local improvements sponsored by Mr. Clinton and his. The peculiar reasons then existing for this feeling will shortly manifest themselves. The mission was unsuccessful, the Congressional committee ruling that the current national situation did not warrant their aid in such a State venture at that time.

Indeed, national affairs of the moment did contribute to a certain inattention. War was in the air, and, as a policy, immensely popular with the gentlemen of the frontier country of the West—with Henry Clay and his followers, who had their eyes on Canada. De Witt Clinton was not of those who sympathized with this trend. He felt—and needless to remark he knew whereof he spoke when he expressed the feeling—that the country was still wholly unprepared for war. His uncle had spent the past few years in raising his voice, where raise it he could, in the cause of adequate defense, believing, as he had long since written to De Witt, "warr was inevitable." But the nephew's personal rather Jeffersonian history did not point to the "inevitability" of war at any time in his thoughts. His watchword was always preparedness, as an aid to peaceable persuasion. Mr. Madison's administration, notwithstanding the popularity of the war faction, had provided no navy to speak of; no army that any potentially great nation would wish to own as such. And, as ever, not enough fortifications, or even enough munitions, to say nothing of enough funds. All this while international conditions had steadily grown worse and worse.

That was why De Witt Clinton, a peace-loving man but a drilled and instructed and an hereditary fighting man for all that, and one who could be counted upon to play his part if belligerence really proved inevitable, did not approve of declaring war at the moment. On the subject of the inevitability of war at some imminent period he was in agreement with his uncle, but only because adequate defensive and offensive preparation, which could possibly avert it, had been neglected. And failing that preparation, he would delay it. Being De Witt Clinton, he did not hesitate to declare that if war should come, he would support the administration; but that if he were the administration he would try to avoid it.

That he soon had a following was, of course, inevitable; but his views, however completely vindicated later, were not presently victorious. The United States went to war against England in the year 1812, when President Madison was running for re-election. And after his country had actually gone to war, De Witt Clinton applied for a military command. He had said his say. The die was cast. He was now ready to defend that which, after all, he loved more than either politics or theories. He asked for the rank of Brigadier by virtue of his previous militia command. The Council of Appointment vouchsafed him the rank of Major-General—but no command. And so he sent to his one-time protégé and friend, Governor Tompkins, a request for a corresponding fighting status. He sent the request by the hand of a mutual friend—Thomas Addis Emmett, whose report of the transaction is on record.

Now Tompkins had owed his original appointment as a judge to the efforts of Clinton. He had had Clinton, still all-powerful in the State, to thank for his election to the Governorship. But Tompkins and Tammany were violently for Madison and war. He therefore did not reply to Mr. Clinton's request, for a while. But guns and men and ships meanwhile moved on. Pressed then, Tompkins gave word by Emmett that older men were awaiting commands, and how could he place a junior (meaning the Mayor of New York, aged 43) before them? These were the Governor's apparent justifications. The true reason why he not only kept Clinton out of an army rôle, but did his best to conceal Clinton's burning desire for one, was different.

Mr. Madison was out to retain the Presidency on a ticket of righteous belligerency. Mr. Tompkins' obvious duty, as a good Madisonian, was therefore to join in the outcry against Mr. Madison's opponent for the Presidential chair—a man who had said the country should not go to war. Madison's opponent was widely dubbed a pacifist, and as such was plastered with opprobrium. It would therefore certainly never do to have it widely known that that opponent, though officially for peace, was ready enough to take active part in the war when it actually came.

For the man who was nominated for President against James Madison in the year 1812 was De Witt Clinton of New York.

13

CONFLICT

1812 - 1817

AS A MATTER of fact, Mr. Clinton had been supported for nomination by a great many people who wished to see a man of action conducting this war. He was also supported by many who did not wish to see a war at all. And further he was supported by those who happened to be badly in need of his aid in obtaining a charter for the Bank of America—the "Six-Million Bank," as it was called—which that year did triumph and open in New York City. That the last-named group of his would-be aides did not receive his help will have been gathered from a previously quoted comment from Clinton that their agents "whispered like Satan in the ears of Eve." Nevertheless it is a fact that some of his closest and most time-honored adherents were interested in the application of that Six Million Bank for a charter, and the most cruel condemnation Clinton ever received arose from the circumstance that he refused to withdraw his friendship from these men. The beginnings of a quarrel between Clinton and Judge Ambrose Spencer arose out of this unwillingness on the part of the former to cast the promoters of the new bank out, personally, when their campaign began, as it did, to show the familiar signs of bribery and corruption. Spencer was now closely related to Mr. Clinton by marriage. On the death of his first wife he had married, in 1807, Clinton's eldest and widowed sister, Mary. She had died in 1808, and in the following year Judge Spencer had taken as his third bride Catherine, her youngest and also widowed sister. Catherine Spencer devotedly loved her famous brother De Witt, but that did not prevent Catherine's husband now from joining forces with Governor Tompkins. Governor Tompkins was opposing the Bank of America with all his might.

He was also opposed to the canal.... In his January, 1812, message he had made no reference to internal improvements whatever, though it was increasingly a burning question. His admirers and followers among the Martling-men were not so reticent. They openly flayed De Witt Clinton for having gone to Washington. They asserted that he did so only to boost his Presidential chances. They avowed that the whole project of a canal from Albany to Lake Erie was an impossible scheme which Clinton and every one else well knew to be beyond the human and financial powers of state or nation. They warned their fellow-citizens against throwing any money into "Clinton's Ditch." And they threw all their own collective weight against it, as also against Clinton's candidacy for the highest office in the nation. They said (and the declaration of war was still pending when they said it) that if De Witt Clinton should gain the Presidency, he would advocate peace (which was then fundamentally true) and that the United States of America, suffering from acts of seizure and acts of impression, scorn of passive resistance and scorn of American mercantile hopes, would be placed in Great Britain's power for good and all. The fact that Clinton's whole aim, and that of his support in the Republican party, was delay, time to place the country in a state of preparedness, time to use that preparedness itself as a weapon, was subtly obscured. Likewise the fact that he fully and actively shared in the popular resentment against the acts complained of. He too thought Britain should be enlightened—but not by any attempt to make war without the means of winning it.

All that went unheard. He became, in the eye of the potential Madisonian voter, a monster who would deliver up the land to the enemy. And though the land was in every possible way unready for war, the fact remained that war was what a majority of its people now desired. The blood-lust flamed from speakers' stands, from newspaper columns and from the hidden back rooms whence already the country's political fate was more or less directed.

In March, 1812, the Canal Commission presented a second report to the Legislature of New York State. Mr. Morris, who drew this one also, had abandoned the notion of an inclined plane east of Lake Seneca, and had raised his official estimate to six million dollars. The report recommended that "*now* sound policy demanded that the canal should be made by the State of New York, and for her own account." In June, through the efforts of De Witt Clinton, a new law gave the Commission the right to purchase the interests of the old navigation companies, and to try to raise five million dollars within and outside the State for the construction of the canal. The investigations went on into the summer of 1813, with Mr. Morris still clinging tenaciously to the last remnants of his inclined plane theory.

But political waters were meanwhile flowing along vastly different channels. On May 28th, 1812, a Republican convention in the State of New York had placed De Witt Clinton in nomination and recommended him to the party throughout the Union as its candidate for President. Mr. Madison was of course the nominee of the regular party caucus in Congress. Many Republicans in the State deplored the action of the Clintonian meeting, undesirous of any new split in the party ranks. Many Federalists approved it, because in effect it opposed the war, and they had already raised their voices to insist that war against England was no more called for than war against France at that moment. Clinton himself perceived no reason why he should not accept the support of men who were unready for war at that juncture, regardless of party. But if Federalist gentlemen voted for him as representing a policy of peace, there is no doubt whatever that they understood him as completely as the Republicans who also supported him. His record was well known. His Jeffersonian view of war had found public expression more than once.

It must also be remembered that Jonas Platt was now in a position to know Mr. Clinton and his character quite intimately —and that Platt carried considerable weight at that moment in the Federalist party in the State. Also, a great deal of campaign work was done by John Pintard, who thus emerged momentarily from the peace of non-political existence. Campaigning enthusiastically through his distinguished kinsmen, the Boudinots and the Bayards, and his many prominent Federalist friends in New Jersey, he helped in a tremendous measure. A change in the electoral law in that State that year placed the choice of electors in the legislature instead of with the people.

The Federalist majority there gave Clinton their vote, and also held a correspondence with members of their party elsewhere which helped to bring about the Federalist convention of delegates from eleven States that likewise voted Clinton its support. Clinton has been damned for promising peace to Federalists while promising a more vigorous war to Republicans, and the cry of corruption against him personally was founded on this alleged duplicity. The letters of the New Jersey gentlemen to Pintard and others show that his personal repute and his record, already beginning to be known outside his State, were his recommendations and the true foundation for his Federalist support as the "peace candidate." The strong refutations by his Republican supporters of Tammany newspaper attacks against his motives and principles similarly show a personal, and not a political or a corrupt, bias. If peace could be won and maintained, Clinton would win and maintain it. If war was unavoidable, Clinton would war efficiently. The Republicans knew this and accepted it. So did the Federalists. It was superfluous for Clinton personally to deny (though he did so) that he had made any promises to any one.

On the other hand, however, Federalists there were ("high-minded Federalists," they called themselves) who, failing to give Mr. Clinton their support, did so because of his strictures upon them in the past and his apparent vacillation on the question of the embargo. Rufus King was at the forefront of this group.

The Republicans who opposed him did so for various reasons: some because they disliked the division in the party; some because they wisely doubted his chances against the present incumbent; others because they adhered to the policies of, or perhaps it should be said the pressures upon, that incumbent; and still others because the name of Clinton was anathema to them, and they invariably opposed him on principle—or for lack of it.

Erastus Root, Assemblyman, was at this time of the second of these groups. He spoke against the Clinton nomination because, he said, he felt that it would spell ruin for Clinton politically. He said the eyes of all New York, the hopes of New York, were centered upon Clinton, and that an overwhelming defeat at the polls would destroy his influence for right doing in the State. "Spare, oh, spare that great man!" he cried—though that was not always to be his cry.... In any case, Clinton was not spared.

DE WITT CLINTON
By Henry Inman

Doubters (Spencer among them) were brought into line. The New York members of Congress came home bringing urgent messages from Gideon Grainger, then Postmaster-General and a disciple of the Clintons, that De Witt Clinton ought to be nominated. And so nominated he was, by what was officially termed the peace party; and eventually only the followers of Tammany supported Madison in New York. Outside New York, those who wanted peace, or were against this particular war or the method of pursuing it, indorsed the nomination of Clinton.

On June 20th, 1812, the United States declared war against Great Britain. The vote in the House of Representatives for war was 79 to 49. Clintonian supporters were of course numbered among the minority. On the instant, the approaching Presidential election became truly a matter of War or No War. The war spirit swept many away from the cause of Mr. Clinton before the summer was over. There was much recrimination. Many of those who deserted tried hard to make Clinton do the same. They said that unity behind the war was now a necessity. They said that nothing would lend so much prestige to Mr. Clinton as a graceful retirement from the scene of action for another four years. A Republican delegation from Massachusetts took the trouble to come to New York to see Richard Riker, who was on the Clintonian committee, and to suggest that the party in Massachusetts might promise their support to Mr. Clinton next time, if he would withdraw from the contest now.

Mr. Riker in reply made public a statement by Mr. Clinton. Mr. Clinton felt that bargains between politicians were inconsistent with the purity and dignity of Republicanism. Mr. Clinton would not withdraw from the contest.

The outstanding feature of the Clintonian campaign was undoubtedly the support of Martin Van Buren, who took a seat in the New York State Legislature for the first time in November, 1812, as Senator from the middle district. There was at the moment a strong Clintonian majority in the New York Senate, a Federalist majority in the Assembly. There was also a complete lack of organization at Clintonian headquarters in the matter of insuring the strongest possible electoral ticket in the State. Mr. Van Buren, new as he was to legislative affairs, took the Federalists and the Madisonians in hand. Largely by his efforts the Senate was persuaded to unite on a complete Clintonian ticket of Presidential electors. In the Assembly, the prevailing choice of the Federalists was for electors of their own party; but on the final joint ballot a number of the Federalists joined in choosing the Clintonian electors.

Nor was Mr. Van Buren's influence confined within the boundaries of his State. It was, however, for the time being at least, metaphorically barred by the waters of the Potomac. De Witt Clinton carried New York, New Jersey, and all New England save Vermont, while Maryland added five of her votes to his total count. Madison won the remainder, north and south. The vote was: Clinton, 89; Madison, 128.

Mr. Clinton went back to his efforts to share in Mr. Madison's war. The New York militia as now mustered were pathetic in their numbers. The Federal Government, moreover, still saw fit to confine itself locally to precautions against invasion from the direction of Canada. No measures had been provided for resisting any attempt to land troops on Long Island or the Westchester shore. A provision for a fort at Hell Gate was the sum total of local governmental protection.

Mayor Clinton now drew up and presented to the Corporation a report on the measures necessary for the defense of the city of New York. He proposed that armed camps be lodged at Brooklyn and at Harlem Heights, with enough militiamen to garrison them, the Governor using his power under the militia law for the purpose. He proposed that the Corporation tender a loan to the State toward these new soldiers' support. And he wanted the attention of the President of the United States called to the necessary cause of adequately fortifying New York. In all these aims he was completely successful. Governor Tompkins' admirers could not well say no to such petitions, and as for the Federalists in the Common Council, their patriotism proved to be above both jealousy and party.

The Governor's response was patriotism personified. He gave New York City twice the number of troops asked for—and he applied to Washington successfully, amid nation-wide acclaim, to be named in person the commander of these new forces.... He was tremendously popular—a man of infinite charm. He was also politically amenable, which Clinton, the originator of the scheme of defense, the Major-General without any troops, never was. And if, in his patriotic zeal, Governor Tompkins neglected to provide further financial support for his troops than the thirty thousand dollars lent by the city of New York, the urgent necessity for such provision was yet to make itself apparent....

Meanwhile the complicated politics of New York State grew a little more complicated than ever, with some Federalists favoring the Clinton faction and others inveterately opposing it; with former Clintonians deserting from the ranks and swelling those that followed Tompkins. The details of the ins and outs, the ups and downs, of Mr. Clinton's friends in these years would fill a great many pages. Suffice it to say that he himself was suffered, as Federalists plus his immediate supporters continued to rule the Assembly and thus most often the Council of Appointment, to remain in his office of Mayor of New York. He failed, however, to be renominated for Lieutenant-Governor in 1813, partly through the now open enmity of his brother-in-law and former friend, Judge Spencer, and partly through Martin Van Buren's desertion of De Witt Clinton's standard. The latter came about in the following fashion: It chanced that the Republican promoters of the Bank of America had attained their ends in 1812 by certain now time-worn methods. There had been, in short, a bargain between some of the would-be bankers and some of the "high-minded Federalists" that if the latter would support the Bank in 1812, the Bank's political sponsors would give their votes to Rufus King the Federalist for a U. S. Senatorship which was to fall vacant in 1813. This bargain was kept. Rufus King went to the U. S. Senate in 1813; but Martin Van Buren, who had put up a candidate against him, blamed De Witt Clinton because that candidate had not prevailed. Van Buren, apparently unaware of the aforementioned machinations on the part of the Bank's supporters, let Clinton know that he thought it was by Clinton's influence that a Federalist had won.... It was the old story—the cry of collusion with that party for his own ends. It mattered not that Clinton was personally as completely opposed to Rufus King as he was to the undue extension of banking privileges, even to his friends. He had no personal vote at the time, save his *ex-officio* casting vote. But Van Buren taunted him with direct insinuations about his associations and his influence; and when the moment for nominating a new Lieutenant-Governor arrived, Van Buren carefully killed De Witt Clinton's chances. Tompkins won the renomination for Governor, and

John Tayler was named to take Clinton's place. Clinton's supporters assailed Van Buren, condemned the Federal government for not prosecuting the war with vigor (which was a just indictment) and accused both Tompkins and Tayler of being the tools of the Madisonians.

As for Mr. Clinton himself, he must have felt well content that the year 1812 was over. It had been a terribly hard year for him. His aged uncle had not survived quite long enough to see him put in nomination for the Presidency. George Clinton died on April 20th, 1812, in Washington; and before De Witt had well got over a loss that was understandably overwhelming —the loss of one to whom he had been almost, in truth, a son— death took his father too.

It was on the 22nd of December, 1812, that this second bereavement took place. James Clinton was 76. He had not, as has been remarked, rested on his laurels since the Revolutionary War. Liking and appreciating the comforts of private life after his long and active military career, he was nevertheless never allowed to remain completely in retirement. He was always an outstanding figure in the State, and the State had constantly required his services. He had been an exemplary husband and father, affectionate almost literally beyond words; for he had always found his feelings difficult to express. He was a soldier always; a legislator by request; a family man to his marrow. With his second wife he had lived in contentment, and by her had had a second family of six children, who fraternized freely with their half-brothers and sisters. The people of the State which he had served so well showed their grief at the loss of him. His son De Witt was marking the occasion by helping, appropriately enough, to insure his native State's security, actually digging up New York earth as well as New York cash for this somewhat listless campaign. A most active member of the Committee of Defense, he was constantly at the Narrows, watching and personally aiding in the erection of the added fortifications there; on Long Island and at points on the East River shore. He was serving his country—under difficulties, but he was serving; by word of mouth, perforce, and by sweat of brow, if not in the military command he craved. New York was in danger of attack more than once. On one of the more immediately perilous of these occasions, Governor Tompkins sent Mayor Clinton word by

Thomas Addis Emmett that if New York should be actually invaded, Clinton would be called, as he desired, to a command. Mayor Clinton received the message with the single comment that he thought it might be desirable that his commission take place a little beforehand, so that he could at least be ready for the invaders....

The invaders never did reach New York. Outside the harbor waters the magnificent sea-battles took place, and the vessels, mighty but few, that the United States boasted upheld United States pride. On Lake Erie, so peaceful a few years since, Perry fought his great fight and won his great victory. On land the commanders continued to fare less fortunately. In the youthful capital city of Washington occurred burning and pillage and flight. In the long run of the war's result, however, neither British nor Americans triumphed, though the diplomats who went to Ghent in 1815 were not exactly worsted over the peace.

And in New York in those fighting years Mayor Clinton was a shining star, for his city in those years was not only in danger from without. The American city of that day effervesced with conflicting elements, who fought whenever opportunity occurred—but not against the common foe. They rioted, in short, revolting against each other and against the authorities. The city of Baltimore in Maryland was currently a case in point. There had been bloodshed in Baltimore. Mayor Clinton decided that there would be no bloodshed in New York. Certain Tammany Republicans had freely and publicly announced their intention of settling ancient scores by disposing of those whom they still called "Tories," and proving themselves patriots in so doing. Mayor Clinton, in one of his current charges to the grand jury, referring to the scenes in Baltimore, sounded a clarion call for sanity. It was a clear statement of the duty of a law-upholding body of men as metamorphosed by the rigors and the internal dangers of wartime. Nor did he stop at words. He reorganized the police of the city, and put both his police system and his plans for keeping the peace through the processes of the Common Council. There was peace in New York—but those who had threatened now denied that they had done so. They said the Mayor was merely trying to stir up alarm....

Meanwhile there was war outside; increasingly and menacingly. And the loan furnished to the State by the city of New

York for the support of the emergency forces had dwindled rapidly, till now there were no funds left. When this crisis came, the New York Legislature happened to be in recess. To apply to the Federal Government was useless, for the Government was experiencing financial distresses of its own. It was a moment when a politician would have thrown the onus where it undoubtedly belonged; but not De Witt Clinton. He presented a further report to the Common Council, and won its approval to pledge the credit of the city of New York to the amount of more than a million dollars. And by public subscription among his increasing number of merchant friends, in a time of national financial stress and embarrassment, he raised his million for defense, and placed it at the Governor's disposal. Both Federalists and Tammanyites again supported him. Rufus King addressed the meeting of citizens that thronged the Tontine Coffee House in favor of the loan.

Clinton worked on, to help the measures of the administration which had administered to him personally such a crushing defeat. And his achievement looms the greater for the fact that in local politics his adversaries held the power ever more completely. It was only because his efforts of the period were nearly all fighting efforts that they could not say him nay; but that did not prevent the patriotic Tammany Society from threatening to devote some of its mass meetings to the cause of "seeing that the Mayor puts through the measures that he proclaims." Tammany was going to have the local credit if it could get it; and of course it would be absurd to say that Tammany was not entitled to a share of it. But unfortunately for Tammany, who begrudged the Mayor his share, the masses were those among whom this vigorous and admirable Mayor actually worked, and for the moment the masses could not be completely deceived.

Nearly all fighting efforts, but of course, even in wartime, not quite all. In October, 1812, he was performing a service for his friends the merchants of New York City by laying the cornerstone of the latest addition to the markets of the city: the Washington Market. In December he was bestowing honor where honor was due. Four months before, Captain Isaac Hull, of the United States Navy, in command of the *Constitution,* after a series of encounters in which his noble ship and his somewhat raw crew had been in the most extreme peril, put out to sea from a reconnoitring cruise to the northward, and fell in with the British *Guerrière,* which he had met before.... When the encounter concluded, the *Guerrière* was no more, and Captain Hull, from off Boston Light, was announcing by dispatch to the Secretary of War that he was carrying into Boston harbor two hundred and sixty-seven prisoners, besides ten impressed Americans found on board who had refused to take part in the fight against their compatriots....

The eastern seaboard promptly burst into a pæan of praise. Boston got ready for Captain Hull with a flotilla of boats garlanded to the topmasts, as a fitting welcoming committee; and ashore that city turned out in its entirety, party differences, even war differences, forgotten, to do him and his fellow-heroes honor. Thence "Old Ironsides" (for she had been so little damaged by the enemy's guns that the name had already been affectionately bestowed upon her) bore Hull and his crew in triumph to New York, which happened to have been peering out for months from the ramparts on the Battery for a sight of the *Guerrière* and of an American ship at least chasing her. New York was also ready for Captain Hull. The citizens had raised a subscription to purchase presentation swords for him and his officers, which were presented amid acclaim. On September 7th the Common Council had come together and "Resolved: That the Freedom of the City be presented to Captain Hull in a golden box with an appropriate inscription. And that his Honor, the Mayor, be requested to forward the same with a copy of these resolutions." And the following week they requested Hull to sit for his portrait, to be placed in the picture-gallery of City Hall and thus "transmitted to posterity."

On December 28th the Mayor, at the head of the Common Council, presented the freedom of the city to Captain Hull in person, in the Council Chamber of the City Hall. And he said:

> ... Deeds of valor and achievements of glory are at all times cherished by patriotism and rewarded by true policy, but when we consider that our recent victories on the ocean have exhibited the American character in the most interesting light, have creaated a new character in the annals of naval warfare, and have been the principal means of establishing our navy on a respectable and permanent basis, it must be universally admitted that actors

> in these scenes of heroism are preëminently entitled to the gratitude of their country.
>
> That commerce is essential to our prosperity, that it cannot flourish without protection, and that it cannot be protected without a navy, are truths too evident to be denied, and too important not to be appreciated by the intelligence and public spirit of America.
>
> We cannot withhold on this occasion our approbation of your generous and benevolent treatment of the vanquished. It demonstrates the natural alliance between courage and humanity, and in mitigating the calamities of war, it reflects honor on our national character.

He then administered the freeman's oath, and presented the "superb golden box, prepared with suitable emblems," containing the certificate. Captain Hull replied briefly. He said he would preserve the box and its contents as an incentive for future "strenuous exertions" which good fortune might offer him. And he added that "to have it believed . . . by so highly respectable a body as the Corporation of the City of New York that an action of his had contributed to so desirable an event as the establishment of a navy on a permanent basis was a source of pleasing reflection which would only cease with life."

But it was so. At the opening of the war, no ships had been added to the twelve war-frigates of varying tonnage that constituted the United States Navy (if one discounts Jefferson's flotilla of gunboats, his only war measure, which were actually never used for the purpose for which they had been built). More, Mr. Madison and his advisers quite patently expected this war to be confined to the land, and it was only at the insistence of the officers of the ships of the line that the navy was put in fighting trim at all. But "Old Ironsides'" victory raised a furore on both sides of the Atlantic.

On October 25th, 1812, the frigate *United States,* Captain Decatur, fell in with the British frigate *Macedonian,* a faster and more heavily-armed vessel, with Americans and Frenchmen impressed aboard her and a brave and experienced British captain named Carden in command. . . . The *Macedonian* came into Newport a prisoner, completely overwhelmed. The city of New York, whence Decatur had sailed, waited in a very turmoil of excitement until he and his frigate and his prize should sail into home waters.

And so it came about that on December 29th, 1812, De Witt Clinton sat at the center of a banquet table in the City Hotel, New York, with Decatur on his right and Hull at his left. The hour was 5 P.M. The banquet-hall was "colonnaded round with the masts of ships entwined with laurels and bearing the national flags of all the world. Every table had on it a ship in miniature, with the American flag displayed." The table at which the Mayor presided, surrounded by the captains and their officers and other guests of honor, was on a dais, and before it was a ten-foot strip of greensward, in the center of which was "a lake of real water in which floated a miniature frigate." Behind the table hung the great furled mainsail of a ship, which at the toast "To our Navy," was slowly unfurled, to reveal a transparency representing the victories of Hull and Decatur and also that of Captain Jacob Jones of the sloop-of-war *Wasp,* who had in October captured the British sloop *Frolic,* but unfortunately was later taken by the *Poictiers,* together with his prize, and carried into Bermuda. Captain Jones was honored, as his fellows were, by the Federal Government and by several of the States independently. Also by the words of the Mayor of New York City, in a luminous address on patriotism and the prosecution of it which he delivered at this resplendent dinner. And lastly, his calling was honored by the official recognition, somewhat tardy, on the part of Mr. Madison and his Cabinet that more warships were a desirability. It was only now that more were commissioned and put into construction.

The Clintons had another son that year. They named him Franklin, for his maternal grandfather. Maria's mother, Mrs. Osgood, still survived, widowed for a second time in August, 1813. When the Clintons were in New York the old house on Cherry Street still saw them often. The education of his growing family kept pace in De Witt Clinton's thoughts with the education of the children of the poor; their education and, in holiday time, their adequate entertainment. "Went to the play," is the diary entry for January 6th, 1813, "with Charles and De Witt." "Went to panorama with the children," "Went to the play with De Witt and George," and in summer, "Went fishing with the children," are important entries. Holidays were holidays, even when the father of a parcel of boys and also a couple of growing girls was as preoccupied as this one.

In his current enjoyment of a single office, Mr. Clinton improved every possible occasion, public and private, to the ends best calculated to improve his own mind, often to the enlightenment also of his fellow-citizens. His many-sided greatness was still, perhaps, best illustrated by his conduct in his more strictly legalistic capacities. His model there was Lord Bacon, and in intellectual pursuit he strove to emulate him, while in adaptation he also flattered him by following in his footsteps.

It was in September of 1813 that Captain Oliver Hazard Perry, at the end of a sanguinary encounter on Lake Erie, sent to General Harrison, in command of the northwestern army of the United States, the message: "We have met the enemy, and they are ours: two ships, two brigs, one schooner and one sloop...." In the following January, Perry—Commodore Perry now—came to New York City at the invitation of the Common Council, and received at the hands of the Mayor the freedom of the city, and was initiated in the presence of the Mayor into the Society of Cincinnati. All these naval heroes found the Mayor of New York a worthy object of subsequent close friendship.

But naval victories to the Americans, and land victories to the British (for such had become the fairly general rule) were not leading to any conclusion of this war, and there were in certain quarters indications that both sides were ready for peace. Russia, through John Quincy Adams, then minister there, offered to mediate. "Lord Castlereagh, as we are told," wrote Clinton in his diary on January 3rd, 1814, "signified to our Government that the Russian mediation was declined, with, however, every disposition to negotiate directly." He himself was still for peace through preparedness, which adapted to the exigencies of a country already at war meant peace through an adequate display of strength. He was contributing his views along these lines, heavily cloaked in disarming pseudonyms, to the New York press at the moment.

> The President is (he wrote), I believe, for peace on any terms, but he dares not succumb for fear of the violent men of his own party.

But still there were sufficient peaceable pursuits. On January 13th the diary has: "Attended a meeting at my office to form a Literary and Philosophical Society." That New York society was formed largely through his coöperation with Dr. Hugh Williamson, the former associate of Rittenhouse in the American Philosophical Society in Philadelphia. Its charter was won almost entirely through Clinton's agency. By that charter he was named the Society's President, and he held that office until his death. In his inaugural address he spoke of the leading lights of legal history, and, comparing Lord Bacon with his brother authority, Coke, observed:

> They were both eminent in their profession, and attained the highest honors and most lucrative emoluments. Bacon became Lord High Chancellor of England, and Coke a Chief Justice. The former had ascended the empyreal heights of literature; the latter had plunged into the learning of Norman lawyers, and had become the oracle of the common law. The works of Bacon are referred to as the oracle of truth and knowledge, and as the revelation of genuine philosophy; while the black letter learning of Coke is an eleusynian mystery to all out of the pale of the profession. The difference between a mere lawyer great in his profession alone, and a great lawyer eminent in literature and science, can never be more forcibly illustrated than in the exhibition of these celebrated men. Bacon enlivened, enriched, and embellished every subject upon which he wrote; even flowers sprang up under his feet in his journey through the thorny paths of legal investigation. But from Coke you must expect nothing but the dry barren weeds of scholastic subtlety and Norman chicanery.

An interesting commentary from the lips of a man whom more than one historian has summarily dismissed with a contemptuous "politician," or with the somewhat reckless assertion that he had no thought in his mind but advancement for self-gain. . . . Incidentally it is interesting that Dr. Samuel Mitchill, who had in 1811 actually served on a Tammany committee to oppose the candidacy of Clinton for the office of Lieutenant-Governor, was proud to be Clinton's colleague in the learned societies at this time. A little later, Mitchill was to be not unconnected with the only recorded instance of the entrance of politics into the choice of members of any of the societies, and Clinton was to be the target at which a purely political exclusion was aimed. The exception, however, does no more than prove the rule, which was that daily Mr. Clinton came in contact socially and culturally with those to whom he was politically anathema. And daily they paid tribute to the fact that socially, scientifically, artistically, educationally, he was beyond even their reproach. In February his social activities ranged from entertaining the gossipy merchant and auctioneer, Philip Hone, to attending the opening of Eastburn's Literary Rooms. In May he was presiding at a dinner in Washington Hall in honor of Hyde de Neuville, the new Minister from France. In May, too, the fort called Tompkins, on Staten Island, was begun....

And still De Witt Clinton found time to read, to study, to note things both great and small. Still and throughout his life an early riser, ever punctual to a degree, he husbanded his time and employed it to the full. If amusement interfered with the improvement of his mind or with his contribution toward the improvement of the lot of his fellow-men, he postponed amusement without any special regret. Hosack declares, with an entirely eulogistic intention, that Clinton thought frivolous amusement wholly unworthy; but Hosack was not vouchsafed access to his diary, which, noting circuses and plays and parties, and relishing a practical joke, seems to belie that view. He took excursions to Sandy Hook with the children with the double purpose of viewing the fortifications and benefiting the children's health, and boys and girls vied with each other to be his companions. They went with him to Staten Island, to "Helegat," and of course always gladly to the summer home at Newtown.

On August 18th: "Went to Harlem Heights. A fort laid out called Fort Clinton. Visited Fort Greene." In September, "Worked with Free Masons on fortifications." In November Commodore Decatur stepped ashore to be again the lion of the hour, and to receive the freedom of the city at the hands of the Mayor, at whose town house he was a very frequent visitor. John Randolph of Virginia, and of the U. S. Senate, was also in town, and shared the honors of the day and the attentions of Mr. Clinton. Decatur aided the Commissioners of Fortifications that year to lay out the fortifications at Hell Gate, and to place a block-house at Rockaway.

Clinton's mother-in-law, Mrs. Osgood, died in October. Maria now came into the residue of her heritage, and the house and farm at Newtown became hers (or, as the law had it, her husband's) outright. Mr. Clinton, as owner through his wife, spent a great deal of time adding to the place and beautifying it, but in December of 1814 he was back in New York for the familiar purpose of honoring one more hero—General Macomb of the United States army and also of New York. At that moment the somewhat inconclusive if frequently dazzling fighting that was called a war was actually giving way to diplomatic negotiation. As circumstances freed him from the necessity of begging money for war causes, Clinton began spending his eloquence and his literary ability once more in framing a memorial and presenting it to the Legislature in behalf of the New York Historical Society. He showed how historical documents and relics were in danger of being lost to the State. Indian tribes were dying out, and their customs with them. Dutch records were in the archives of the Dutch West India Company. Records of Colonial times were largely in England. Revolutionary data, newspaper pamphlets, lay neglected. Important manuscripts gathered dust in the closets of unidentified private owners. Mr. Clinton asked that New York City's duly chartered Historical Society be officially financially fortified. The Legislature responded with an appropriation of twelve thousand dollars from lottery revenues.

By those he thus aided, and by those who heard his eloquence, he was sometimes regarded with affection and always with admiration. With most men outside the principals in the long fight for political supremacy, public differences of opinion did not, still, cross the borderline of private intercourse. Witness Gouverneur Morris, politically opposed and temperamentally as different as could be; of another generation, moreover. Clinton and Morris were on the most cordial visiting terms throughout the latter's lifetime, and if they had interests—a majority of interests—that diverged, they had plenty more in common. The fighting men who heard him speak (Commodore Macdonough and General Brown were honored in January, 1815, by the city of New York) avowedly treasured the recollection as well as the chance acquaintanceship. Nor did he ever forget old friends, or fail them. Thomas Eddy was suffering reverses of fortune that winter, and extreme physical disability in addition. De Witt Clinton it was who procured him a hospital bed, and took him there and visited him constantly. No mere hollow honor was Mayor Clinton's membership in the medical and charitable societies.

On February 13th, 1815, there arrived the news of peace

—a word that was shouted from the housetops in the jubilant days that followed. The Common Council met in special session to designate the proper means of celebration, and weird and wonderful were some of the means they chose. A mournful event, however, caused the rejoicings to be put off. On February 24th, the Historical Society met to mark the death of a distinguished member—Robert Fulton. Mr. Clinton was at Fulton's funeral on the 25th, and the delayed illuminations in celebration of the peace, which were displayed on the 27th, were rather dimmed by the loss of one who had been both an ornament and a benefactor to his age. But the magnificent City Hall did belch forth artificial fire and rockets and fountain displays, and transparencies and other luminous fruits of ingenuity blazed on every hand.

That year Mr. Clinton gave his aid to his friend John Pintard in the latter's three-year effort to bring all the learned societies together under one roof with the general title of "The New York Institute." When Pintard had first broached the subject in a letter in 1812, Clinton had observed that "the request was too impudent to be submitted to the Corporation." But he had not forgotten that request, and in 1815 he was not only talking to the Corporation about it, but writing advice to Pintard on how best to present it. In 1815 the disused but spacious almshouse at the rear of the City Hall became The New York Institute, home of the growing group of literary and artistic and historical societies and also of an attractive museum which duly became a favorite resort of the Clinton children among a great many others. It was a convenient arrangement for a number of people. Men like Clinton and Pintard and Mitchill were members not of one but of all or nearly all the groups; and they were busy men outside them. Mr. Clinton was more amazingly busy than ever that spring, dining with the Friendly Sons of St. Patrick on March 17th, attending with his fellow-trustees the examination of girl applicants for admission into the Free Schools; dining with Mr. Astor; playing host to Philip Freneau; meeting Edward Everett of Boston at a party; moving his family into the Cherry Street house; and running up to West Point to enter his son James as a cadet. With his son De Witt, already showing signs of following in certain of his father's footsteps, he became more and more companionable. In summer at Newtown they rode together daily, and were constantly in each other's society. Small Mary was also dear to her father's heart.

In town he was rather more remote, though not to the grownups. Edmond Genêt was still a welcome visitor. So, though this was somewhat surprising, was Mr. Martin Van Buren....

By those others who remained his more active and immediate political adversaries, however, he was increasingly and unceasingly detested. These gentlemen had risen on the electoral wave of 1814 in New York. And as the year 1813, by their machinations, had seen Clinton no longer Lieutenant-Governor of the State of New York, so the year 1815, by similar and proportionately more intensive means, saw him no longer Mayor of New York City. The war-party had carried on a war and by this time had made a fairly satisfactory peace. It was restored to popular favor; and the former opponent of the war-party was now to find one of his own former triumphs recoiling on his head. It was, it will be remembered, largely he who had officially bestowed on the Council of Appointment the last word in appointive power. Now a Council composed entirely of his political opponents, swept in on a Van Burenite wave, cleared the public offices within their province of their adversaries, good or bad, in the accepted political manner, and in doing so robbed Clinton, with what pleasure may be imagined, of his last remaining executive office. The Bucktails loudly proclaimed again that he had opposed the war; and they said he had been "lacking in patriotism during its course."... In sweeping him into private life they were jubilant, and did not bother to hide their jubilation. Gulian C. Verplanck, who was already making his mark with a poetic and scintillating pen, adopted the pseudonym "Abimelech Coody," for the purpose of belaboring Clinton in the Van Burenite press, ridiculing his love for the learned societies, criticizing his knowledge of the classics, condemning in general his public and private course. Clinton's friends and supporters, rising to his defense, strove to outdo Mr. Verplanck and his followers, whom Clinton himself dubbed "Coodies."

But the Coodies had not scared him away from his favorite pursuits. They had made him a private citizen, but not by any means an idle one. Robert R. Livingston, the President of the Academy of Arts since its inception, had died in 1813. De Witt Clinton succeeded him in that office, inducted in 1815 when

America was at last at peace and able to consider the arts at leisure once more. That year Clinton coupled with his spoken memoir of Livingston a similar eulogy on Livingston's friend and protégé, Fulton. Both men had left a heritage to art as well as to science. Clinton's discourse, replete with classical and poetical allusion, traced the association of these two men for the betterment of humanity; told how Livingston's means and discernment allied to Fulton's inventive brain gave to the world the practical adaptation of the principle of navigation by steam; told how Fulton had aided in the question of defense, how he spent his time and exhausted his strength in meditating and experimenting with innumerable devices, so that he was "cut down in his prime," and had gone too soon to join the kindred soul who had not only seen eye to eye with him but actually worked hand in hand with him in a glorious venture.

And meanwhile De Witt Clinton had never let his own interest in the question of travel, of transportation, by water lapse in the slightest. The Canal Commissioners had met with fair regularity in spite of the war; but of course in wartime their hopes of progress were at zero. As early as 1812, however, Mr. Clinton had re-borrowed Jesse Hawley's essays, and he did not return them until 1820, when much water had already flown literally as well as figuratively under a number of bridges. And on March 8th, 1814, the Commission had actually submitted a new report. This one, drawn of course by Morris, exhibited a desire on the part of the Commission to be held as not committed *exclusively* to an inclined plane.... There was also some revival of enthusiasm for taking the Lake Ontario route, the outcome of an optimistic view of the probable results of the current warfare. Peter B. Porter and his circle of friends at Black Rock, now a somewhat war-torn frontier village, were prominent in this. But the war was then still on. The net result of this 1814 report was that the Legislature repealed the act of 1812 authorizing the borrowing of five million dollars for canal purposes. Any five million that could be raised was at that moment needed for other purposes; and manifestly no part of the five million could then be obtained, as had once been hoped, from England.

In 1815, however, the face of national affairs was serene again. The friends of the canal in New York City came together and organized a great mass meeting in the City Hotel. Clinton returned an earlier compliment and called Platt and Eddy to the aid of the project for reviving public interest in the canal scheme. William Bayard, leading merchant, presided at the meeting, which took place in December, and John Pintard acted as secretary. It was Platt who addressed the audience and urged the abandonment of the inclined plane theory in the interest of the success of the whole project. He also proposed that a committee be appointed to prepare and present a memorial to the Legislature in favor of a Hudson-Erie canal. Four men were duly named to this committee—Thomas Eddy; Cadwallader D. Colden (grandson of the earlier Cadwallader, friend and patron of Fulton and Livingston, adopted son of Tammany but the only Tammanyite to give himself wholeheartedly to the canal measure); John Swartwout (who now appeared ready to bury old differences); and De Witt Clinton, who was placed at the head.

The country had never been riper for expansion to the westward. But such was the state of political parties in New York in 1815-16 that only a superlatively convincing work on such a subject could have prevailed. It must be a paper that would make men not only read but think; and not only think, but see. It must be a plea that would make men grow in stature, for what it asked was a stupendous, a gigantic thing. Above all, it must be a work that would cause honest citizens, interested in their State, to insist upon that which was advocated, and to insist upon it forthwith.

The memorial was written by De Witt Clinton—he who had lately been abandoned by both friends and enemies in political life; whose very name ambitious politicians avoided because those who sympathized with Clinton were paying for their sympathy. Some, indeed, turned against him because he would not woo the accepted political gods, but insisted on staking his future and his fame upon such a controversial—many still said chimerical—project. This memorial was his answer. It told of the land, the proposed undertaking and the general conditions under which it would have to be effected. It told not only why the canal should be built, but how it should be built, and exactly where, with reasons; and just what it would probably cost. It demonstrated beyond further argument the superiority of the direct Erie route over that of Lake Ontario in terms of the future. It envisioned the great dream of that future, linking it up characteristically with the story of the past. It described not only what the canal would mean to New York, but what it would contribute to the nation and to a closer union between the States. There have been many since to say that had this memorial been De Witt Clinton's only contribution to the canal project, it would have entitled him to his place at the pinnacle of the history of that project. It was adopted by acclaim by the citizens of New York, and, printed in pamphlet form, was broadcast throughout the State.

Forthwith, canal meetings were held in almost every place between Albany and Buffalo. On March 1st, 1816, the memorial, signed by the New York City committee, was presented to a joint committee of the Legislature, which had been called together to act on that part of Governor Tompkins' February message which ran:

> It will rest with the Legislature whether the project of connecting the waters of the Hudson with those of the Western Lakes is not sufficiently important to demand the appropriation of some part of the revenues of the State to its accomplishment, without imposing too great a burden upon our constituents. We may rely on the coöperation of the States of the West in any judicious plan in that direction.

Governor Tompkins was still and always personally persistently cold toward the canal scheme; which fact renders certain current political behavior of Clinton's rather more notable. When Tompkins ran for reëlection in the spring of 1816, and Rufus King was put up as his opponent, Clinton supported Tompkins, "not as a positive good," he wrote, "but as a less evil." Nevertheless, only tremendous pressure of public opinion, it will be increasingly apparent, had called forth Tompkins' earlier and somewhat tepid recommendation. All the many meetings following on the publication of Clinton's memorial had produced reports; the citizens of New York had officially indorsed it by a second memorial; all had advocated the building of the canal in no uncertain terms.

But now some public opposition reared its head, and mounted. Some of the counties along the Hudson valley and upon Long Island did not look kindly at all toward possible strong competition in the matter of farm produce from the western part of the State, difficult of access and therefore of development hitherto. On March 8th, however, the Canal Commission presented its annual report to the joint committee. It pleaded that, the late war having interfered with its sanctioned operations, immediate action was now a necessity if only to "prevent the trade of the West from passing down the St. Lawrence." Gouverneur Morris drew this his last report, but this time all the Commissioners added their corrections and emendations. The result was that all the Commissioners save Morris signed it, and De Witt Clinton went to Albany to plead for its adoption. The inclined plane theory had been formally abandoned.

On March 21st, the joint committee rendered its own report. It favored an immediate start on the construction of the canal, and offered a bill to that effect. Immediately there was a battle. The representatives of the river and Long Island counties offered the strongest opposition. Amendment after amendment threatened the favorable outcome of the proceedings; but it was one of these amendments that finally lessened the resistance of the canal's detractors. By this it was agreed that along the middle section of the proposed canal, the lands on either side, to the extent of twenty-five miles in width, should be taxed toward the expense of the undertaking. This policy was not sustained in actual practice, but certain it is that it here served its purpose. The prospect in other respects was a limited one. Only the middle section was to be sanctioned, for the time being. A bill for the construction of that portion, with provision for the expenditure of two hundred and fifty thousand dollars per annum, and a limit of two million dollars as the cost of the entire section, passed the Assembly on April 12th, and thirteen men were named as a new Commission.

Martin Van Buren, in the Senate, killed that part which authorized immediate construction. Clinton and others were questioned as to whether the line had been physically and decisively marked out. Upon their replying in the negative, Mr. Van Buren insisted that the Legislature had insufficient information to justify it in authorizing the canal undertaking at that time. . . . A motion was made to throw out the bill altogether; but it passed with an amendment offered by Van Buren, striking out the part which authorized construction, and calling merely for an exact course to be located, and for the probable cost to be officially based on such exact location and course; also for the gathering of information as to whether and in what quarters and to what extent loans could be obtained. Eight of the Commissioners named by the Assembly were negatived by the Senate, and the new Commission which now came into existence consisted of Stephen Van Rensselaer; Joseph Ellicott, of Batavia (the agent of the influential Holland Land Company); Samuel Young, a Tompkins man and a political choice from the north; Myron Holley, member of Assembly from Ontario County; and De Witt Clinton. Their duty was to report to the next session of the Legislature on such measures as might be devised to connect the Hudson River with Lake Erie and also with Lake Champlain. A grant of twenty thousand dollars was made for the expenses of their task.

This Commission met and organized itself in May. Mr. Clinton was immediately named President of the Board, with Holley as Treasurer and Young as Secretary. The five gentlemen spent the summer in going over the entire route again, in obtaining the further surveys and the further estimates called for by the Bill, and in sounding out possible sources of financial aid for the scheme. The last-named task had fallen to Clinton's lot, and there was something ironical in that fact. His personal finances had never been lower. The defense of a lawsuit in connection with the title to some lands which had been sold to him by his mother-in-law prior to her death had sapped his resources, and he is to be observed, on the eve of his journey westward, disposing of his Manhattan Company stock. For he was of course receiving no salary from any source, and his meticulousness in paying his bills was as complete as his anxiety that the canal when it came should likewise pay its own way. In the latter connection his current studies convinced him of the desirability of creating a fund for the repayment of the loan which must be raised. A mere pledge of faith had too often been considered enough, and too often failed of redemption. Clinton wanted lenders to be both confident and lenient, and knew that only cash on hand would make them so. This was his study for that summer —this and a new earnest glance at the country where the whole promise was to be fulfilled. A letter from Clinton to Henry Post upon his return from the West in August, 1816, says:

> ... *Buffalo* is to be the point of beginning, and in 50 years it will be next to New York in wealth and population. We have looked at all the difficult points, ascended mountains, penetrated forests, descended into widespreading and deeply excavated ra-

> vines, and have, upon the whole, encountered more fatigue than I thought I could bear. The result is most satisfactory. The work can be easily effected, and the utmost cost will not exceed our calculations. The public sentiment is also fixed in its favor....

He was a little too sanguine about the choice of Buffalo as yet, as will be seen. But only about Buffalo, and that was not to imply a permanent failure. All his other hopes were to bear, under his fostering, golden fruit....

In November, the New York Legislature held a special session for nominating Presidential electors. Mr. Madison's second term was drawing to a close. Governor Tompkins, addressing both Houses, made an extremely chilly and fleeting reference to the expediency or otherwise, during the session then commencing, of employing inmates of the State prisons, "either in building a new prison at Auburn, erecting fortifications, opening roads, constructing canals, or in making other improvements." In January, 1817, when the Legislature met again for its regular session, he made a stirring speech in recommendation of the gradual abolition of slavery in the State of New York, which recommendation was turned into fact by official enactment that year; but he did not refer in any way to the question which was now on more people's lips and in more people's minds throughout the State than any other.

In February, nevertheless, the Commission presented its report, covering all points authorized, and praying that the work might begin at once. Four hundred and forty miles of the actual route had been traced upon the land, and carefully including every conceivable contingency and expense, the Commissioners had estimated the cost of the work at six million dollars. Incidentally a new light had been thrown on the financial aspect of the scheme at that moment by a bill then in debate in Congress for apportioning among the States the dividends on the stock owned by the Government in the duly resuscitated Bank of the United States. Had this bill become law, New York would immediately have become the richer by about ninety thousand dollars per year. It passed both Houses of Congress and came before President Madison for final action. And as one of the last acts of his second and final administration, Mr. Madison vetoed this bill.

If (and it must be reiterated that there were a great many

who believed that way) this action was aimed partially at least at Clinton, who was still remembered at Washington as one of the suppliants for the canal, it only served to prod him personally to greater efforts. In declaring the bill unconstitutional, Mr. Madison had at the same moment approved a law bestowing Federal financial aid on the Cumberland road and on a road in Tennessee. But Clinton did not waste his time in complaining. From now on he cried that the canal was the State's affair; that the State must carry it out and also finance it. He entered into a lengthy and detailed and persuasive correspondence with the heads of the Holland Land Company in a successful effort to obtain from that body, in view of the enormous potentialities inherent in the canal scheme for the future development and advantage of its holdings, a grant of land for the benefit of the canal. He interviewed his wealthy friends among the merchants of New York in an effort to ascertain how successful a loan floated by the State would be. And he continued to work out his plan involving the different sources at which money for the repayment of the loan by the State could be obtained by taxation. In his plea to the Holland Land Company he was of course aided by Joseph Ellicott, the Company's agent and a fellow-member of the Canal Commission, who admired Clinton wholeheartedly.

But there was still the little matter of authorization from the State to be secured. The joint committee on canals now backed Clinton to the extent of recommending that the section between the Mohawk and Seneca Rivers be commenced without delay. This was something of a personal triumph for him. He had been occupying himself in trying to batter down opposition; to kill indifference among politicians by proclaiming the growing enthusiasm of the public; to instruct and to enlighten. The joint committee now asked for a draft canal law, including a system of finance. Mr. Clinton drew up and presented that which it asked.

In April, the Committee of the Whole considered a bill along the lines of the joint committee's report. The usual fierce opposition and the still more inevitable amendments promptly evinced themselves. There were men who would never be convinced until they saw it with their own eyes that in their day an artificial waterway across the entire breadth of the State could be not only dug but made to work. There were others who would never cease to fight it because of the man who loomed largest behind it. Nevertheless, something tangible at last had happened in the greater body of this school of thought. Clinton's report had been hammered home in the sections where it would do the most good, and some of the river counties were beginning to be swayed by the thought that if a new competition came out of the West in the matter of traffic in produce through the port of New York, a new demand would also be created in that quarter for commodities arriving there. Some eloquent advocates of the canal arose in the river counties....

The new bill passed the Assembly on April 11th, 1817, and was battled over in the Senate until the 14th, when Martin Van Buren's voice was to be heard in strong approval of it. Mr. Clinton was a visitor in the Senate that day—just how deeply interested a visitor may be imagined. He heard the voice of the man who had once upheld him but had since consistently opposed him, favoring his dearest dream of all; and when Mr. Van Buren sat down, Mr. Clinton moved through the buzz of excitement which the speech had engendered, and seizing the hand of the man who had given the bill this unexpected weight—the man who never failed to see which way the political wind was blowing,—pumped it hard.... The bill passed the Senate, and went to the Council of Revision.

And here Governor Tompkins plays a singular and quite unofficial part. He becomes the extremely unwilling instrument of the fondest hopes of the canal. Mr. Tompkins had, on the 4th of March, become Vice-President of the United States under President James Monroe. John Tayler was acting Governor of New York when the Canal Bill came before the Council of Revision, and he presided over the deliberations of that body on the subject. The other members were the Chief Justice, Smith Thompson; the Chancellor, James Kent; and two judges of the Supreme Court, Yates and Platt. Tayler and Thompson were adamant in opposition to the canal. Kent was in favor of it on general principles, but, like Jefferson, feared that the time was not ripe. Yates and Platt supported it with all their might. But it looked as if all their might would be insufficient. Chancellor Kent was visibly wavering to the side of the canal's opponents, and acting Governor Tayler was visibly awaiting the chance to settle the question by his casting vote, when Vice-

President Tompkins, holidaying in New York, arrived to sit in at the deliberations.

Tompkins raised his voice—quite unofficially. He said, with all the weight of a former executive who had loyally supported the measures of the late administration,

"This peace with Great Britain, gentlemen, is a mere truce. There is no doubt whatever that we shall soon be again at war with that country. Instead of wasting the credit and resources of this State in this chimerical project, we ought to employ all our revenue and all our credit in preparation for war."

It was, of itself, an extremely short-sighted pronouncement. In the first place, none knew better than the late Governor of New York how much the war forces themselves had suffered for want of easy and rapid water transit facilities for artillery and reënforcements. In the second place, there still remained men in public life who thought the late war had been a mistake, and feared the very attitude that lingered still in the quarters that had urged it.

Chancellor Kent was of the latter classification. He sat up, considerably aroused.

"Do you really think so, sir?" he inquired.

"I do," said the Vice-President with conviction. "Depend upon it, England will never forgive us our victories. Take my word for it, we shall have another war within two years."

The Chancellor rose.

"Gentlemen," he said, in a decisive tone, "if we must choose between the canal and war, I am in favor of the canal."

And thereupon, on April 15th, 1817, the Canal Bill became law.[1]

It now remained for Clinton and his colleagues to reveal their schemes for financing it. As Jesse Hawley remarked:

> The great merit of Mr. Clinton in relation to the Canal consists in his having put his powerful mind to the subject and, probably with great labor, comprehended the magnitude of its utility and the splendor of its enterprise; and failing to render it a national work, he conceived the idea of rendering it a state undertaking and property—an idea which had escaped all others from the supposed inadequacy of the state resources to accom-

[1] The authorities for this incident are Judge Jonas Platt and Chancellor Kent himself.

> plish it—resolutely shouldering the responsibility of the measure at the hazard of his popularity and reputation—while others were confronting him with the assertion that it would require the revenue of all the kingdoms of the earth, and the population of China, to accomplish it.

It would seem that here indeed did lie the very root of Clinton's greatness. He argued not on points with which he was unfamiliar; he never guessed. He had taken the trouble to investigate the financial resources of the State for himself, as he had investigated the possible success of the physical undertaking; he had carefully ascertained the probable investment and the possible return. In De Witt Clinton's mind, the Erie Canal had now become New York's canal in every possible particular—and he had sold it, in effect, to New York. True, New York, in an appalling measure, was still dubbing it "Clinton's Ditch." His political enemies—and their name was legion—continued to fight it with all their strength, by every means, fair or foul, that lay within their reach. A New York City representation that was considered too friendly toward the scheme had been replaced by one totally inimical to it, and still more so to Clinton. The only undeviating political opposition throughout the canal legislation, as a matter of fact, came from New York City and the southern district of New York in general. That it was largely an opposition personal to Clinton has never been disputed. But the crowning irony of it is that in ceaselessly forcing personal responsibility on him, his enemies ultimately helped to establish him in all his canal glory. In assuming that personal responsibility so gladly (and he continually insisted that he was proud to assume it), he stood indeed alone. Others were cautious. He alone accepted the challenge to "sink or swim" with this his major dream. More than forty years later, his eldest surviving son, Charles, was to recall the fury and the mercilessness of that fight. Charles, a mere boy at the moment, was being initiated into the duties of private secretary to his father—a position he was to enjoy till the end of Mr. Clinton's life. He knew all the participants in that great canal battle, friend and foe—but it was mostly foe. He saw that his father's political fame was not to be turned to immortality if the "Bucktails" could prevent it. He saw that even some of those friendly to his father had been terribly hard to win. Money was precious, land was precious, vision was a quality that many, even among the true statesmen, still lacked. But politics, above all, was an acid that could be thrown to blind men to the possible good of internal improvements, of commercial growth, of State achievement, of any advancement at all save that of self. This was the acid deliberately flung in the eyes of many who might otherwise have seen much clearer. A distrust of official estimates by men who urged this public improvement or that was deep-rooted. These Commissioners were no experts, said the skeptics. They might well prove to have been far too sanguine. It might even be that they had manufactured their figures in order to commit the State to a project which, if begun, would have to be completed whatever the cost. New York, even apart from the politicians, still felt extremely young, and in finance was extremely timid. The war just ended, reconstruction time was surely a time for pulling in the strings; particularly the period of such a peace as this, which, now that the first excitement was over, was rather widely mistrusted.

But above all considerations which had weighed with his adversaries politically in this contest, and continued to weigh, was the fact that De Witt Clinton was personally established as a Presidential possibility. This fact made it thrice important that his name should not be immediately associated even with a potential improvement. So citizens were encouraged to recoil at the magnitude and at the cost of the proposed feat of engineering, and to believe that, especially for such a young country, it was impossible of achievement. Comparatively few, even yet, had actually grasped what success would mean to their youthful State; the potentialities of the golden West.

In this light it becomes clear that Clinton's achievement, even thus far, in presenting a winning argument, was the triumph of a master personality. Certainly he was the most talked-of man of the hour, in one way or another, and as his enhanced reputation trickled out beyond the boundaries of his state, the alarm within those boundaries was proportionately magnified.

Men called the Presidential day of James Monroe "the era of good feeling." And indeed the hatreds and the intrigues of national party politics as such appeared to have been suspended. The last remnants of Federalism had perished in the waves of war feeling. The factions in the nation were at peace when the actual fighting ended, and seemed to be working shoulder to shoulder, in a refreshing and novel amity.

But there the era of good feeling found its boundary. Among parties it bloomed, but among individuals the good feeling seemed to have turned inward. It was really the era of each man for himself. It was the day of Henry Clay, of John Quincy Adams, of William H. Crawford and also of De Witt Clinton. The only novelty was in seeing lone men play politics, instead of parties, as theretofore. Adams was by all odds of tradition now the "heir apparent." So much was of custom recognized in a view of the man who occupied, as he did now, the Secretaryship of State. But Clay's supporters, Crawford's supporters, De Witt Clinton's supporters—each group was already grooming its candidate and setting up its howl. The era of good feeling had its limits ever more clearly defined.

It would be idle to state that Clinton was a passive onlooker at this aspect of his affairs. Politics were in the breath he drew; ambition was a ruling factor in his make-up. But he never really learned to play the game of politics as the game of politics was played. He invariably balked at direct conciliation and intrigue. As for his ambition, it was a complex thing, with components as divergent as petty politics themselves and, on the other extreme, sheer love of country. He was tremendously aware of the political forces always working in his favor, as well as those which, failing his complaisance, were increasingly against him. He was even more enormously aware of the natural forces that were being harnessed to make some of his ideals come true.

For work on the Erie Canal began that year. Mr. Clinton's plan of finance included a twelve-and-a-half cents tax per bushel, for the benefit of the canal fund, on salt manufactured in the western part of the State. The fund was vested in a board, and the faith of the State was pledged that it would not be diverted. The final disappointment in regard to Federal aid having rendered a revision of the original scheme of finance necessary, Van Buren suggested that the general credit of the State be pledged for the redemption of the loan, in addition to setting aside a fund for that purpose, and this suggestion was adopted. Senator Tibbits, of Rensselaer County, one of the four men (all drawn from the ranks of Clinton's political opponents) who were charged with the administration of the canal fund, added the plan whereby all duties upon auction sales in the State, save $33,500 a year which was reserved to other causes, likewise swelled the fund. These, plus the proceeds of sale of the property of the old navigation companies and the actual tolls as and when the waterway became navigable, were the financial policies actually adopted, though others were at first enacted. The salt duties alone very quickly brought in an enormous revenue, and the auction duties also in due course afforded a sizable income. Above all, Clinton's insistence that a canal fund should be established, instead of a mere pledge of faith, was to prove a benefaction to the entire country. New York paid the interest on the canal loan, which was subscribed to by merchants and bankers and private individuals both here and abroad, with ease. As a consequence, the credit of the United States in general was greatly improved, and the raising of funds everywhere facilitated.

The Commission, as aforesaid, was authorized by the act to construct the middle section of the canal, and also a canal from the headwaters of the Hudson to connect with Lake Champlain by way of the northern Wood Creek. On June 3rd, 1817, they met to receive proposals and make contracts, and Myron Holley, Benjamin Wright and James Geddes were placed in charge of the work, the details of which obviously have their place in other writings than the present. On July 4th, 1817, De Witt Clinton had the honor and the happiness of thrusting a spade into the ground at Rome, which was exactly at the proposed center of the first section of the canal, and thus actually setting the project in motion in both directions. All the Commissioners were present; but particularly for the head of the Commission that Fourth of July was a very great occasion. His State was coming into its own. He was coming into his own. That was the order, undoubtedly, in which he would himself have put the two eventualities, ambition or no.

Both publicly and privately he was coming into his own. That year he became President of the New York Historical Society, in place of Gouverneur Morris, who had died in the preceding winter. His inaugural discourse is described by Hosack, his fellow-member and ultimately his successor in the office, as "comparable with the Treatise *de Moribus Germanorum* of Tacitus." Incidentally Hosack further remarks that throughout the whole course of his career, Clinton's devotion to the arts and the sciences was such as to lead one to the impression, did one not know him in other aspects, that these were his sole occupations. At the height of his administrative labors and in the depths of his disillusioned, black hours alike, his scientific work and his scientific knowledge assumed proportions that could well have been deemed full employment and full accomplishment by many a man. "He excelled," says Hosack, "in zoology, botany, geology and mineralogy. In ichthyology and ornithology his knowledge was minute." And always he was adding to the collection of mineral specimens that was later to rank with the finest in the country. As honorary member of the Linnæan Society of London, and as regular correspondent and personal friend of most of the prominent naturalists and scientists of his day, he was sufficiently a master of their subjects to shine in the most rarefied of such circles. In his letters to John Pintard of this period he is medical student, art connoisseur, banking expert, canal man, historian, friend, family man and a great many things besides. In one of them he writes:

> ...I like a correspondence that enters into details of what happens in the circles I esteem, and to the institutions I cherish. Even the tittle-tattle letters of Swift to Stella have chained my attention, although they treat of remote events and of unknown persons. When you write, therefore, tell me of everything that occurs in our literary institutions, etc., and excuse the want of reciprocity on my part. What, indeed, can I write to you about? The clashes of politicians are nothing to you—and it will afford you no entertainment to hear the history of my studies, vacillating between political economy and mineralogy, and now and then enjoying a *bonne-bouche* of poetry....

As it happened, most of the fare that year was to be politics for Clinton. In the first place, a reconciliation had taken place between him and his brother-in-law, Judge Spencer. This meant rather more than family approval or even personal mutual satisfaction (for they were really devoted). Spencer happened to have enormous influence at that moment with the party; Clinton, officially, very little.

Unofficially, however, he had gained a new and an especially pleasing predominance. In the first place, his personality, though not always winning in the softer sense, was unfailingly commanding. When he had entered the Legislature as a special pleader on behalf of the canal, many new young legislators who had never come in contact with him before were charmed by his oratory and his mien. With the public, his name was already a household word in connection with the canal.

On the other hand, Martin Van Buren, influential with the Tompkins men and the "Bucktails," speedily made it clear that there had been nothing personal in his support of the growingly popular canal bill. A successor to Governor Tompkins was due to be chosen. Ambrose Spencer and his allies now decided that that successor should be De Witt Clinton; and Van Buren fought against this move with all his might and main. This was no matter of the way the wind was veering. It was political ascendancy, for better or for worse, that was the stake this time. So Mr. Van Buren, who since 1815 and his party's triumph had held the office of attorney-general in addition to his State senatorship, bent every effort to prove constitutionally that former Governor Tompkins could be present Governor Tompkins until his proper term expired in 1819, notwithstanding his concurrent tenure of the Vice-Presidency. Governor Tompkins wisely did not lend himself to the trial of such an issue. He resigned, and the Van Burenites turned to an attempt to continue the Lieutenant-Governor in office, under the Constitution, for the remainder of the term. This also dying a more or less natural death, they tried to raise alarm by pointing to the patent desire of the leading Federalists for the nomination of Clinton, reviving the ancient charge of collusion with that party. They also had great hopes of defeating the nomination by virtue of the still existing mode of selecting the candidates, which was by caucus in the Legislature. Van Buren had many of the Republican members of the Legislature in the hollow of his hand; and the shadow of Vice-President Tompkins lay upon a very great many more.

But Ambrose Spencer enjoyed a very close friendship and an equally great influence with three of the four members of the existing Council of Appointment. Thus considerable weight was lent to Spencer's and his followers' plea that the caucus be abandoned as leaving out many honest Republicans who happened to be represented in the Legislature by Federalists. They proposed instead an innovation—a revolution in State political procedure: a system of primary elections and county conventions, to choose delegates to a nominating convention. It was well understood on both sides that many Republicans in the counties represented by

Federalists favored Clinton, and thus this became the crux of the battle.

Spencer won. He obtained the support he wanted for a nominating convention. Van Buren was left to the necessity of naming and gaining support for a worthy opponent in the contest for the nomination; and Peter B. Porter duly agreed to stand as the candidate of this faction. But it was a losing fight now, so far as both Van Buren and Porter were concerned. In the State Convention the nomination of Clinton won easily. The Federalists put up no candidate in opposition, but Tammany continued to send leaflets into every county in the State, with "Peter B. Porter for Governor" upon them.

In spite of Tammany, however, and in spite of Van Buren, it was De Witt Clinton who took the oath of office as fifth Governor of the State of New York on July 1st, 1817.

14

GOVERNOR

1817-1822

THE CLINTONS lived, temporarily, in the Yates mansion, that stood at the corner of Broad and Westerlo Streets in Albany—an attractive house soon enriched with many books, with some little artistic treasure and with infinite affection. The successful termination of his legal fight for his real estate holdings, which had sapped his financial resources to such an embarrassing degree, this year made him once more a comparatively wealthy man; which meant that his personal life knew graciousnesses that had been lacking, and also that others profited again by his inability to say no to distress. Albany at least saw him free from financial worry at the beginning of his gubernatorial career. And those who came to Westerlo Street were lavishly welcomed as of old. Here, as at Newtown, at Richmond Hill, Mr. Clinton's hobbies and interests betrayed their ubiquitous presence, plants and test-tubes, stones and fish-fossils rubbing elbows with State paper and political cachet. Here foregathered the cronies who, let him say Clinton was cold and unloved who will, lavished such affection on him as few men have been privileged to receive: the Bloodgoods, the Gansevoorts, the Van Rensselaers, all the young men who had been won by his personality and his aims. Of the latter was James G. Haines, who had played an enthusiastic part in the late campaign by bombarding the press and the voters with letters and pamphlets in support of Clinton.

In his new public capacity, though nervous tension was never to desert him when speaking or even appearing before any large group, De Witt Clinton showed that, consciously or subconsciously, he had always been preparing in his mind to stand upon some such eminence as this. His first message to the people of the State of New York was a message of congratulation on the commencement of the great canal. It also embraced all the ills as well as the blessings that New York had been heir to—all his fondest themes, the schemes he was forever to aid: agriculture; colleges and common schools; the arts; the militia; the reform of jurisprudence by the reduction of the enormous number of justices' courts, which had become centers of corruption and abuse. Marshals acted as counsel; counsel made it a practice to purchase the claims of needy clients and prosecute them for their own benefit. Clinton asked that these things be abolished also. He pleaded for improvement of the condition of the poor; the control of banking; the preservation of historical treasures; and above all, the system of internal improvements. All the things that had been bottled up in his heart against such a day as this came pouring out. His speech was published far and wide. It was recognized as a State paper of rare excellence, and the name of De Witt Clinton began to be voiced in the remotest regions as well as in all the old capitals of the Atlantic States. In the English newspapers his messages as Governor were to be presented to British readers, and admired by statesman and man in the street alike. His efforts in behalf of the canal, and likewise his antagonists' personal attacks in the same connection, had made his name familiar to countless thousands. His speeches, however formal and devoid of artifice, were to render his mind an object of general respect. And the schemes he sponsored, such as the aforementioned reduction and reform of the justices' courts, which was effected during his first term, impressed by their excellence and by the fearlessness of the sponsor.

The canal, however, was the keynote, not only of his initial oration, but of all the years of this his first essay at Governorship. It was to be, for him, otherwise, a time of gloom both personal and political. It was to be a span filled to its limits with disappointment. The honor, the office, the sense of achievement, were there. But frustration overshadowed them. The birth of the canal, and the smooth flowing of the work being done upon it, formed the one bright spot. Clinton did not—could not—truckle to any man, or even to any system; and it is here, incidentally, that his detractors most misunderstand him. They point to that faculty for sarcasm which was not, indeed, his happiest trait. They rightly describe him as in public austere. They tell how, angered, he flayed his adversaries, and pronounce it as not in any degree surprising that his adversaries should lie in wait for the chance of flaying him.

Even among those groups usually friendly and congenial to him, this spirit was not, it appears, absent. That year the Lyceum of Natural History was founded, under the presidency of the ubiquitous Dr. Samuel L. Mitchill. Now there was no distinguished lay scientist of his day who had more pretensions to membership in such a society than De Witt Clinton, and surely nobody knew that fact better than President Samuel Mitchill, even though the latter functionary had actively and in concert with Tammany opposed Clinton in matters of politics since 1813. But the Lyceum happened to have been born of dissensions that circled round Clinton's name. Politics, in a word, had filtered into his beloved societies at last. And so when the name of the then candidate for Governor came up for honorary membership in the Lyceum in April, 1817, it was negatived. In August John Pintard took it upon himself to write as follows to Dr. Mitchill:

> Respected Sir,
>
> ...I understand that it is in contemplation to reconsider the nomination of Governor Clinton as honorary member of the Lyceum, who was *rejected* at the last meeting. As *his friend* and *in his absence,* I think it a duty to request it as a special favor not to call up this question until Mr. Clinton's return, which I understand will be this week. I consider it indecorous that a personage so elevated in civil society and who fills such distinguished offices in the scientific and other Institutions of our State, should be exposed to the *mercy* of a juvenile Society without being consulted. I will take upon myself every responsibility for this interposition, which arises from the high sense I sincerely entertain for Mr. Clinton's personal merits, without the most distant possible reference to his political rank and sentiments....

Mr. Pintard sent a copy of this letter to Clinton, who, touched, nevertheless replied that Pintard was far more exercised over the affair than he. He begged him to trouble himself no further. But the honorary membership was bestowed on the Governor in the subsequent course of events; and that the Governor bore no malice is plain from his unfailing efforts in this Society's behalf as in that of all the rest.

Likewise from the moment of this his first assumption of the Gubernatorial chair, he refused to lower the dignity of his office or of his person by answering public attack by public refutation. His retaliations, his sarcasms, his counter-attacks were all on paper and they were all private. And such was the patent quality of their veracity, the irrefutable nature of his essays at vindicating his conduct or his course in the matters for which they were constantly blaming and frequently slandering him, that the recipients of his letters in this classification were only too glad to keep them as private as he wished. The drawback to this procedure was of course that the attacks remained public. The refutations still repose mainly in old letter-books; in anonymous newspaper articles and pamphlets difficult of identification and still largely confused with those of his friends; and in the manuscript collections of the State. The slanders have often entered into history and remained there. The refutations, hardly ever.

It is also necessary to consider that the old oppositions, greatly magnified, were ever present and ready to fight. In the Assembly, Tammany, as personified by the members from the city of New York, ceaselessly assailed the canal. They condemned it to speedy and inevitable ruin, and Mr. Clinton with it. In the Senate, Van Buren, though committed to the canal, openly and vindictively led an unremitting personal opposition to the Governor. That Van Buren should emerge as the acknowledged leader of the "Bucktails" was a foregone conclusion. That he should evince the utmost ability in such leadership no less so. Before the first year was out, all the little Bucktails, all the bigger Van Burenites, were spitting and snarling at Clinton, the increasingly magnificent Clinton, dubbing him, in derision, "Magnus Apollo." They might have dubbed him "colossus," for colossus he was. He bestrode indeed their petty world, he loomed gigantic beside their cheap combines, he thought large thoughts and performed big deeds. He shunned small actions, shunned the darker ways. Above all, and most disastrously for the equable political flow of his Governorship, he distributed such offices as lay within his gift and that of a fairly friendly Council of Appointment according to his own judgment and, right or wrong, his own political principles. This it was that really doomed him. He stepped into office while Spencer's Council had still a half-year to go. Immediately, those Republicans who had supported him deluged him with demands that he oust all those who had thrown him and his followers out of office in 1815, and reinstate the latter. Federalists besieged him with calls for recognition of their aid.

He refused to be a party to any such wholesale system of removals. He maintained—as far as he could, in view of that peculiar status of the Governor in such matters which he himself had long ago helped to bring about—his old views of a fair division of the spoils. There are in existence letters of his in reply to office-seekers that are unshakable expressions of his determination to keep his administration pure and free from either fear or favor. Toward Van Buren and the Bucktails generally he was personally cold and sometimes, in the bosom of his circle of friends and sympathizers, violent. But even as regarded the representation of the city of New York, and the office-holders in it, he would not approve either wholesale removal or wholesale reward.

From that moment his immediate doom was sealed. From that time onward, Federalists fought him and Republicans fought him too, the Van Burenite ranks swelling with each new disappointment. Their sole aim became his overthrow, and all the mud they could scrape together they scraped, and what they could not scrape they manufactured. He scorned them. "The little satires of literary buffoons . . ." he wrote in 1820, "render nobody ridiculous but themselves." But unfortunately the "literary buffoons" were having their day unchecked by the devastating quality of his own literary ability. His own pride helped them to effect that which they desired. And that which they wrote in their newspapers and their pamphlets and distributed far and wide, disdained by him and perforce by the more weightily influential of his friends, has too often since become acceptable biographical data in the eye of the not-too-curious historical chronicler. Thus Beveridge, in his life of Clinton's noted contemporary John Marshall, disposes of Clinton briefly and somewhat scornfully as "politically corrupt" because both Federalists and Republicans voted for him for President in 1812; quoting somewhat remote authorities for the already exploded charge that Clinton promised the Federalists an "honorable peace" and the Republicans a vigorous war.

Thus also Henry Adams compares De Witt Clinton with Aaron Burr, and by no means to the latter's disadvantage. Henry Adams has recently been hailed anew as a giant among historians.

Yet his pronouncements regarding Clinton include the astounding reflection that "no one ever explained why Burr did not drag De Witt Clinton from his ambush to shoot him, as two years later he shot Alexander Hamilton with less provocation." He charges the Clintons with vicious combines against Aaron Burr; and he not only swallows whole the corruption cry of 1812, but adds, "no man of common sense who wished to preserve his government and the Union could longer refuse to vote for Madison." It is a typically Adams view, derived from typically Adams sources: Rufus King's correspondence; Albert Gallatin's estimates.... Grandfather John Quincy Adams had said of De Witt Clinton that he prostituted his great talents for the sake of political aggrandizement. Incidentally De Witt Clinton said of John Quincy Adams that he was unfaithful to his heritage and his party. They were both wrong. Both were above party; each was faithful to his patriotic ideal. Clinton was not a man to be dismissed with the epithet "Father of the Spoils System" or of any political system. His whole life-story shows him too big, too concerned with human affairs to father any machine. And the story of the years following 1817, the first of his Governorship, shows disappointed Republicans and Federalists alike damning him because he would not help to distribute the spoils in any common or accepted deal, but only to men who possessed his confidence as well as his gratitude. Tammany still was unable to control him, and so opposed him. Likewise there were Federalists who supported him and, waiting in vain for their compensation, showed too clearly that they regretted having done so.

For if De Witt Clinton was prominent in a political group that had made largesse a rule of the game, it must be borne in mind also that the Clintons themselves were honest men. In fighting for themselves, they unquestionably deemed themselves worthy, deemed themselves of tremendous potential use, as indeed they were. Elevated, they almost invariably pulled worthy men to their level. The Clintons' quarrels, no less than the Clintons' appointments, prove this. "Graft," in the modern colloquial sense, was completely foreign to their natures. They expected to spend money and brains in the course of their political lives, and they did both ungrudgingly. As for the uncompromising character of De Witt Clinton's personal political faith, the very puerility of the accusations leveled at him by his disappointed erstwhile supporters in 1817 alone place it beyond all doubt. He played for power plus worth; not for "pickings."

This was the man whom the "Bucktails" desired to unseat from the Governor's chair. And so numerous were they, and such were their political artifices and strength, that before his administration's second year had passed, his enemies had achieved a majority in both houses of the legislature, and a Council of Appointment inimical to his interests. From this vantage-point they harried him at every angle of his administrative work. And when it comes to his work, no one, even among his detractors, has ever denied that, if he let others work for him, he himself never labored for anything but the public good. This fact it was that saved him, for the moment, from the effects, if not from the bitter taste, of his adversaries' machinations. This alone, effort for country, love of country, and the resultant confidence of his portion of the country, saved the canal scheme, for instance, from being shelved after all. He proved, even in impending defeat, a little too big for his attackers. Hammond, who was near him and friendly towards him at this period, says he could still have saved himself politically by playing politics with one or two key members of the opposition, and blames him for not following the now accepted rules of the game, which Hammond describes himself as pointing out to Clinton once or twice. Clinton was invariably cold to suggestions that he might make advances even to those who were, so to speak, sitting on the fence.

His achievements were many, among the most eminent his agency in the founding of the State Library. In his message advocating such an institution, he declared that New York, the greatest State in the Union, was also the least known. He also inaugurated the annual custom of setting aside a day for Thanksgiving in the State.

He had, however, small cause for personal thanksgiving just then. Since his tenth child, Julia Catherine, was born in 1817, Mrs. Clinton had been in extremely delicate health. He took her and the children to Staten Island in the summer of 1818, going down by sloop from Albany in four days early in July. The vacation began well, with friends by the score dropping in to dinner and supper and even breakfast, as of old. On July 28th, however, a plague of mosquitoes—"noxious in places," as Mr. Clinton, wise in his generation, remarked,—infested the Island, and Mrs. Clinton became so much worse that her husband removed her to the northern outskirts of New York—to Pearsull's Inn at Mount Vernon.

But the mosquitoes were there too—a plague such as had not visited the vicinity for upwards of sixteen years. Mrs. Clinton grew weaker. Dr. Hosack came in his professional capacity, and Mr. Pintard hovered round because his interest in one of the Clinton children—James Henry, the second boy, who was his godson,—had made him more welcome than ever in the family circle. Some three years before, James had entered the navy, sponsored by Pintard who had interests and connections there. From that date Mr. Pintard had made himself responsible for James, acting as Mr. Clinton's agent in the matter of supplies, and almost as a second father in the matter of correspondence and advice. Mrs. Clinton was affectionately grateful to him, and when she knew her time was upon her, she commended her young son anew to his good offices, so many and so youthful were the brothers and sisters of James, fluttering sadly under their father's wing. James at the moment was aboard the *Franklin* at Leghorn, rejoicing at news that Jackson had seized Pensacola, and boasting boyishly that the "snug and gallant little squadron" to which he belonged was ready to fight Spaniards or Englishmen whenever either should wish it.... But he was not ready for the news his father had even then sent him. On July 30th, 1818, Mr. Clinton wrote in his diary:

> This night, a few minutes before 10, witnessed the final departure of my dear wife. She retired to another and a better world with characteristic fortitude, leaving an *immedicabile vulnus* in my heart which will be felt with the continuance of life.... 42 years, 8 months and 22 days....

He had loved her devotedly, and she him. Ten children, of whom seven still survived, had been born to them in the twenty-two years of their happy married life. All of the surviving children—Charles, James, De Witt, George, Mary, Franklin and Julia Catherine—were minors still when their mother died. They clung to him, and he cherished them, but both he and they were lost. The little Julia in particular attached herself to him "as though," he wrote, "she fears I would leave her too." The children needed a mother, and he needed such a friend and a confidante as only his wife had been. He was sad and forlorn, in spite of the almost ceaseless procession of people from every walk in life who called to lighten his loneliness. His lists of visitors at this period include Noah Judah, Stephen Van Rensselaer, Theodore Sedgwick, as well as the faithful of the closer circle. He was intimate with Bishop Hobart of Trinity Church, and a chronicler of the period, Dr. John W. Francis, states that the saying was, "New York City rests on three columns: Hobart, Hosack, and Clinton." The three names, or one at least, could be found on every charitable, medical, ethical or educational list of the time.

But De Witt Clinton was not yet done with personal trials and tribulations. Soon after his wife died, he suffered a fall and fractured one of his legs, being obliged to go on crutches for a considerable period thereafter. He never walked without a limp again, and the violent exercise, the horseback rides, which he had so enjoyed all the days of his manhood, were over for him forever.

There was, however, one thing that not even fractures or crutches succeeded in preventing—his personal inspection of the work as it progressed along the canals. "I have just come from the North, and set off tomorrow for the West," he wrote to Pintard that same summer. "The Canal comes on gloriously." His son De Witt accompanied him to the north, where the waters of Lake Champlain were to be diverted to flow into the Hudson. With Saratoga Springs as their headquarters, they visited Whitehall, Sandy Hill, Waterford, all alive already with canal activity. Then General Van Rensselaer accompanied them to view the greater Western Canal, meeting the remainder of the Commission at Utica.

And in Albany, in New York, he was busier still, with members of the Legislature joining him at breakfast; with the Chief Justice inviting him to take tea; with the military giving him dinners, and even his supper-table never anything but crowded. The very nature of these occasions made the gap in his gracious household more real, the necessity for a loving hand to tend his brood more urgent. As the year 1819 began, he was questioning himself as to whether he should take a second wife; questioning his heart and questioning his need, and reasoning out his feeling, as of course he would. In March his son James wrote to Pintard from Albany that he wished he could remain there "till Papa is

CATHERINE JONES CLINTON

married. He said he would be down in about a month, and I suspect it is for that. However, I tell you this in confidence."

On the 21st of April, 1819, De Witt Clinton married Catherine, the daughter of Dr. Thomas Jones, of New York, and niece of that famous Dr. John Jones of Philadelphia who had been Surgeon-General under Washington. This lady gave him companionship; she gave him a background of considerable and rather specialized social grace; and she gave him a fierce loyalty unsurpassed even by that of the loving Maria. But Catherine Jones was no Maria Franklin, modest and retiring, though they shared a meed of beauty. Miss Jones had been a figure in society before she met Governor Clinton. And after she married him her feeling toward society seems to have resembled nothing so much as that of a conqueror. "Mrs. C.," wrote Clinton, in the second month of his marriage, "has just past thro' the ordeal of ceremonial visits, and is much pleased with Albany. . . ." Albany laughed a little at "Mrs. C.," but her new husband was eminently satisfied with her. If she never quite filled Maria's place, particularly with his children, at least she took his daughters affectionately under her wing and proceeded to groom them in the gentle arts. She was interested in his sons, and in their advancement and welfare. And she relieved her husband of a considerable share of his more ceremonial duties, for ceremony she adored.

He needed the relief. One significant development in the political life of New York State at this period is to be noted;—all things considered, a promising development. The Council of Appointment, owing to its persistent use as a tool for patronage and often for vengeance, was becoming more and more unpopular. That is, honest men were dodging election to that body because honest members of the Legislature viewed it increasingly askance. Hammond, who was a member of the Council in 1818, tells how reluctant he was to accept the nomination, and how he often labored in vain at the deliberations of that body that year to support an honest desire to uphold the worthy wishes of the Governor. . . . And Hammond was at heart no political friend of the Governor.

In 1818 Ogden Edwards, a member of the Assembly from New York City, introduced a bill for the calling of a State convention to consider a revision of the Constitution with reference to the appointive power. The Clintonians disliked extremely the source of this suggestion, and while they also joined in the wish that the Council should be abolished, they opposed the bill in fear of ulterior motives on the part of Tammany. Since the Clintonians in 1818 still possessed a winning voice, the measure died.

The outstanding developments, politically, of Mr. Clinton's first four years as Governor appear to have been the increasing efforts of Martin Van Buren to organize and consolidate a strong opposition to his reëlection; the efforts of the same gentleman to prove collusion between Clinton and the Federalist party; and the unswerving pronouncement on the part of Clinton that as far as he was concerned, "Federalist" and "Republican" as a political division no longer existed, coupled with his unceasing efforts to win the confidence of both. In commenting on Clinton's probable principles and motives in this connection, even Hammond, who was soon to give up in disgust his political support of a man who would not toe the political line, concedes him a probable desire to amalgamate all parties, "which," says Hammond, "in a free state is chimerical." With the leader of his ancient Federalist opposition, Rufus King, Clinton had become reconciled by that gentleman's current outstanding efforts in Washington, and when King's term as United States Senator expired in 1818, Governor Clinton united in supporting him for reëlection, in which he was successful.

The Bucktails continued their efforts meanwhile. So did the Clintonians; but the political protests of the Clintonians became noticeably fewer as the Governor's immutability in the matter of his political behavior threw more and more victims of blasted hopes into the ranks of Van Buren's following. The excellence of Van Buren's political generalship is of course unquestionable. The details of his campaign against Clinton are completely documented in the various political histories of the State of New York, which taken together give a fair view of the situation, though that of Alexander leans a little too heavily on Henry Adams. Van Buren's loyalty to former Governor Tompkins was still complete, and Tompkins was as popular as ever in New York Republican circles. As for Van Buren's personal ambition, it was constantly beating itself against the rock of Clinton's personal eminence. But that he managed by devious ways to prejudice an increasing number of Republicans against Clinton by reason of the latter's alleged favoritism toward the Federalists, even while

Clinton was losing his Federalist support by refusing to favor that party, is beyond refutation and worth emphasizing.

In 1819 the Governor in his message adverted again to the canals; reported excellent progress on the northern span and on that of the only section yet authorized of the western. He recommended that the entire undertaking, from Lake Erie to the tide waters of the Hudson, be authorized by law.

Now it happened at that moment that an unmistakable wave of sentiment, emanating from no less a body than Mr. Van Buren's supporters in the western part of the State, was supplying many indications that continued opposition to the canal was not good political business. The western part of the State was actually watching the canal take shape, and dreaming dreams. Intelligent politicians out there already knew that a party based on opposition to this patently great undertaking was already doomed. And since Mr. Van Buren, whose support had helped the passing of the original Canal Bill, had never since then coupled personal opposition to the canal with opposition to Clinton, it was easy for him to take a hint and to pass it on to his following. The party's opposition to the canal began to be more circumspect. The party's hatred of Mr. Clinton went on; grew, indeed, more violent as that executive's wholly worthy administration continued.

There was, for instance, the matter of the Governor's recommendation of the completion of the entire route. Some of Mr. Clinton's own friends evinced a certain reluctance to endanger confidence in the whole project by an excess of zeal before the time should be ripe for wider action. Would it not be better, they asked, that the section already authorized should first be completed? Then, with public confidence won, the public would support a further pledge of the financial resources of the State. Tammany promptly seized upon this expression of sentiment, which was in no way subscribed to by the Governor, as proof that the Governor was no longer interested in the completion of the canal. It was the entering wedge of a political strategy by which the entire Van Burenite faction intended to garner the credit, if credit there were to be, for the consummation of the scheme. The newspapers, pro and con, carried on this somewhat sham battle. But what was rather more important, the "Bucktails" managed, in 1819, to secure a majority on the Board of

Canal Commissioners itself, through the resignation of Mr. Ellicott and a subsequent able campaign which gave his seat to a Van Burenite. The ultimate aim of this was political patronage in Van Burenite hands from Lake Erie to Lake Champlain, and the transformation of Clinton's greatest achievement into a weapon for Clinton's downfall. It will be seen in how far, and in how deadly a fashion, all these machinations bore fruit.

It was at this precise moment that Tammany gave a dinner at Tammany Hall in honor of General Andrew Jackson, who was visiting the city. Tammany had lately been suffering from another of its periodical scandals, and this patriotic display was in the nature of a customary sequel.... It was a Tammany man who proposed the toast: "General Jackson: so long as the Mississippi rolls its waters to the ocean, so long may his great name and glorious deeds be remembered." This was Jackson's cue to tender to his hosts a verbal pat on the back. He had learned a great deal from his hosts of the political situation in New York.... He had seen the Tammany papers, that described the Governor of New York as a plotter, an autocrat, a base self-seeker.... There were even those who sought to tell him that Clinton had dubbed him, Jackson, a "mutineer" for his recent exploits in Florida, which had lately been the subject of official questioning. But Jackson had also, it seemed, made some other contacts in New York; seen some other versions and also drawn some other conclusions as to the relative worth and honesty of New York's prominent men. And so, when twenty-two toasts had been drunk, to Tammany's selection of Presidents and patriots, exploits and ideals, General Jackson took his glass in hand and responded to an invitation from the chairman that he render a toast of his own. The chairman was Cadwallader D. Colden, now Mayor of New York, friend of De Witt Clinton—and growingly anathema to the sachems here assembled.... General Jackson's toast was: "De Witt Clinton, the enlightened statesman, Governor of the great and patriotic State of New York."

Then pandemonium broke loose in the dining-room of Tammany Hall. The General had missed his cue, to the subsequent delight, not only of the Clintonians but of all non-Tammany or non-partisan New York.

Of course, the wits of the day burst forth. The poets Fitz-Greene Halleck and Joseph Rodman Drake sent "squibs" to

William Coleman's New York *Evening Post,* under their current joint *nom-de-plume* of "Croaker." A poem of Halleck's was entitled, "The Secret Mine, Sprung at a Late Supper" and affords a piquant glimpse at the occasion:

The songs were good, for Mead and Hawkins sung 'em,
  The wine went round, 'twas laughter all and joke;
When crack! the General sprung a mine among 'em,
  And beat a safe retreat amid the smoke.

As fall the sticks of rockets when you fire 'em,
  So fell the Bucktails at that toast accurst,
Looking like Korah, Dothan and Abiram,
  When the firm earth beneath their footsteps burst.

Another *nom-de-plumed* bard included in his version of the affair:

...Then proudly triumphant the conqueror rose,
And smiled at the Governor's chop-fallen foes—
He loves to kill Indians wherever he goes....

In 1819, the Van Burenites decided to request Vice-President Tompkins to enter the Gubernatorial lists in New York again in the elections of the following year. As it happened, in 1819 the accounts of Governor Tompkins as agent for the Government during the late war had undergone a review by the State Comptroller, Archibald McIntyre. A shortage was discovered which was apparently imputable more to the shortcomings of Mr. Tompkins as an accountant than to any lack of honesty on his part. Tompkins' supporters now neatly put through the Legislature a bill which virtually wiped out the former Governor's responsibility and also his indebtedness for this amount, and threw the deficit upon the State. It was a shrewd political move, and coupled with the continuing enormous popularity of Tompkins personally, made him at once an official with unsullied hands and also a dangerous opponent for the present incumbent in the Governorship.

But the outstanding political event of that year, as far as the present chronicle is concerned, was undoubtedly the removal from the office of Attorney-General by the last of the Clintonian Councils of Appointment, of Martin Van Buren. The wonder now does not appear to be that he was removed, but that he was continued in so important an office for so long, in view of the fact that he openly opposed the administration at all points save the canal. T. J. Oakley, a Federalist, was appointed in his place, and the Van Burenite press, which was growing in power and virulence, promptly gave tongue. Mr. Van Buren did not complain in person. He was engaged in warding off the Clintonian fires that raged over the Tompkins accounts and the Tompkins candidacy. Comptroller McIntyre possessed almost as great a degree of popularity in the State as former Governor Tompkins, and the detractors of Tompkins were the supporters of McIntyre and also of De Witt Clinton.

Mr. Clinton was reëlected Governor in 1820, when New York was preparing to join in the celebration of the two hundredth anniversary of the landing of the Pilgrims at Plymouth. But the New England dinner which Clinton ate that December tasted little of either celebration or hope. The spring campaign had been an uncommonly bitter one. Vice-President Tompkins had heard the call of his party and returned from Washington to enter the lists as a foil for Clinton. And Tompkins, for all his current critics, had almost proved himself once more the man of both party and people. He still knew how to be popular. Clinton, never. Clinton's friends loved him. His acquaintances were sometimes a little afraid of him. His enemies loathed him with a whole-heartedness that matched his complete and undisguised contempt for them. To the general public he seemed, to be sure, at moments, a sort of demigod. But this was not one of those moments. A spell-binder was working on the general public, and temporarily blinding its eyes to Clinton's more godlike qualities. It was a weary and an almost completely disillusioned man who found, at the end of the elections of that year, that he had won something less than fifteen hundred more votes than Tompkins. The campaign had been particularly venomous. The newspaper wits had poured such ridicule on Clinton and his societies that he who took his cultural affiliations with a never-failing seriousness, had resigned from the head of the Academy of Arts and the Historical Society out of respect for their dignity.

And even in politics, although he was in, most of his supporters were out. He had presented himself to the voters that year with a little more than his usual courage and confidence. Rancor against himself on the part of the Bucktails had taken on the aspect of a battle so patently unfair that he was certain his friends the New York public would manifest their disgust. "If

Bucktailism does not receive its death-blow at the approaching election," he wrote, "I will renounce all pretensions to political sagacity." But Bucktailism triumphed—though political sagacity, in a certain limited measure, was his. The trouble was that he trusted too much. He angered too quickly. He measured others by his own stature. In 1820, however, the small men, by small measures, were almost too big for him. What some of those measures signified he was soon to learn.

It was the farmers, the prospective settlers along the canal to the west, who had saved him personally from the general fate of what must now be termed his own party. The southern district had voted solidly for Tompkins. The farmers, plus such of the Tompkinsites as stood committed to the canal, and also a majority, still, of the old Federalist party, had chosen Clinton. They recognized him as a man who had moved Heaven and earth to bring about a great internal improvement, which had already taken on the aspect of a partial vindication of the hopes of the faithful. But it still had its virulent and vindictive opponents, mainly in the Tammany ranks, who still vowed that Clinton's final ruin would come when the uncompleted two-thirds finally proved the whole venture a complete fiasco. It is easy to understand that those who gave Clinton their votes did so because if Tompkins should come back, the canal project might yet be abandoned as canal projects had been in the past. The bill for constructing the remainder of the work had finally been debated and won; and in 1820 the middle section was actually completed. But money still had to be raised by loan to effect the eastern and the western ends; and enthusiasm still had to be kept alive, if the new law was not to stagnate.

De Witt Clinton, above all others, kept it alive. That year he contributed a series of letters to the New York *Statesman* over the nom de plume "Hibernicus," with the general title: "Letters on the Natural History and Internal Resources of the State of New York." They were, and are, interesting letters, full of light and of anecdote, covering all phases of travel through the Mohawk country and about the Lakes; all resources, as the title implies; and all possibilities. They were campaign literature for the popular support of the canal, and later, when the canal was almost completed, Clinton sent a set of them to ex-President Jefferson, at Monticello. Jefferson acknowledged them with considerable appreciation, and added that there must still be many who agreed with him that Clinton had anticipated the natural course of progress by perhaps a century.... He asked what quality it was, of mind or maybe of climate, that had enabled New York alone to carry through that which other States could just as easily have accomplished....

Governor Clinton's supporters in the Legislature now found themselves in a rather embarrassing political juxaposition to their former enemies the Federalists. That the two did not form a fusion party goes to prove that their only common ground was a preference for his personal presence in the executive chair. His immediate following still desired power, but not at the hands of the Federalists, whose superior numbers would have placed them in the ascendancy in any coalition. So the Clintonians tried to remain a separate political entity, and in effect Clinton's support itself was composed of warring factions.

He continued his usual governmental courses. That year his recommendations included the institution of savings banks and the formation of a board to help agriculture and the raising of livestock. The following months were to see the consummation of both these recommendations. He also wanted the inspection laws altered with a view to raising the quality of New York flour, and this hope too was realized in part, to the great advantage of the wheat farmers of the State.

But for the rest, all was conflict; indeed all victories were tainted with gall.

The Bucktails, with a highly practical majority in both Houses, pursued their advantage to the full, and Tammany is to be seen in August of 1820 resolving, in full meeting, that a convention "with unlimited powers to amend the Constitution" should be called, the proceedings of such a convention to be submitted to the people for confirmation or rejection. The Republican press sustained this resolution with great vigor. So did a vast proportion of the general public. So, in spirit, did the Clintonians —save that they would give no vote for "unlimited power" to any Tammany majority.... The need for amending the Constitution had long been apparent. The Clintonians now announced it as their belief that the people themselves should vote on the question of a convention and also of the extent of its powers. Tammany should not wield "unlimited powers" as a means of getting rid of Clinton if Clinton's supporters could prevent it.

That autumn a new Presidential election was due to take place, and the New York Legislature held its special session to choose its particular electors. But public dissatisfaction was growing against this method of choosing electors, and Governor Clinton had placed himself on record years before as being interested in the passage of a law providing for the choice of Presidential electors by the people, by general ticket until the United States Constitution should be so amended as to provide for a choice by States. Mr. Clinton now addressed a largely hostile Legislature with a recommendation to that effect, and at the same time lifted his voice in a valiant attempt to combat some of the political usages that had placed him in his present position and might conceivably place others there. He sounded a note of alarm against the growing practice of the influencing of State elections through Federal patronage. Some of his most bitter critics admit that there was justice in his plea; that pressure from Washington had indeed insinuated itself so subtly that its practical results had been rather more effective than the indignation it aroused. Since the Presidential day of Jefferson himself, who had systematically refused to remove customs or other Federal officers without cause, deaths and the growing requirements of the departments had created vacancies, which were duly filled by men who had served their party in elections.... These had continued active. In the southern district of New York State, the campaign work of Federal employees had played a large part in Clinton's local defeat there in 1820, and it was well-known that not one Federal officer had given him his vote. In his message of November, 1820, Mr. Clinton said:

> Our government is complex in its organization, and it is essentially necessary to preserve the State governments in their purity and energy. A free government could never exist in a country so extensive as the United States without a judicious combination of the Federal and representative principles. The apprehensions which some of our wisest statesmen entertained, at the formation of the Constitution, that the State governments would constantly encroach on the powers of the national government, appear not to have been realized. The practical tendency has been in the opposite direction. The power of the general administration has increased with the extension of its patronage. And if the officers under its appointment shall see fit, as an

> organized and disciplined corps, to interfere in the State elections, I trust that there will be found a becoming disposition in the people, to resist these alarming attempts upon the purity and independence of their local governments; for whenever the pillars which support the edifice of the general government are undermined and prostrated, the whole fabric of national freedom and prosperity will be crushed in ruin. I have considered it my solemn duty to protest against these unwarrantable intrusions of extraneous influence, and I hope that the national legislature will not be regardless of its duty on this occasion.

He then recommended that a State convention be held to amend the State Constitution, on the condition that the people first approved it by popular vote, and later approved its proceedings and resolutions likewise.

It was the voice of Tammany, under the guidance of Martin Van Buren (a Van Buren officially inactive but very, very busy behind the scenes) that answered the Governor. The voice of Tammany, as represented by a Van Burenite majority in the Assembly, managed to select a Council of Appointment composed entirely of men completely opposed to Clinton. It also poured out a volume of righteous wrath at what it chose to consider his direct accusation that the officers of the general government "as an organized and disciplined corps," had interfered in the State elections. The State Senate passed a resolution calling on the Governor to produce proof. The Governor promptly replied in the following words:

> Gentlemen:
>
> Fully appreciating the patriotic solicitude of the Senate to prevent all unwarrantable intrusions in the political affairs of the State, I have received their application for information on this subject with great pleasure, and I shall, in due time, make them a communication which, I trust, will be satisfactory in its nature and salutary in its tendency.
>
> De Witt Clinton.

But sarcasm did not avail him. Ten days later the Senate, obviously piqued by the implications of his answer, passed another resolution attacking his attitude toward the Federal government as "highly improper." Senator Pierre R. Livingston even went so far as to term it treason against Clinton's "liege lord, the President of the United States." Mr. Clinton's friends, taken a little unawares, gathered themselves together to insist that the Governor's statement had not been an indictment at all, and had not called for proof; but that if proof were to be insisted upon, sufficient time had not elapsed in which to gather it from the many quarters of the State. The original resolution passed, however, and was transcribed for the benefit of the Governor. He replied once more:

> Gentlemen:
>
> I have this moment received a resolution of your honorable body, which, as well as the one to which it refers, I shall fully notice at the next meeting of the Legislature; and shall therefore, at this late hour, pass it over with the expression of my sincere regret that any branch of the Legislature should, in so unprecedented a manner, lose sight of the respect due to itself, and the courtesy due to a coördinate department of the government.
>
> DE WITT CLINTON.

On the day this message was received, the Legislature adjourned. A few minutes before adjournment, the Senate voted to return the Governor's message to the Governor, which was done. . . .

Meanwhile a very great deal of recrimination and vituperation had been spent upon the debates on that part of the Governor's November speech which recommended a Constitutional convention, and after a bill calling for such a gathering "with unlimited powers" had passed both Assembly and Senate, an unexpected defection in the Council of Revision made it necessary for the Governor to cast his vote in settlement of the affair. He cast it against the bill. The unlimited power condition was against his lifelong principles and his policy. And there certainly was no secret made of the fact that "unlimited power" in the hands of the Bucktail majorities, however salutary their other changes in the Constitution might be, was to be principally directed toward the removal of Clinton's friends in the Council of Revision, his sole remaining prop of any strength, by a sweeping reform of the State judiciary system, on the ground that the judges' position in the Council impaired the purity of the Bench. Clinton's friends in the Council of Revision happened to constitute one of the few remaining groups of great and humanly disinterested figures in the State, including as they did Chancellor Kent, Ambrose Spencer (now Chief Justice of the Supreme Court) and Jonas Platt, a judge in the same body. It was patently more in the punishment and isolation of Clinton than in the purification of the judiciary that the Bucktails were interested, even though their avowed aims possessed merits that could not fail of appreciation.

A Van Burenite Council of Appointment went speedily to work meanwhile. McIntyre was removed from the office of Comptroller, which he had filled with distinction. Thomas J. Oakley, who had succeeded Van Buren as Attorney-General, was ousted to make room for Samuel A. Talcott, a "high-minded Federalist" who had opposed Mr. Clinton's reëlection. Stephen Van Rensselaer was swept out of the post of Adjutant-General; and Gideon Hawley was inexcusably removed as Superintendent of the Common Schools. These gentlemen, all able, were all friendly toward Clinton. Hawley had worked heart and soul with Clinton for the formation and the success of the public schools, and his removal caused a little storm even among the Van Burenites. But these were only a few of the removals, which in total did away with Clintonian office-holders in almost every case to which the Council's powers extended. Governor Clinton did not sign the minutes of this session of the Council of Appointment.

He did, however, submit to this session of the Legislature the proof of Federal interference in State elections which he had promised at the last. On January 9th, 1821, he sent to the Assembly a capacious green bag containing a vast quantity of correspondence, certificates and affidavits, all showing proof of interference on the part of Federal officers in the State elections, and particularly with his own reëlection as Governor. Among the contents of what came to be known as the Green Bag Message was a letter from Martin Van Buren to Henry Meigs, a member of Congress from New York City, dated April 4th, 1820 (which was at the eve of the election), giving the names of four Clintonian deputy postmasters, recommending their removal, and suggesting by name men of the opposition for appointment to their places. The letter urged the utmost haste and the great need for "alarming them by two or three prompt removals." Two removals were made as Van Buren requested, and as promptly. No misconduct in office was charged as the reason for the removals, as had been the case almost invariably before.

This and all the other "Green Bag" documents were referred to a joint committee which was ordered to render a report on their merits....

The three outstanding events of that session, however, were, first: the passing of the Convention Bill, duly amended by a provision for the previous submission of the whole question to the people of the State, which left no party any sound reason for opposing it further, whatever underlying fears may have possessed certain interested persons; second, the election of Martin Van Buren as a Senator in Congress in place of Nathan Sanford, whose term had expired. This, in effect, placed Martin Van Buren in the same position of State and national prominence as Clinton had held in 1803 and might have retained; and third (and perhaps most significant for Clinton) the addition of one more member to the existing Canal Commission. The newcomer was William C. Bouck, Senator from Schoharie County and an ardent Van Burenite. He was a man of popularity and of considerable ability, and his career as a Commissioner was smooth and energetic. Nevertheless it was a foregone conclusion that he would not add to the smoothness of the lot of the head of the Board, and indeed he did not.

In March the joint committee reported on the Green Bag message. It produced a number of affidavits impeaching the evidence offered by the Governor, and it again strongly censured him, delivering the bold collective assertion that no extraneous influence had been evident in any of the State elections. They even attacked him for reminding them of an ancient resolution which held it improper for a Federal officer to be concurrently a member of the State Legislature, though only a few months later the resolution was to be repeated and incorporated in the Constitution of the State of New York, as amended by the State convention. That convention, largely composed of delegates of the Van Burenite persuasion, met at the end of August, 1821. Van Buren himself was selected as a delegate by the people of Otsego County, of which he was not a resident. Vice-President Tompkins was chosen by Richmond County. Rufus King now came from Queens as the selection of the Republicans there. James Kent, Stephen Van Rensselaer, Ambrose Spencer and Abraham Van Vechten were selected in Albany County; Judge Platt from Oneida; Erastus Root, once Clinton's eloquent eulogist, now established as one of Clinton's most implacable enemies, from Delaware; and General James Tallmadge from Dutchess. These as a sample of the more scintillating selections, of both political complexions, though so adroit had been the management of the affair that the quality of the Clintonian representation far exceeded its quantity. The Governor presided officially over the convention. Tompkins was chosen Chairman. Men of decidedly Van Burenite sentiments soon largely composed the duly elected committees.

But that convention conferred a lasting benefit on the State of New York by abolishing the Council of Appointment and placing the power of nomination in the hands of the Governor and that of appointment in the hands of the Governor and the Legislature jointly, save in the case of local county officers who were to be elected by the people, and justices of the peace who were to be nominated by the local boards of supervisors and appointed by the Governor. This last was a political move on the part of Mr. Van Buren, who presented the resolution. It was to live only a few years, and it was Clinton who was to sweep it away. Mr. Van Buren, however, was the chairman of the committee which reported the resolutions upon which this entire and most salutary enactment was based. In abolishing the Council, it destroyed a weapon which had been wielded by many, not excepting De Witt Clinton, as a means of consolidating their own party positions, and by but few (but here Mr. Clinton must be included in the more beneficent minority) for the good of the State. It had always been the center of contention, a focussing point for envy, hatred and malice.

The existing judiciary system was abolished, and a new one substituted; the State was divided into definite judicial districts; and other sweeping reforms, including an extension of the voting power, were made. But the most significant action of the convention as far as Mr. Clinton was concerned was that it also did away for ever with the Council of Revision, and gave to the Governor the veto, and to the Legislature, by means of a two-thirds vote of both houses, the power of overruling the veto. The Governor's term of office was reduced from three years to two, and made to run from January 1st instead of July 1st as theretofore.

By the same token, a period had been put to the existing Governor's term, and apparently to his entire political career. With the powers of the executive apparently extended and re-enforced, the powers of Mr. Clinton as such had been actually reduced to the vanishing point. He held no control of the law-making privilege, with anti-Clintonians lustily ruling both Senate and Assembly. He held none in the matter of appointments, for the striking out of any nominations of his, without need for comment or review, was a foregone conclusion.

He had had one major triumph at the late convention, however. The canal law was made inalienable by any act of the Legislature, and the canal fund was established by a clause in the constitution as revised.

Mr. Clinton met the Legislature on January 2nd, 1822. He stood in a House of Assembly manned by representatives whose power and influence, whose place and voice, had been advanced or checked by one standard of concerted action—the proscribing of all who had so much as dared to support De Witt Clinton, no matter how, or how remotely. They had, in effect, robbed him of the last vestiges of his power, and by officially adopting the irresistible canal policy as their own they had left him without a political leg to stand on. The men he faced might include many secret sympathizers and furtive and reluctant admirers; but only a pathetic handful dared to avow themselves Clintonian by preference now. He was equal to the occasion. He congratulated the Legislature on the "civil revolution" effected by the late convention, whose findings and resolutions were now in the hands of the "only sovereign power . . . among us—the people themselves." He reverted to trade, and advocated protecting home manufactures by duties upon imports. He praised the rapid progress that had been made on the canals. He was quite radiant about them. He spoke of the current canal projects of Ohio and Illinois, and urged that the members of Congress from New York State should be requested to use their best efforts to procure grants from the Federal Government to these States, to aid them in the work. He referred to the request of the city of Washington that the State of New York likewise use its influence in the Government toward helping improve the capital city. He recommended certain improvements and revisions of the New York criminal law. And he looked at his fellow-legislators of New York, and said,

> Whatever diversity of opinion may exist, I am persuaded that we will all coöperate with a sincere and entire devotion to our solemn and momentous duties, in cherishing a spirit of conciliation and forbearance, and in cultivating that respect which we owe to each other and to ourselves.

The Legislature, through the medium of a committee, made due comment on the Governor's message. The comment was couched in the following terms:

> RESOLVED that this House approves of the declaration of the late Assembly: "that the custom of delivering a speech by the Executive to the Legislature at the opening of the session, and of returning an answer to the same, is a remnant of royalty, not recommended by any considerations of public utility, and ought to be abolished."

This statement, though confined to the record (no direct reply to the Governor being vouchsafed) was rendered a trifle more personal in its aim by the fact that Governor Clinton on first assuming office had announced that he would not require the Legislature to answer any of his messages, but that he preferred delivering those messages in person to sending them by messenger, because the former procedure appeared to him more respectful to the representatives of the people....

In the year 1822, De Witt Clinton refused to renew his candidacy for the Governorship of the State of New York.

15

THE DARK YEARS

1822-1824

AMBROSE SPENCER, Pierre Van Cortlandt, and Archibald McIntyre came as a delegation from his respectable band of faithful friends and supporters to express its admiration of his character and his deeds, its undiminished confidence, and its fervent hope that he would reconsider. But both he and his friends well knew that reconsideration would be both idle and degrading. The long arm and the predatory fingers of Tammany had pushed him definitely into the discard, a menace no longer, a bar to complete power no longer—for the time being. ... The canals, the golden note of his fame in the pæans of an increasing pioneer army, were firmly controlled by a strongly Tammany Board, and hence by strongly Tammany patronage along the way. The public schools, with whose amazing growth to date the name of Clinton was hardly less associated, had been delivered into the jurisdiction of the Secretary of State. Measures which Clinton had advocated with all his heart and soul emerged as Tammany measures and passed and redounded to Tammany's credit. The name of Clinton had become a difficult one to utter in the halls of the Legislature. In those halls, it seemed, he was already the forgotten man. Outside—?

In January, 1822, a delegation of New York citizens had come to him direct from a mass meeting held to express public confidence in him. In February, March, April, his friends and supporters added their pleas. He was firm. But he remained, when his other public service was apparently at an end, the god of the canals, attending the meetings of the Commission constantly; ever and again at Utica, at Sandy Hill, at Rome. He knew every step of the work and its remarkable progress, weighed every suggestion and consulted with experts for its smooth completion.

Also he was busy in a like fashion in behalf of the State of Ohio. He had, at the request of the citizens of that State, lent his ear and his advice to their own projected canal. He had persuaded Mr. Geddes to direct the engineering work in that undertaking, and was giving his own experienced mind to the solving of this sister State's improvement problem, and generously expending himself.

Mr. Clinton's diary for the end of May and the first half of June in the year 1822 reveals perhaps better than any other portion the condition of his mind, the status of his reputation, and the many-sided character of the man. It begins on May 23rd:

> Set out in a hack to attend a meeting of the Canal Board at Buffalo. George[1] accompanied me, on his way to Hamilton College. Arrived at Schenectady at 3 o'clock, where dined. On my way, saw dames and damsels, attended by knights, squires and dwarfs, as would be supposed in days of chivalry. An old man at Halfway House, a great talker and declaimer, grew quite familiar, and was astonished to see so little pride—as the whole country rang with my arrogance, and among other stories of my having taken up money at the Utica and other banks to carry on elections. There were great rains last night, which rendered the roads worse and the weather cold and windy. The approach to Schenectady was as usual beautiful.
>
> After dinner set out in a light covered waggon got from Powell who accompanied me to indicate the Canal, on the south side of the Mohawk. The road becoming bad, and the night dark, we crossed the river at Vedder's ferry, 10 miles from Schenectady, and arrived at 10 at night at Conyne's Tavern, 40 miles from Albany, stiff with fatigue and cold. The storm and fatigue of the night was lightened by the calls of the solitary whippoorwill and the concerts of the amphibious animals in the water and marshes.
>
> Mr. Powell says that the stages employed by his company pay annually $3,000. in turnpike tolls—and that the quantity of produce at Schenectady is so great that it cannot be conveyed to Albany in all June.

[1] This son George was later to be prominent in the development and public life of Buffalo, where members of his family still reside. He was a high-ranking member of the judiciary and sometime Mayor of that city. His hobbies and a great deal of his training were, like his father's, along scientific lines.

24th May. Set off in same vehicle at half after 5 and arrived in 3 hours at Burtis from Palatine Bridge (14 miles from Conynes), where breakfasted. Mr. Powell left us at the latter place. The morning was cold and the whole day continued windy and unpleasant. The boats in the river—the carriages in the road—and the operations on the Canal exhibited a scene of bustle and business. The scenery was beautiful and picturesque. The country was filled with crops of pease, rye, wheat and Indian corn. We were regaled with the music of the Groves. We saw the king bird, blue bird . . . boblinkus . . . crow, blackbird, robin . . . and the kingfisher. Among other shrubs, a superb lilac in full blossom was remarkable on account of its size and beauty.

There follow the technical details of certain variations which have been made in the original plan of the Canal in order to carry it through the heart of Schenectady.

. . . Wrote letters home at a fire—the weather being so cold—and opened a Bible which was in the room. St. Paul seems to delight in witty conversation. In the 4th Chapter, 6th verse of his Epistle to the Colossians, he says: "Let your speech be always with grace, seasoned *with salt.*" Does he mean Attic salt?

Dined at Little Falls, 20 miles from Palatine Bridge. Viewed the Canal and slept at Herkimer Village, 7 miles. Our dinner at Little Falls was composed of pike of the Mohawk and wild pigeon.

The flower of the mandrake or may apple is white.

Viewed the old and new canals—another contemplated aqueduct. . . .

Where the new canal enters the old one at German Flatts the new lock is said to be 14 inches too high. There is a palpable difference between the materials and workmanship of the lift lock of the new and the guard lock of the old canal.

The sliding banks at the Dug Way, as it is called, are based on quick sand and are frequently choking up the canal.

The bank swallow, the smallest of the hirundine tribe, has perforated the banks for its nest, and has exhibited great art in selecting the stable and firm places, there being solid gravel both above and below their holes, and they carefully avoid the quicksand. They also indicate unwearied industry in their operations—50 are sometimes employed in making the same hole. Each species of hirondel has an appropriate call or note.

The alluvial matter at this place makes an excellent material for puddling.

The West Canada Creek might be used as a feeder for the Canal. It comes from the north and strikes the Mohawk at right angles. Whenever an occurrence like this takes place, flats and islands are found in the principal stream . . . and the German

> Flatts, which extend from the Little Falls to upwards of 6 miles above Herkimer village, were produced in this way, and being granted by Governor Burnett, were formerly called Burnett's Field.

Here he runs into a discourse on the history of the village of Herkimer, and follows it with some detailed observations of the natural history phenomena revealed in the excavation work on the canal, and the varied excellences or otherwise of the different contractors.

> ... Vast quantities of produce stored on the banks of the Canal at Herkimer. Slaves brought down flour retailed at 5 25/100 a barrel, and ground gypsum 5 per ton in bulk.
>
> Pike and chubb have entered the Canal here from the Mohawk. Saw two kingbirds in close pursuit of a crow, and force him to light on a tree.
>
> A snapping turtle devoured young goslings....
>
> Mr. Spinner, the German clergyman at Herkimer, says that Clinton has conquered his head; Tompkins his heart....
>
> A loaded canal boat can go 25 or 30 miles a day. A loaded waggon but 20 or 25....

On the 27th of May he was boat-riding on the canal, and finding out more about feeders and locks and their capacities:

> ... The old leaven of nature still ferments against the Canal. John Huff told General Van Cortlandt in New York, in a triumphant manner, that the Canal had all broken up and gone to destruction.
>
> The number of lift locks in the whole Canal will be 81. Guard locks are not included....
>
> It now costs only $20 a ton to convey commodities from New York to the head of Seneca Lake or to Geneva. It formerly cost $50.
>
> Saw a great number of ascending and descending vessels, among the rest "Lady Clinton." ...

Wool and cotton and glass were passing down the canal, as far as it yet went. Vessels, and likewise tolls, increased in number.

> ... In 20 years, says Engineer Wright, there will be a canal on the north side of the Mohawk.

He returned to Utica by way of the canal, greeting, as everywhere, a host of visitors and passers-by *en route*. He viewed the locks at Little Falls, and the fish there, too, and detailed both for his own information.

He saw the villages, farms, factories that were springing up in a myriad places where grass and weeds and stones and swamps had flourished undisturbed. It was he who had made men see that progress lay this way. That much they could never take away from him, and in its light his zeal in recording the state of things along the course of his canal in 1822 becomes human and attractive. But he has zeal in all things. At Olden Barnevelt,[1] for instance, he had already made the acquaintance of Francis Adriaan Vanderkemp, with whose conversation and processes of mind he was speedily enchanted. This New York country gentleman was Dutch in manner, appearance and blood. Master of many subjects of antiquity, he was dubbed by De Witt Clinton[2] "the most learned man in America." Clinton it was who had procured the services of Vanderkemp in editing the Dutch records of the State for the State Library at Albany. Clinton it was who never failed thereafter to sit at Vanderkemp's board when his journeyings took him westward, or to act as his host when the Dutchman's new duties bore him east. "A man of pure morals and unaffected piety," wrote Clinton. "His family agreeable but ugly. Something fascinating in personal beauty."

He winds up his entry for that May day with some observations on Indian corn:

> ... The silk ... is like a Fallopian tube, to convey the male dust or pollen to the cob. Whenever the grasshoppers destroy this silk, there is no corn; only a cob. In like manner, cut the tops and there is no pollen, of course, and the same results....

And meanwhile he was traveling forty miles a day. But while he surveyed the fruits of his hopes and the growing justification of his confident advice, certain major disappointments may still be seen to have rankled. Thus on the 31st of May:

> "What a thrice-double ass was I,
> To take this drunkard for a god,
> And worship this dull fool...."
>
> The gulled Electors of this State may exclaim as above, with Caliban in "The Tempest," when he understood the real character of Stephano and Trinculo.

Nevertheless he was, in spite of himself, at last on holiday—the kind of holiday he most enjoyed. He was studying fish

[1] Later Trenton Village, Oneida County, N. Y.
[2] In one of the "Hibernicus" Letters, N. Y. *Statesman*, 1820.

alive in river and canal, and dead in the twice-a-week market in a steadily-thriving Utica. He hovered over plants, and worked out botanical puzzles. He used his pocket thermometer to watch the daily temperature. He traveled, with the Board, to Syracuse, which Joshua Forman had founded. He noted that forty boats, on an average, passed Syracuse each day. He inspected lockage and he familiarized himself with the sick and the casualty cases of the canal construction camps. On the 4th of June, he went in a boat called the "American Water Coach," drawn by four horses "like the Troy ferry-boats," to survey the innumerable rivers and streams that watered the country on all sides. He studied their sources and the causes that originated them. He examined and noted the formation of rocks along the banks. He was familiar with the different species of wild game. "Prodigious large trees," he noted; "particularly black walnut." He came to Lockport, and hardly recognized the primitive outpost of his earlier call. "This place has sprung up like a mushroom. It has 60 houses." When he returned in the following year, the number of houses was two hundred, and the canal was not yet finished.

> There is a black walnut here 21 ft. in circumference, which William Britton, former keeper of the State Prison at Auburn, had cut down in order to make a canoe to go to New York in, after the Canal is finished.... Slept at Molyneux, 7 miles from Lockport, 13 from Lewiston. The roads bad. The stage broke down. Had to walk. Heat intolerable and mosquitoes most annoying.

On the 7th of June the party arrived at Niagara Falls, and made a leisurely sightseeing journey down to Buffalo.

> Arrived at Buffalo at 7 p.m. (Clinton notes). Received with a salute.... Saw a steamboat at Black Rock, taking in a cargo for the Fur Company.

Buffalo was interesting and occasionally amusing. The town was packed with sightseers, come, like Clinton and his fellows, to see what was going on. Porter was hospitable in his neighboring home at Black Rock. Influential men on the Canadian side extended invitations, which were accepted. On the 10th of June: "Received a message from the Seneca Indians requiring an interview." The interview took place in the Buffalo Court House, in the presence of a large audience, and Clinton, who was as completely interested in the well-being of the "pagans" as he was in that of the rest of humanity, made the acquaintance of the famous chief Red Jacket. The high spot of the interview seems to have been the announcement of an Indian named Corn Planter that he had "had a visit from Jesus Christ, warning the Indians not to turn Christians."

So home, via Batavia, Canandaigua and Auburn by road, with the word "canal" following them on the summer breeze. These lands were pregnant with expectation—and alas, with speculation too. Land jobbers were racing each other along the route, and *bona fide* owners were often not above following some of their methods. The procuring of the ground for the waterway and its operations would contribute a history in itself. ... So in a boat called the *Myron Holley,* sailing all night for Utica; and in like manner to Little Falls, and thence in a stage for Schenectady, and home to Albany on June 16th. It was a year of journeys. In July he returned for a brief visit to the scenes of his childhood. That is, he went visiting along the banks of the Hudson in company with his wife and her mother. They called on the surviving De Witts at Kingston, where Clinton as a boy had known a second home. The old Dutch family Bible —indispensable adjunct and record of an old Dutch home— brought memories. It was thirty years since Clinton had seen it last, or the old Dutch homestead either; or the invincible institution at which he had prepared for his college training.

His holiday was an interlude between canal duties. He went with Van Rensselaer, attended this time by his youthful son Franklin, to view the works to the north, dining with the Schuyler family at Schuylersville along the way

> Arrived at Sandy Hill next evening, at Baird's Tavern, where slept. Frightened to death by the spontaneous ringing of his house bells. Cause unknown—electricity—mice—ceiling examined.... The house well kept. Females for waiters—very smart, and very active in arranging their long curls....

Next day he inspected the feeder above Glens Falls, Clinton the botanist at the elbow of Clinton the engineer, cataloguing the flora and fauna of that attractive countryside. At White Hall on the 31st he wrote again of the swallows, describing their nests in detail. There is scientific evidence that among his more concrete contributions to ornithological knowledge were his discovery of a new species in this family of birds along the route of his canal travels; to botany his finding in the region of Utica of the wild wheat previously described; and to ichthyology his discovery of a strange fish in the upper Hudson and his identification of a species of salmon, which he called "Salmo Otsego" after the lake in which he found it.

August was vacation time again, with his family at Saratoga Springs. More than twenty years later, Philip Hone recalled in his diary how Clinton appeared on these too-rare holiday occasions. It was the farmhouse near Saratoga of a Hollander named Barhyte that was "a favorite resort of Governor Clinton, whose moments of ease and hilarity," says Hone, "I have often shared. Many a joke of his have I enjoyed, when he laid aside his state to be a boy once more, and many a good dinner have I helped him to eat in the old Dutchman's house."

In September he went west again, for another meeting of the Board. James H. Clinton, the midshipman, went with him. A great many of Clinton's fondest hopes were centered in this particular son, now twenty years old, who had dedicated himself to his country's service. And his friends, and Mr. Pintard's, in the navy were pleased to further these hopes where they could. Commodore Chauncey had young James under his command, and so, later, did Commodore Perry. Mr. Clinton's ambition for his boys was always as consuming as his ambition for himself, and far less complicated. He wished James, in his chosen calling, to shine as his superior officers had shone. He warned James' sponsor against encouraging the lad's too-urgent fondness for a game of chance, a merry day ashore. As for James himself—he tried to be a Spartan, to please his adored father. He tried to live up to his father's dictum that "constant employment is necessary to restrict the ardor of his temperament and to keep him in the straight uneven road to virtue." He yearned heartily enough for active service, and was known to wish that there would be another war, so that he could be in it. He never saw active service of that kind. But in his brief span of life, if he snatched at pleasure and was hungry for it, he managed to achieve place and the beginnings of an excellent record. In his way perhaps a hero, James, loving home and friends and sport, but sailing to far places and trying hard to stick to his duty because his father esteemed time as a commodity not to be wasted.

In the winter of 1822, his father was setting him an example along those very lines. Mr. Clinton had said good-by to his high office and to those who had thrust him from it. He had all the time in the world to waste, if he so desired. It is needless to remark that he did not. Retiring to his farm, he applied himself with energy to all those pursuits so dear to his heart. He also devoted himself, as a refreshing change, to his family. On October 10th he took his son George to his college at Clinton, New York.

> 12th October. Arrived at Clinton at 9 a.m., where breakfasted at Mr. Foote's Inn. Viewed the village. Old Squire Foote settled in Clinton in 1787. Utica in 1785 a wilderness. Old Governor Clinton advised him to abandon it on account of the weight of timber—beech, bass and elm—it being, as he thought, impossible to conquer it....

And still the canal, for a great variety of reasons, remained the center of his life. Not the least of these reasons, however, was the choice of professions of his third surviving son, De Witt, Jr. Young De Witt had elected to become an engineer himself, and on April 1st, 1822, Mr. Clinton had noted in his journal with pride: "De Witt went on the Canal." From this time on, the diary is studded with notes of visits to "the Engineer" at Middletown, which was on the route of the northern waterway. And as that northern waterway was a branch and an offshoot of the great Western Canal, so was the second De Witt Clinton a sprig from a familiar tree. In September Charles, George and Franklin accompanied their father to see their brother engaged on his new job. In October Mr. Clinton conducted his friend Samuel Jones, Jr., on a similar errand. Young De Witt could be a proud youth, as he was apparently a competent one. His work was to extend itself into the period and the pioneer labor both of the railroads and of modern water supply. His father's was not, by the narrowest of margins.

But the canal and its glory were still De Witt Clinton's. And that was what the Bucktails could not bear—that his benefactions, his personality, should still loom so amazingly large. On the 28th of November, 1822, he was at Waterford again with James, the guest of honor at the opening of the canal at that point. In June of 1823 he was off again to tour the whole route, his destination Buffalo, where the question of the ultimate western outlet was to be decided at a meeting of the Board. It was an exciting, even a furious, meeting. Black Rock was fighting Buffalo for the prestige and also for the riches that would come into the arms of a terminal harbor; and in Peter B. Porter, son and resident of that village, it had a canal luminary who could and did put in a powerful word. Clinton was opposed to the added cost and labor of artificial construction necessary to effect a harbor and a canal outlet at that point, and was in favor of the natural resources along that line of the more easily accessible Buffalo. But Porter, still in political life, was also strong outside it, particularly in these parts. And thus a familiar political struggle followed Clinton into the wilds.

Both he and Porter won it, but the final victory was to be his. The Black Rock harbor came into existence, but not as the ultimate outlet of the Erie Canal. Which is why Peter B. Porter nursed a grudge against Clinton even beyond the grave. Clinton opposed the Black Rock project as impracticable. Tammany methods at first flush put it through—and impracticable, as built, it proved. Yet it was Peter B. Porter who ever after led the cry of "impracticable," of "no engineer," against De Witt Clinton. For at first, let it be repeated, Porter won. On June 19th, 1823, the Commission, after repeated balloting and a great deal of violent debate, passed its vote against Buffalo, with one dissentient and one Commissioner not voting. Clinton was the dissentient. Van Rensselaer was the non-voter.

But Clinton continued to think about Buffalo, open later in winter than Black Rock; housing, already, a great many people who had settled there on the strength of the general expectation that the Erie Canal would extend thither; and on his journey home his mind was busy with the fight that he had determined should continue. It did. He rounded up support for his contentions and beliefs; he besieged the Legislature with petitions. His active friends in both Houses helped. The engineers who favored Buffalo told why they did so. The citizenry of Buffalo charged corruption in the securing of a majority vote for Black Rock, and Clinton was called as a witness in the investigation that ensued, which did not endear him the more to Porter and his friends. Clinton's evidence was that he had long thought Buffalo the more practicable place for the harbor, and still did; that he had thought the vote for Black Rock ill-advised, and still did. He had, however, no evidence that it had been obtained by corrupt means.

The immediate *dénouement* was that the two harbors were voted for—one at each of the disputed points. But Clinton went on agitating, and the cost and later inadequacy of the Black Rock works helped him in his cause. The seal of actual utility was duly put upon Buffalo and the cutting of the main line of the canal through to that point. The canal was more and more "Clinton's Ditch," but not in the Bucktail sense. On his journey home, he had "scratched gravel" (a term that the canal people used to describe a walk on the towing-path) at Rochester. He had looked at the thriving township, standing where the wilderness had reigned in 1810. Here was an aqueduct seven hundred and ninety-two feet long, with hundreds of men at labor upon it.

> A sublime work.... A growing place.... The hum of men—the bustle of business—and streets crowded with building stone. ... Squire Durfee and Wilson took boat with us at Palmyra on a jaunt to Lyons. The former moved from Rhode Island when a boy thirty years ago. He drove eight cattle and traced his way by an Indian path. Gave 75 cents an acre for his land, which is now worth $30.... From Rochester to Lockport 62 miles by canal. The tendency of the Canal has been to ameliorate the neighboring roads. People turn out to work. It draws business there and banishes heavy teams.... Night aboard uncomfortable. Crowds of women and three children in the next cabin, divided from us by a baize partition.... Although like going from an oven into an ice-house, got up at night—wrapped myself up in my cloak—and stayed on deck until we passed from Oneida Creek to Rome—16 miles through gloomy swamps. The moon was luminous—the fog heavy—the air cold.... Arrived at Rome at 1 a.m. and took good lodgings on the Bridge.... Breakfasted at Rome—a good salmon. Went with the citizens to view the proposed change of the Canal, and arrived at Utica at half after 2 in a waggon....

And so in a canal-boat to Little Falls, and home thence by the stage.

Late in August he was traveling again—to the new summer resort in a pine orchard in the Catskill Mountains, in company with his wife and his youngest daughter and a party of friends. Here the evenings were enlivened with center-dances and cotillions "performed with elegance" in a ballroom lined "with branches of the tree vulgarly called balsam of fir, whose resin is sold as a salve under the name 'Balm of Gilead.'" Here in the dawn he climbed noble summits to watch the rising sun.

In October he went, by special invitation, to New Jersey, to view the projected route of a canal from the Passaic to the Delaware. Vistas were opening to the southward. The eyes of the neighboring States were upon New York. In this State of New Jersey rival factions were warring for rival canal schemes. Clinton was enthusiastic and lavish in his coöperation—for in him, as the god of the New York canals, was concentrated the regard of his hosts. Indeed, requests for investigatory visits, for advice, were multiplying in his regular correspondence. Trade that had trickled southward down the Mississippi and northward into Canada was now beginning to be turned into New York as the promise of cheaper transit from the interior to Albany grew greater. Peaches and other choice fruits from Philadelphia were beginning to find their way already along the Northern Canal to a market in Vermont. The United States was beginning at last to realize the value of facilitated communication and the desirability of easy intercommunication.

> In forming a judgment as to the benefits to be derived from a canal [Clinton wrote at this time], it is necessary to consider if there be in its vicinity articles inexhaustible in quantity and of indispensable necessity, bulky in their nature, of low value at the place of transportation, such as salt, gypsum and coal. Auburn crackers have sold in New York 10 for a cent.
>
> Politics: Dennis H. Doyle's toast: "D. W. C. like an old brass kettle. The harder he is rubbed, the brighter he will shine."

But he is in New Jersey, studying the fish in the Jersey rivers as he takes his way along, the nature of the land about the Passaic, the stones, the birds, the trees. At Paterson they gave him a public dinner which was attended by a hundred guests. He was interested in Paterson, already a highly industrial town. He was shown over its factories and conducted through its mills, noting incidentally that the mill-hands worked eleven and a half hours a day. He went to Morristown, where he was the guest of Governor Dickerson. Four private fishponds on Dickerson's bachelor estate testified to that executive's interest in a subject likewise dear to De Witt Clinton's heart: the re-stocking with suitable fish of those lakes and rivers and ponds that had been denuded by reason of the use of their waters to supply mill-power. Both Clinton and Dickerson conducted extensive experiments along this line, and also a pleasant correspondence upon their mutual discoveries.

Clinton had, apart from his sought-after canal advice, been vouchsafed new worlds to conquer. He went to Easton in Pennsylvania, and observed that "the banks of the Delaware are lined with limestone." He had brought along with him the transactions of the Philosophical Society bearing on the topography of this region. He read them and endeavored to put them to use. He found out the comparative prices of Lehigh coal in varying places, and the uses to which it was being put. He noticed that the apple-trees in the New Jersey orchards leaned toward the southeast "owing to northwest winds. Ought to be planted with a north-west dip." He went to Trenton, to Newark, and of course on extensive surveying tours; and he came to the conclusion that not only was the Passaic-Delaware canal scheme practicable, but also its rival the Raritan-Delaware route. He actually drew up a report on the subject, and accompanied it with a verbal message to the New Jersey Legislature.

But it was 1823. It was October, late. And in the following year the electors would be choosing a new President to succeed James Monroe. Clinton, at home again, emerges as a candidate hopeful of a nomination by reason of dissensions and splits in the Bucktail ranks and a growing knowledge of his deeds and his reputation throughout the country. His gossip, *vide* his diary, grows freer:

> A Bucktail said that the good combined vs. V. B. because he had sold his State.... Calhoun ready to break with Adams. Alarm of his friends here about me. He told Haines he wished to be considered my friend... Dr. Everett, the President's secretary, told Dr. Hosack that he believed Clinton would prevail; that he had seen enough to convince him.
>
> "Timid men succeed; timid measures, not."... Ingraham confident of success. Says that Dukins says all is right to the south—that the ticket will carry; that Emmott says all his friends are against Adams; that Gallatin will come out for Crawford—that he and Eckford are for Clinton, and that to be stemmed is to rise—and that Crawford speaks highly of C(linton). A young man told Weeks that C. is more respected in England than in this country....

But even Presidential aspirations and venom-filled campaigns cannot keep his mind on politics exclusively. He writes of Crawford and of crawfish almost with the same stroke of the pen; of electricity and Dr. Franklin. Then he is back in politics again:

> V. B. told Cruger, a young lawyer at Albany, that in 10 days I would be nominated at Washington.
>
> When J. Q. Adams was here (he) asked what was to be done for C(linton). His services ought to be secured to the U. S.... Hone says that the North River Squad is friendly.

That autumn he visited the flourishing group of New York City Free Schools. A miracle in public education had been performed in the years since Clinton had first solicited the Legislature for a charter for this great new undertaking; a miracle in the performance of which he himself had been an unwearied and invariably successful medium. When money was to be asked at Albany, it was Clinton who pleaded for it and won it. When the Corporation was to be approached for appropriations, it was Clinton who approached them and persuaded them. And in all the steady developments of the school system; in all the changes and progresses in its charter; through the extension of school privileges from children who were proper objects of charity to all children who stood in need of help in gaining an education, from scholarship rolls exclusively male to the apportionment of school space for girls as well; from curricula lacking in provision for religious teaching to the setting aside of hours for that study, he had played his part. As the greatest benefactor, without doubt, that the schools had yet known, he could be proud as he surveyed, in 1823, no less than five public schools in flourishing action: No. 1, in Chatham Street; No. 2, in Henry Street; No. 3, in Rivington Street; No. 4, in Hudson Street; No. 5, in Mott Street.

At this time his thoughts were also much upon slavery. People said that upper Canada was full of fugitive slaves, and Clinton, an anti-slavery legislator from his youth, went into statistics as usual: "Expenses of bringing up a slave to 18 in Virginia —$468."

But he continued to revere a Virginian—his lifelong hero, Thomas Jefferson. "Monticello," he wrote in his diary, "is the Mecca of Virginia." Jefferson was an aged man now, but his acolyte girded himself for battle in the true Jeffersonian style.

> Calhoun's letter to Haines states that Adams is out of the question. Adams falling off in the West....

But Adams it was to be, this time, and not even a party nomination for Clinton. There were compensations, however, if only spiritual ones:

> Story of Jefferson: Pumped by his neighbors, said the President ought to be the greatest man in America. Afterwards asked who was, he said D. W. C.

That winter preceding the year of the most venomous Presidential campaign to date, he entertained Jefferson's son-in-law, Governor Randolph of Virginia, and went with him over the public institutions of the State. All New York gave parties for the distinguished visitor, and all New York appeared to please him. He and Clinton sat up late together, discussing Jefferson and his religious beliefs, or his lack of them. (Clinton had once written a paper, under the pseudonym "Grotius," to prove Mr. Jefferson a Christian.) They also discussed people and things in general, and even politics, warily. Governor Randolph said politely, if somewhat noncommittally, that he "hoped New York would do her duty." And that was recorded in the diary too.

But if Mr. Clinton was hungry for praise, for encouragement, he did not fail to recognize its emptiness on occasion. His journal also bears a note that when Governor Randolph returned home from his triumphal visit to New York, he described De Witt Clinton as "taciturn...."

In national politics, in 1823-24, the Bank of the United States was again the burning question of the day.

> The object of the national bank [wrote Clinton]:
> 1. To equalize currency;
> 2. To transmit public moneys.
> The bill for internal improvements to gild this pill.

But internal improvements were only momentarily to gild the pill he personally had to swallow. On the 10th of September, 1823:

> Went to visit the first passage of sloops through the lock and dam at Troy, in company with Chancellor Kent. Passed the lock in company with the "Firefly" and five other vessels to Waterford. Returned to Lansingburgh, where dined, and returned in the evening with the addition of E. Jenkins, Esq. A splendid day.

The splendor continued, temporarily for him, permanently and gloriously for the State of New York. On the 2nd of October he wrote to John Pintard from Albany:

> On the 8th instant, the first boat will enter the canal at this place. Will you honor the celebration with your attendance? Remember that you were secretary of the meeting at the City Hotel in 1816, when the measure was first brought before the public in an emphatic manner.

On October 8th, 1823, the city of Albany, where were so many who knew De Witt Clinton and admired him, celebrated with joy the completion of the canal works at the Hudson River end. And it was Clinton, dining with the citizens, crossing the Aqueduct proudly in the packet-boat named for him, leading his wife out to dance a cotillion at the great Albany Canal Ball on the 9th, who was the hero of the hour.

To triumphant Van Burenites then he loomed as a continuing and quite impossible political menace—a denuded pillar of strength, but still a pillar. Presidential material, and the idol, through the canal, of the man in the street. He must, they decided, be finally overthrown.

Joseph C. Yates had succeeded him as Governor of New York, and Clinton had thus far been left to his "ologies," to his horticultural experiments, to his history and science and sociology, to his charitable, artistic and educational propensities, to his home, his farm and his family. He would have continued to be left to them, had it not been for the canal.... And many strictly private circles and enterprises would have gained—indeed, had gained. His second wife's social gatherings, more lavish and far more formal than his first wife's, were more often graced by his commanding presence. Her calls were more frequently made in his company. They went often to fashionable Saratoga, to Ballston Spa. Clinton was more than ever accessible to friends and acquaintances, to those with a tale of want or of progress to tell. He saw much of his widowed sister-in-law, Hannah Clinton, and her family. He indulged a little, with other men of his years, in what he liked to call "anecdotage." He walked with Mary and the baby, Julia.

These, plus a legion of other men and women and children and causes, had gained because Clinton had lost. They had gained his full efforts and his full attention, which meant that they increased in prosperity both financially and spiritually. He was on terms of increasing friendship with Chancellor Kent, and they foregathered at his own house or the Chancellor's, or at that of some kindred spirit, at least once a week to talk of books and science and art, the subjects they both loved and of which they were both students. They talked of men, but not of politics. Indeed men joined them who might have let politics stand in the way, had they not been above it. Kent tells how John Quincy Adams was one of the group whenever a rare occasion brought him to New York. . . . Clinton was intimate with Astor and his son William, with William James Wadsworth and with James Roosevelt, with the old Patroon Van Rensselaer, and with the "young Patroon," General Stephen, his son. All these were his constant visitors, and many more.

Letters had gained. He was ardent in support of every library movement.[1] He read, with a pencil in his hand. In July of 1823 he delivered the annual address before the Alpha of the Phi Beta Kappa Society at Union College, Schenectady. And in urging the young men to seek knowledge, to cultivate the sciences, to further art and love of country—in tracing, as he loved to do, the history of these things, and also of good government and of man himself through the darkness and into comparative light—in coupling religion with cultivation, and both with civilization, and in proclaiming liberty in all these branches the keynote of man's success; in touching on geography and topography, on faction and fiction and fact, to illustrate his points, he concluded:

> Pleasure is a shadow, wealth is vanity, and power a pageant; but knowledge is ecstatic in enjoyment, perennial in fame, unlimited in space and infinite in duration. . . .

Certainly the pursuit of knowledge was the spice of life to him. He had none of the popular vices. His political opponents had more than once tried to put down his ruddy complexion to the bottle; but his private letters proclaim him an anxious believer in temperance and a practitioner of it at all times, and friends and children could and did testify to his abstemious habits through life. He was a faithful husband and a singularly devoted father,

[1] Including the Mercantile Library in New York City, which soon after his death was housed in a building of its own, named for him, "Clinton Hall."

particularly in view of the extreme fullness of his days. His son Charles, for years now his private secretary, said later that though men called him vain, no man ever walked in greater humility. This son presents him as kind and forgiving even to his enemies, and magnanimous even to those who had deliberately injured him. His ambition was unswerving and inflexible; his tendency was to dominate politically, and to pass over those who failed in devotion to his cause. But grudges he did not bear, and striking back blow for blow at his enemies, he could forgive them when the battle was over, whoever was the victor.

Not so those enemies themselves. His enemies were still uneasy. As the canal grew, so grew Clinton—so De Witt Clinton emerged from the disguise of impractical visionary with which so many of them had enshrouded him. More, scandals among the personnel of the Commission had rather enhanced the general view of his own integrity. There had been questions about Holley's accounts in the west, and about Young's choice of contractors in the north. Both men blamed Clinton that their conduct was subjected to investigation; but others than Clinton had put the searchlight on them. Clinton, however, remained a thorn in the flesh of the Bucktails. All their victories still failed to satisfy them. They sought more—and wrought their own undoing in the seeking. For had they left him with his laurels at this time, he might well have remained the god of the canal, yes; but a strictly private deity.

They did not do so. His cup, to them, was not quite full. There was a deeper bitterness to come.

In the year 1824, Mr. Clinton found himself with his Presidential hopes fading. The forces that had put him out of the Governorship had managed to keep him out of the Presidency. There was no longer a Clintonian party, and the Van Burenite majority of the Democratic party, as it now emerged, had pledged itself in caucus to support William H. Crawford as its candidate. Mr. Clinton as usual had done nothing to foster his cause with these wielders of power. On the contrary, the previous April he had been occupied in expressing the continuance of sentiments that had long annoyed a number of the recruits to that faction:

> With regard to the Bank Tax, etc., I can only say that it is a most pernicious measure, which meets with my open and unqualified reprobation—but it will pass—The Van Burens and

other would-be great men of the day are in favor of it—but nothing is more easy than to prevent the recurrence of similar calamities and to extinguish this evil. Opulent men must guard the rights of property. Wise men must uphold the substantial interests of the country—and influential men must appear in the electioneering struggles, not by the application of corrupt influence, but by the use of those honorable and enlightened measures which Providence has placed in their hands for the protection of the Republic against the harpies of faction and the votaries of jacobinism. . . . I rather believe that I will be in N. Y. at the meeting of the Bible Society—but shall I address the assembly? Give me your opinion candidly. If it will be of any service to the cause of genuine religion, I shall not hesitate. . . .

The letter is to Pintard, founder and recording secretary of the American Bible Society, who had recruited the willing Clinton into the membership of that body. The sentiments, both peaceable and fighting, reveal a consciousness that prestige, power, influence, had indeed been wrested from his hand.

He still had his one public office in the State of New York, however,—that of head of the Canal Board. Today, in the perspective of more than a hundred years, it would seem that that office, and particularly the man in that office, at least must have been unassailable, whatever the political complexion of affairs. No one had in fact done more to project or to perfect the entire canal scheme. No one had been more active in working, in campaigning for funds and in metaphorically clearing the ways. Not many, indeed, had been more closely connected with the literal clearing of the ways, for engineers and construction workers, diggers and builders alike, were working largely on Clinton's suggestions, formulated from a close and comprehensive and a continuing study and an understanding communication with practical engineers.

All knew this. The public knew it, and lauded him accordingly. His friends knew it, and valued it truly. His enemies knew it, and deplored it because it would continue a speculative weapon against their political plans. For the immediate moment, it was his enemies who triumphed. If men had come to think that the word "canal" and the word "Clinton" were inseparable, they were speedily to be shown, to their undying amazement, that they were mistaken. There was nothing but his canal office that the Bucktails could rob him of. And though he was, without the shadow of a doubt, in his connection with the canal above even the suspicion of selfish gain or error—though he had never drawn one penny for expense or salary, never gained a cent by exploiting land or right of way, as indeed he had never been known to take advantage of his high office in any way—the Bucktails speedily proved that they could rob him nevertheless. The Bucktails (Crawford men all) still feared Clinton's canal strength as it related to the approaching Presidential election. The canal, in spite of gloomy prognostications, was practically completed, and laden to its banks with the highest commercial hopes. The people, the voters, knew that Clinton was responsible. And there was nothing the Bucktails could do about it—nothing fair, that is. They therefore proceeded to a grossly unfair action. A bill calling for his removal from the Canal Board went into the Legislature —and it came out of both houses triumphant. No charges of misconduct or unfitness; no charges of any kind, were made, or could be made. No speech was uttered at all in support or explanation of the resolution. Indeed, no member of the State government, then or ever thereafter, could answer the question: What was the basis for this action? If the canal enterprise had failed, the Bucktails would have heaped contumely on Clinton, the responsible. There is ample indication of that. Since it had succeeded, they were by no means equally ready to heap on him the glory. To the contrary. They were terribly anxious now to deny his responsibility, his vision and his leadership; to nullify them if they could; to take, in brief, the power and the glory unto themselves. So it was that in the year 1824, the powers that were in the State of New York removed De Witt Clinton from his office as Canal Commissioner, and rejoiced that thus they had summarily disposed at last of the final vestiges of his once great power.

Indeed it seemed—and certainly it was fully intended—that the day of De Witt Clinton was forever in the past. But appearances deceive. The end, after all, was not to come in frustration or disappointment. The end was not yet.

16

VINDICATION

1824-1825

WITH MR. CLINTON'S exit from State and city affairs, the tenuous column of his supporters had not been absorbed by the Van Burenites. Rather they had gradually tended toward following the fortunes of those Van Burenites who from time to time became dissatisfied. The policies of that group which had come to be known in certain quarters as the Albany Regency, and which included William L. Marcy, Benjamin F. Butler and Samuel A. Talcott among others, did not by any means please all the Tammany-Van Buren rank and file. Those who rebelled against such policies, uniting with a remnant of the former Federalists, became known as the People's Party, and was greatly reënforced when Governor Yates led a stubborn opposition to that increasingly necessary change in the mode of choosing Presidential electors which had been discussed since the days of Clinton.

There is no room for doubt, such was still the reputation of Mr. Clinton outside the boundaries of State politics, that fear of him and his potentialities in connection with any choice by the people themselves of a general electoral ticket was a strong reason for the defeat of the electoral reform bill in the New York Legislature at this time. And yet it is a curious fact that the Clintonian remnant, following more or less the People's Party, had so far evinced no desire to bring Clinton out of his enforced retirement. Too many smoldering fires could blaze as they always blazed around the aspirations of this man. He was far too difficult a candidate now for a minority to promote, and his former henchmen had too weak a hold on the so-called party of the people to risk dragging him back and thus possibly reuniting the warring factions of his erstwhile opponents in a new campaign against himself.

By 1824, Governor Yates had become so unpopular that even the Albany Regency finally abandoned him. The faction headed by that group nominated Samuel Young for Governor by a legislative caucus. The People's Party satisfied themselves by registering a protest at the continuation of caucus nominations, and announced their intention of holding a covention at Utica in September to vote for a nominee of their own. For President they mostly supported John Quincy Adams, though some of their number took part in a separate meeting which voted support to the latest comer in the Presidential entry list: General Andrew Jackson. The rancor grew. The Van Burenites accused the People's Party of plotting with the Clintonians, and by taunting the hottest anti-Clintonians and calling them converts to his following they endeavored to scare them back into the ranks of the faithful Van Burenites.

The dismissal of Clinton from the Canal Board was a direct outcome of all this. It had been moved in the Senate a few minutes before the time for the final summer adjournment, and it was made plain that all who opposed it would automatically confess themselves not only "Peopleish," as Hammond puts it, but sympathetic toward Clintonianism. Only three Senators—Morgan, who came from the West, McIntyre, of Montgomery, and Cramer, an ardent but apparently not a bigoted supporter of Young—voted against the removal resolution, which went to the Assembly and was immediately passed by a majority of thirty votes. Among the thirty was that of James Tallmadge, erstwhile friend of Clinton. And this was rather foolish of General Tallmadge, because at the moment he himself happened to be the almost certain choice of the Clintonians for the Gubernatorial nomination at Utica in September. . . . But the resolution had been intended to scare recalcitrant members of the party away from a declaration that might be construed as aligning them with the Clintonians, and the result of the vote showed that it succeeded fully. Protest was vain. The measure had been rushed through both Houses before the totally unprepared Clintonians could catch their breaths. One of them—Cunningham of Montgomery County

—did arise in the Assembly and with passion give tongue, lauding Clinton, challenging criticism of Clinton's conduct as Commissioner, recalling his years of unrewarded devotion to the canal project, and declaring the whole thing a plot to sow discord—a plot that would disgrace every member of the Legislature in the eyes of his constituents. It was—and it did.... The voice of Clinton's friends in the Legislature had been as one crying in the wilderness. The voice of the people, however, had not yet spoken....

It is not too much to say that the entire country was electrified by the shock of this crowning act of injustice on the part of the ascendant party in New York. A perusal of the newspapers of the next few days—nay, weeks and months—affords the impression that something like a bombshell had burst upon the American public. Far and wide Clinton was known as the benefactor of his State, and of other States, through the canal. Far and wide his canal conduct was an open book, and his fame securely written there for every man to see. The proceedings of the citizens of Albany represent the occurrences in countless cities and towns throughout the State, and many more throughout the Union. The citizens of Albany, in numbers, actually rushed to the Capitol when the news became known. They organized a gigantic protest meeting, at which John Tayler presided and General John H. Wendell, Revolutionary veteran, acted as secretary. Colonel James McKown, former Assemblyman, moved a series of resolutions, drawn by Alfred Conkling, and a committee of the leading members of the community was named to call on Mr. Clinton at his home and present the feelings of the meeting—the very high feeling of admiration for his meritorious services, his unimpeachable integrity; of indignation at the act of rank injustice that had been committed against him; and of gratitude for all the great good he had done. In New York City a similar meeting was planned to be held in Washington Hall. But such was the response to the call that not only Washington Hall, but every public hall in the city proved too small to hold all the sympathizers, and the gathering ultimately came together in City Hall Park, and ten thousand indignant citizens of this ancient seat of Clinton's most violent opposition paid him the tribute of their presence and their confidence, and were addressed by the speakers from the City Hall steps. Colonel William

Few, hitherto one of Clinton's ardent political enemies, but now among the many won over to his cause through this signal act of injustice, presided as chairman. Twenty-five of the most prominent citizens, Cadwallader D. Colden and Thomas Addis Emmett among them, went at the behest of this meeting to wait upon Mr. Clinton in Albany, with New York City's vigorous expression of indignation and personal admiration.

It was a deluge. From along the route of the canal, the banks that were studded with new-born villages that looked to Clinton as their patron saint; from Ohio and Pennsylvania and Virginia, from near and far, from friend and even, often, from former enemy, the letters and parchments and committees and messages and resolutions came pouring in on Clinton, who in a somewhat admirable calm and an obvious pride and joy, replied to them all, with dignity, with gratitude, and absolutely without rancor. He had, he said, trusted to God to vindicate his conduct, and God (in whose embrace were the common people of the United States) had not disappointed him.

From that moment he became the revived hope of the common people for Governor—of the people and also of the so strangely resuscitated Clintonian minority who, seeing through the ruses of the Regency, failed to shut their doors to those erstwhile "Peopleish" members who had been blackjacked into voting approval of Clinton's ousting. Tallmadge, however, at the head of this last-named group, was definitely "out," as far as the Clintonians were concerned; and in spite of the continued aversion to Clinton on the part of many of Tallmadge's colleagues, they had no other man to offer of equal calibre and sufficient political appeal.

So Clinton it was, at Utica, in September. And Clinton it was, by a landslide, at Albany in January. The New York City delegation and the People's Party as such, it is true, disowned the nomination and joined in support of Young. But that rather strengthened Mr. Clinton's position than weakened it in the eyes of the voters. At least it proved an absence of "deals" or collusion. The result of the November elections was a wholesale triumph for the Clintonians. They now outnumbered the Regency supporters by three to one in the Assembly, and of the eight new Senators elected, six were out-and-out Clintonians. Mr. Clinton's personal majority was 16,906 over Colonel

Young; while General Tallmadge, upon whose nomination for Lieut.-Governor the Clintonians had reluctantly agreed, was elected by a majority of 32,409 votes over Erastus Root, the Van Burenite candidate.

This was what the Regency party had done by dismissing De Witt Clinton from the Canal Board. Thus did the people of the State of New York bring him triumphantly out of the slough of despond into which his rivals had thrust him. All he had ever desired, as Philip Hone once remarked, in return for his patriotic labors was the appreciation of his fellow-citizens. All he desired in life was to do the greatest good to the greatest number. And his fellow-citizens had not in this instance misunderstood him. Contumely, disaster, at last were showing their silver linings. A crushing and totally undeserved blow had been turned into a signal stroke of confidence....

Once again, he needed the joy of such a reversal of ill-fortune; for privately, ill-fortune had dogged him once more that year. He had lost the son who was rarely absent from his thoughts—his sailor son James. On July 10th, 1824, Mr. Clinton received the news that James had become ill of yellow fever, at sea, and had died on the journey home. It now becomes apparent once more how dearly Clinton loved his children. Indeed, in all his Spartan adjurations to one or other of his sons there is a vein of indulgence, of understanding, that is tremendously appealing. In the State Library at Albany there is a series of letters which he wrote to his son George while the latter was at Hamilton College. They show him, even while he scolded, pleaded, advised, still understanding well, and showing it; while he complained of demands on his pocket, reaching into his pocket and outdoing the demands. Hence his boys not only feared but adored him. And hence the loss of James was one more of the shattering blows that punctuated his existence; the end of another dream. The boy was twenty-two. He had seen a great deal of the world—far more than his father ever would. He had striven hard to please his father and to show his gratitude to Mr. Pintard. "He is not," Clinton had written then, "cursed with the sin of ingratitude." And he had done well. For all the father's earlier doubts and fears, it was a most promising career that had been so summarily cut short, and a world of hope destroyed in Clinton's breast.

As always in his moments of such need for warmth, for comfort, his friends the citizens of New York, the country people of New York, made their contribution. His personal friends had never ceased to support him by their confidence and trust. The names of the great and the honest and the powerful and the well-born never ceased to adorn his visiting-list, were he in office or out of it. But it was the common people, when all was said and done, who had insisted on keeping him in office, and that was the aspect of his affairs that appealed to him the most. Politically, this was the beginning of his golden era—an era, however, that was not to be without its tragic disappointments. The acknowledged and undisputed leader of a reasserted and powerful party, he now indeed could carry all before him, both within the State and, to an extent, throughout the nation. Hosack says that "as Governor of the State of New York, he was scarcely less conspicuous than the Chief Magistrate of the nation." Certainly his friends' and supporters' ambitions for him were never more to be limited by the boundaries of the State. In this the hour of his triumph he emerged once more as likely Presidential material—but not for immediate presentation. It was too late in the current campaign for that. "King Caucus," true, at that moment was in the death-throes, and so, almost, was the actual caucus nominee, W. H. Crawford. The "era of good feeling," the era of each man for himself, was drawing to a close; and Monroe's second administration likewise. But peace did not reign in the ranks. It was a bitter and not too clean fight for the succession to James Monroe that the impeccable John Quincy Adams, the rampageous Andrew Jackson, and the diplomatic Henry Clay now brought to a climax. Adams, the "heir apparent," proved the victor. He triumphed, unmoved and, amazingly, untrammeled, amid a muddy stream of vituperation. "Bargain and corruption" was the cry of the mob when a deadlock in the vote as between Jackson and Adams, thrown into the House of Representatives, emerged as an Adams victory. But years of effort failed to bring forth one iota of evidence that Adams had, as the Jacksonians asserted, bargained with Clay, the Speaker of the House and, as it chanced, the wielder of the final voting power, for first place. He gave to Clay, regardless of universal howls (and incidentally regardless of the suggestion of the friends of De Witt Clinton that the appointment of that gentleman, instead, to the chair of the "heir apparent" would stifle the slander at its birth), the office of Secretary of State. He offered to Mr. Clinton, whose worth he did not deny though their political aims were inimical, the portfolio of Minister to the Court of St. James's.

Now Mr. Clinton had used all the influence of which he had still been possessed at the time of the elections in behalf of General Jackson. For not alone was the admiration between him and Jackson mutual, but independence of action was also a quality they shared in common. Also Clinton was against both the practice of nomination by caucus and the political inheritance of Mr. Adams. It was whispered that had Jackson been chosen, Clinton would have been tendered, and have accepted, the Secretaryship of State. But Hammond, who went to Washington as the agent of New York State in December, 1824, to settle the State's account with the Federal government, carried with him a message from Mr. Clinton to General Jackson. Mr. Clinton wanted Mr. Jackson to know, according to Mr. Hammond, that he then entertained no doubt but that Jackson would be elected. He also wanted to request Mr. Jackson to form his Cabinet, in that event, without any relation to Mr. Clinton.... Mr. Clinton would not leave the State of New York, and his only hope for Jackson's Cabinet was that it would be such as to insure to the new executive a prosperous and successful administration.

The new President, however, was Adams; and certain of Clinton's friends in New York, encouraged by his new rise to power there, nursed definite hopes for 1828.... They therefore encouraged Mr. Clinton in his unwillingness to leave New York for foreign parts. Others there were of his friends who begged him to accept the President's offer. Stephen Van Rensselaer, who had strained but not broken the bonds of their friendship by failing to cast his last-minute ballot for Jackson in the House of Representatives, where he then had a seat, wrote begging Clinton to say yes. Thomas Addis Emmett, who was trying a case in the U. S. Supreme Court, wrote also from Washington urging him strongly to do so. Hammond observes:

> I was among the number of Mr. Clinton's friends who thought he ought to accept, and advised him to accept.... He never stood better in the State and nation than at this moment.

> If he should then go abroad, I believed he would escape the dreadful tornado which evidently was approaching; would afford time for political prejudices against him to subside; and would, no doubt, retain all his present friends. He would be before the nation, in the service of the nation, in a position which could hardly, by any possibility, subject him to blame; and if at the next, or a subsequent Presidential election, his friends should feel warranted in bringing him forward as a candidate for the Presidency, he could not be better situated to receive and command support than he would be should he accept this mission....

That was the narrower, political point of view, and those who held it were not the only ones who would have liked to see De Witt Clinton on his way to a foreign post.... As it transpired, the whole question was academic; but as for Clinton personally, there does not seem to be room for doubt that the sentiments he expressed in the following letter to President Adams were utterly sincere:

> Albany, 25th February, 1825.
>
> Sir,
>
> I feel most sensibly the honor conferred upon me by your communication of the 8th instant, and I receive this expression of your good opinion with a corresponding spirit. But having recently accepted from the people of this State the highest office in their power, I cannot, consistent with my sense of duty, retire from it until I have had ample opportunity of evincing my gratitude and my devotion to their interests.
>
> I assure you, sir, that it will afford me the highest gratification, in my present situation, to aid you in your patriotic efforts, and to witness the auspicious influence of your administration on the best interests of our country.
>
> I have the honor to be, with perfect respect,
>
> Your most obedient servant,
>
> DE WITT CLINTON.
>
> The Hon. JOHN QUINCY ADAMS,
> Washington.

It is nevertheless true that in London, in a diplomatic post, he would have been at home, at ease, untrammeled. His country's luster would have lost nothing by the presence of such a man in such an office. And the welfare and mutual good feeling of both countries might well have gained.

But the people of New York had called him, and he chose to remain at their service. The "tornado" referred to by Hammond continued to threaten, mainly in the person of Erastus

Root, to whom the Clintonian papers fairly consistently referred, from this time on, as "the Root of all evil." The Senate, still enjoying a Van Burenite majority, put through a law on the eve of Clinton's accession to the Governorship, bestowing on the Senate the right to continue civil appointees in office if it disapproved the Governor's nominees for their successors at the end of their terms. The civil office-holders at the moment were of course nearly all Van Burenites. . . . Likewise the People's party, as a party, still remained inimical to Clinton, and ready enough to curb his power, and Clinton himself was as rigid as ever in refusing to do anything to court their favor, despite the pleas of his closest advisers. He never once lent himself to the making of such personal overtures, and it is for his continued unwillingness along these lines that certain political contemporaries and later historians continued to condemn him. He wanted to be followed on his own merits; not because by political promises he had forestalled opposition. He wanted to fight opposition and, more than anything in the world, to conquer it. That is why he has been called arrogant, but if that be arrogance, it compares favorably with the political sense of which he has been called, and undoubtedly was, devoid. His motives and his aims were invariably pure. By "arrogance" they at least remained pure. By "politics" they could not but have been sullied.

His other chief enemy was now Tallmadge, who, as it happened, had turned against him through a disappointment in the matter of patronage. Clinton's supporters did what they could to lure Tallmadge back into the fold; but not all their blandishments were enough to entice him.

Governor Clinton's inaugural message recommended the passage of a law for popular choice of Presidential electors by general ticket, the election to be decided by a plurality of votes. This was one more project on which he had pledged himself to the people, and he did not fail them. He recommended an extension of the suffrage to all male citizens, and the election of justices of the peace by the people. The suffrage, as amended by the Constitutional Convention of 1821, no longer was limited to freeholders, but extended to all taxpayers, militiamen, firemen and laborers. Governor Clinton wanted to see it further extended to all citizens of a certain residence in one voting district. He advocated the formation of a board of internal improvements and an extension of the canal system by means of feeders to the smaller lakes and waterways. He rejoiced that former objects of contention, with special reference to the now obsolete Council of Appointment, no longer existed. . . . He condemned "the thraldom of patronage," and said the abolition of petty "aristocracies" and "factious combinations" and the restoration of political power to its authentic source, the great body of the people, had "dissolved the union between personal interest and political subserviency."

> The people [he said], rising in the majesty of their power above the debasing trammels of names and the obnoxious dictations of combinations, have sustained and vindicated a system of disenthralled and independent suffrage.

But obnoxious and factious combinations did not cease to work against Mr. Clinton personally, and their efforts extended to all the new Governor's friends. Thus Ambrose Spencer, lately Chief Justice, lost the vote of the Legislature for U. S. Senator that year largely by the efforts of Lieut.-Governor Tallmadge, and still more largely because of his relationship to the Governor. Thus Alfred Conkling's appointment by President Adams to the office of District Judge on the recommendation of Clinton and Van Rensselaer was condemned because Conkling was a Clintonian, and because he accompanied the Governor that year on what Clinton's enemies were pleased to call "an electioneering tour for the Presidency through the Western States." But the Governor himself was far less vulnerable than of old. Of old, his enemies had placed upon him the curse, as they supposed, of the onus of the vast canal improvement. Now, their curses were coming home to roost. Theirs was now the onus, for criticizing his early and sustained belief. His was the honor. In his aforementioned inaugural address, he had announced with pride that the income of the canal fund, plus the tolls, exceeded the interest on the loan by nearly four hundred thousand dollars. The waterway then lay open from the Hudson to within a few miles of Buffalo. The quantity production of salt had kept pace with the enormous increase in demand. The settlements along the canal line were calling for more and more staple commodities and luxuries. The city of New York was fast gaining the lead in the import trade of the United States. Sales at auction had increased, and upon the canal the tolls for vessels carrying goods and passengers had reached a figure beyond the dreams of the most sanguine, even though Lake Erie and the trade that lay there had yet to be physically included in the system.

It was in May, 1825, that Governor Clinton traveled to Philadelphia on the first of what his adversaries called his "electioneering tours." He went at the request of the citizens of Pennsylvania, to lend his support to their own desire to promote by legislative action a system of internal improvements. He was, it is not too much to say, lionized on the occasion. Philadelphia turned out to do honor to a very great man, and all her citizens, from the Mayor and Corporation to the remotest worker, from rich to poor, honored him in unequivocal terms. He met the Pennsylvania canal commission, and toured the proposed route of the waterway.

He talked constructively of methods by which a Pennsylvania canal system could be linked with that of New York for the benefit of both. And when he returned to his home State his honor had, if anything, grown.

Later that summer, he went to Ohio, to help in the inaugural ceremonies of the canal from Lake Erie to the Ohio River, which was to be built largely in accordance with his earlier-tendered suggestions. His journey, which extended, by invitation, to Louisville in Kentucky, was a triumphal progress. Everywhere the cream of society and the common people whom he loved cheered him along his path, and looked upon him with admiration unalloyed. The growth, the promise, of New York was a fact that was spreading to the far corners of the land. New York City was experiencing a real estate boom, a mercantile boom, a wave of roseate promise unprecedented. Albany basked, at the outlet of the Erie canal, in the sun of a bright new day. And all those little villages that had grown into towns, all those empty wilderness lands that had sprouted houses and churches and schools and shipyards and granaries and mills and factories, were thanking Clinton, who had persisted in the belief and the statement and the proof that such a miracle could be. Here is Clinton, said Ohio now. Let us show him that he has opened a vista for us too. And they showed him. From the shores of Lake Erie, where he had the honor of turning the first spadeful of earth, to the Ohio and beyond, they gave him a welcome such as few Americans had ever received before.

It still remained for New York to show a similar appreciation. New York, in a kaleidoscopic variety of ways, continued to experience good reason for such feeling. Under Clinton's sway the lot of the Indians in the State, which had continued miserable enough, was vastly improved. Through his efforts the negroes, their brothers in distress, were likewise further aided. He had never ceased his efforts to lighten the burdens of the slaves, to remove the curse of slavery. "An Act to Prevent the Inhuman Treatment of Slaves" and "An Act to Prevent the Farther Introduction of Slaves" were both emanations from his pen. He never was to cease to do the kind of work he had always desired to perform. He helped agriculture in his State—the tilling of the soil, that he had been heard to say was linked with the cultivation of the mind and the heart of man. During his earliest and most disturbed administration, he had conceived and worked on a plan for the formation of a board of agriculturists whose duties should be to disseminate the latest ideas and improvements in connection with the land; to report discoveries; to encourage the use of labor-saving machinery; and to look into allied conditions of nature that might benefit or instruct the farmer and the horticulturist. He was for establishing a professorship of agriculture in some prominent university, and for making it include chemistry and geology, mineralogy and other departments of natural history, as well as botany. He was equipped tc voice such theories and such pleas. More, he was equipped to apply them, or some of them at least. In 1819 the New York Legislature had passed an act for the formation of agricultural societies. And though not all the fair dreams of Mr. Clinton were realized, even in an agricultural age, his contribution, which was all that he had time or leisure to give, was characteristically constructive. The Board lived in fact only till 1826, which was the limit of the term for which it was appointed. In that period it did its work efficiently, to which fact its three-volume report bears witness.

Also he became an exceedingly active member of the Society of Arts and Manufactures. He was interested in promoting prosperity as a means of promoting true independence. It was this that made him active also in matters affecting internal revenue. He was sponsor of the act for the abolition of imprisonment for debt, which had long cluttered up the English law and in America had played havoc with the existence of many honest men who were too trusting of the ability to pay and the integrity of those requiring backers for their business and personal notes. He was a vigorous foe of the still widespread system of raising revenue by lottery, and had raised his voice at the 1821 Constitutional Convention in favor of having that system abolished, which it was. He worked for the poor, unceasingly; and for the betterment of conditions in the prisons. No man ever approached him in vain in the interests of such causes. He continued to recommend laws to restrict the undue multiplication of banks. He recommended a revision of the militia code, which was adopted.

He dwelt now in a handsome mansion at the corner of North Pearl and Steuben Streets. That it had graciousness and charm we know from an English traveler, J. S. Buckingham, who occupied it in 1838. That it borrowed magnetism from its master is evidenced by the hordes of visitors who daily made it their goal. Buckingham says, "It was equal in size and accommodation to some of the best houses in Baker Street, Harley or other similar streets in the northwest of London." No mean tribute, in an age when the British traveler in America found little to praise. The beauties of Albany at that period were in any case mixed. Clinton's handsome mansion faced the honest dwelling of an old Dutch burgher, "bearing the date of 1732; its yellow and ill-cemented bricks, its small windows and doors, its low body and immensely disproportionate sloping roof, covered with tiles of all shapes and sizes, showing what description of city Albany was likely to have been a century ago, and enabling one to judge of the amazing advance in opulence, taste and comfort which had been made since that humble dwelling had been first reared." [1]

De Witt Clinton thus had reason at last for a certain contentment with his lot, embracing as it did all these satisfactions. But there was a greater satisfaction to come—the greatest of all. In the disillusioned summer of 1824, when he had been striving to make his other interests fill the seemingly final gap in his daily life, he had written the following observation in his diary: "Canalling more popular than banking." He had, of course, ample reason already for personal rejoicing over that fact. In September, 1825, however, the note of satisfaction rises as he writes of the arrangements for Albany and New York com-

[1] J. S. Buckingham in Albany; Annals of Albany.

mittees to proceed to Buffalo for the purpose of making arrangements for a great occasion.

For that which had been his dream of years had eventuated at last. That which he had worked for, fought for and argued for was now an accomplished fact.

The Erie Canal—the first great canal in the Union; from the Lake all the way to Albany and so to the sea—was completed.

17

ACHIEVEMENT

1825-1827

ON AN October day in 1825, Governor Clinton boarded a bedecked and garlanded canal-boat at the port of Buffalo, in company with his wife and several of his children, the personnel of the Commission and, in procession of accompanying vessels, vast numbers of his friends. Dr. Hosack describes him at this period of his life:

> Thin and slender in his youth, in the latter part of his life his frame became expanded.... His head was well-formed and particularly distinguished for the height and breadth of his forehead. His hair was brown, his complexion brilliant, his nose finely proportioned and of the Grecian form; his lip thin and of that peculiar configuration that some critics have deemed indicative of eloquence. His eyes were of a dark hazel color, but peculiarly quick and expressive....

This was the man who symbolized in his own magnificent person, for the many thousands who had heard the call of the West, the shimmering pathway to the future that was called the Erie Canal. Standing erect on that bedecked canal-boat, drawn New York-ward by four white horses, Mr. Clinton was to be seen gazing along that potent pathway, and doubtless finding an October day on the waters more than passing fair.

The outward journey had been gratifying enough. At Schenectady, Utica, Rome, Rochester, Lockport, Buffalo, at all the old and growing townships, all the new and mushroom would-be cities, the population had come out to meet him, to dine him and wine him and to thank him. But his own was the greatest thanksgiving, as he told the citizens of Rochester in his reply to their committee's address of welcome. He had been privileged to pass this way when all this land was waste. To him had been given not only the vision that other men had had before him, but the power to put that vision into words so compelling that not all the jealousy, enmity, fear and ignorance and strife that came after had availed to quench the fire of popular imagination which he above all men had managed to kindle and, more, to foster. He had reason on this day to be proud, to hold his head so high, to square his great shoulders, as he passed these shores where industry and population were growing almost as one watched; these lands that in less than ten years from that day would be the richest agriculturally in the Union. And indeed he did well to savor the hour of triumph unalloyed....

Fittingly enough, it was Jesse Hawley who uttered the first speech of thanksgiving from the Buffalo end.

> But this is all the notice that I have ever received (wrote Hawley somewhat later) from the State or people of New York for it in any wise; nor would I complain of that, having in the mean time, by laborious industry attained from bankruptcy to a comfortable moderate competency, and pleasantly located within a mile of this village (Rochester) and the Canal.

In worldly goods, indeed, he was better off, ultimately, than Clinton, who won the praise, the day, as he so richly deserved, but never, from now to his death, that "comfortable moderate competency" of which Hawley was to boast. Hawley, who claimed the title of true progenitor, whose exact route from Buffalo as far as the Mohawk at least was now being traced by the boats, confessed that when he wrote his articles, he had not thought to live to see the canal an accomplished fact. It was to Clinton the greatness. To Clinton the wonderful day.

Never, surely, was a procession more literally triumphal. At strategic points along the canal had been placed great rocket guns from ships of war. And as the boats moved in their slow course between the close-packed, shouting throngs along the banks, one by one the guns boomed forth, sending the news from emplacement to far emplacement that the Governor, the ceremonial, was under way. Not yet had the famous artist Samuel F. B. Morse, whose acquaintance Mr. Clinton cherished

Courtesy of the Metropolitan Museum of Art

DE WITT CLINTON

By Samuel F. B. Morse

and who painted his portrait that very year, evolved his invention that would one day carry news hundreds, nay, thousands of miles in the flash of a few seconds. The booming guns, echoing along the stages of the waterway, were themselves an innovation, and an effective one; symbolic of the explosive excitement that filled the air for all the days that it took the boats to make the lengthy journey; signaling the suspension, for this vital moment at least, of political jealousies and hates; bringing to that tall figure on the deck of the *Seneca Chief* the fervent recognition of those who already were experiencing the blessings he had brought them; who looked for greater blessings to come, and knew they did not look in vain.

And when it was done—when the procession had reached Albany; an Albany resounding with acclamations, packed with distinguished citizens and visitors from near and far, including a welcoming committee from the city of New York headed by Philip Hone, who had become Mayor that year; when the *Seneca Chief,* with its companions, had entered the Hudson and, joined by a flotilla of bunting-clad steamboats, had been taken in tow by the flagship *Chancellor Livingston* and proudly drawn down to the sea, between crowded banks and amid continuous cheers—there was a brimming keg of the waters of Lake Erie, which Clinton, before the applauding multitude, (Corporation, military, public authorities and citizenry, in water craft of every description) emptied with ceremony into the Atlantic. And that ceremony too was a thrilling one. A committee of the Common Council of the city of New York rode out on the steamship *Washington* and hailed the *Seneca Chief* with a "Whence come you, and where are you bound?" The answer was: "From Lake Erie—and bound for Sandy Hook!" Then the Governor and the assembled gentlemen went aboard the *Chancellor Livingston,* and the ladies went aboard the barge *Lady Clinton,* which was garlanded with flowers and graced by a sculptured head of Clinton with a laurel wreath on the brow.... The Governor emptied the keg into the sea, while in the harbor the guns boomed and the cheers rang out; and in the streets of New York men offered "Clinton kerchiefs," "Clinton hats" and "Clinton glassware" for sale, decorated with his picture. And upon the houses transparencies and fireworks waited for the nightfall, ready to depict all over again this stirring scene of the day. They called it "the wedding of the waters," but it might have been called the baptism of New York State.

For from that day the Empire State emerged. From that moment the modest merchants of New York began truly to come into their own. There had been merchant princes before on Manhattan Island, but never before had the sons of Manhattan flourished as they began to flourish now, because De Witt Clinton, by a masterpiece of leadership, had opened the illimitable West to their commerce and their wares. In an amazingly short time the city of New York, which had existed as no more in truth than a small town, a provincial town, since long before the Revolution, began to take on the unmistakable aspect of a metropolis, foretaste of the glittering towers of the future. It was indeed as though a hand had strewn the actual seeds of prosperity along the banks of the new waterway; as though "Clinton's Ditch" were an irrigation system in fact, nurturing the garden of the future, bearing upon its bosom the materials for a golden harvest. The little city of Buffalo, for instance, which by the grace of Clinton had won the battle for pride of final exodus from the neighboring hamlet and new harbor of Black Rock, was already changing from a city in name, a village in reality, to a city in figures and in fact. So Rochester, Rome, Utica, Schenectady; so all those former sleepy wayside villages, those isolated houses and barns, those swamps and those forest lands. Steamboat traffic on the Great Lakes had waited for its full development till now. So had the future of those Lakes themselves, upon whose shores the primitive outposts and the villages yet unborn would blossom forth into mighty centers of industry, culture and wealth—Cleveland, Detroit, Chicago. So had the unborn states of what would come to be the Middle West, and they in their turn would see pioneers on the way to new fields that were bounded only by the Pacific. This was the ultimate vista, the change the Canal had wrought. The immediate vista was New York's. Where men had toiled on the long, long portages, carrying staggering loads of merchandise for infinitesimal profit and at a snail's pace, the broad canal bore salt and cement, wools and cottons, lumber and grain and hemp—the canal now bore, in effect, gold. . . . Where Clinton himself, with his colleagues, in 1810 had spent seventeen days in transit from Schenectady as far as Geneva, the packet-boats now performed the same journey in a matter of thirty-six hours. Flatboats with fifty tons of cargo only took a dozen hours more. These waters were cleaving not only land but time and also prices, and the answering tides were bringing swift demand and swift result. The waterway was the way to the future indeed, and New York's future was already insured for wealth and for preëminence. Toward that future Mr. Clinton had contributed in more ways than one. As he and his canal were destined to be followed by a son of his who would be a builder of even speedier iron roads and of a different kind of water course, so the princes of industry whom the canal would create would beget others; and they, in turn, through industry, would foster humanity and the arts and sciences. The future as assured was a complete cycle of all the hopes that Clinton held most dear.

Meanwhile the gratified merchants of New York proceeded to show their gratitude in kind. The business men of Pearl Street, Manhattan, of all political parties, caused to be made and to be suitably engraved a pair of massive and handsome silver vases, of classic design. These they presented to the Governor through a distinguished committee which proceeded to Albany for the purpose. The vases were placed on display in New York before the committee's departure, and in Albany, by request, after the presentation at the Governor's mansion. An almost endless line came to view and to admire.

He ought to have been riding the wave, and in many respects, of course, he was. But a man with so numerous, so long-standing, and so well-organized an opposition as he could not conquer it even by ascending to the pinnacle of public adulation. His major blessing was still his family—his secretary son, Charles; his engineer son, De Witt; his scientifically-inclined son, George; and the fledgling, Franklin. Also his two girls, so dear to his heart; and his wife, the very model of a Governor's lady. In science, in the arts, he continued to dabble and to enjoy. His friends there were legion and his friendships quite serene. In education he was recognized as a benefactor. Queen's College (later Rutgers) had bestowed on him the honorary degree of Doctor of Laws in 1812. Columbia had paid the same tribute in 1824. In 1824 also, General Lafayette had come over from France to visit the scenes of his youthful ardor and bravery. And amid the almost overwhelming plaudits of his tour, he had sought out the son of James Clinton, who had been his Revolutionary comrade. He sought him out for the sake of old friendships, but, as he later wrote to Dr. Hosack, it was De Witt Clinton's own friendship that Lafayette prized from that time on.

Indeed in friendships Clinton was eternally secure. But politically he could never be at peace—completely at peace. True, there were current trends in politics, particularly as they inevitably related to the next Presidential election, which were working toward a reconciliation between Clinton and Van Buren. Van Buren never overlooked the main chance. He weighed the full force of Clinton's popularity with the masses and with the West, and was ready to adapt his own ambitions always to a course that would best promote them. Moreover, there is evidence that he had lately learned that some of the things for which he had roundly denounced Clinton in days gone by, and condemned him to eternal strife, were not of Clinton's doing at all; were nothing else but dead Tammany campaign material.

So Mr. Van Buren began to be personally conciliatory toward Mr. Clinton as the 1826 Gubernatorial elections approached; meanwhile continuing, however, to work along well-tried lines for a strengthening of his own hand. He encouraged the citizenry to abandon individuals and support the party; to vote where the plums fell thickest; and to cast out Adams and those Federalists—those ghosts of Federalism—who had supported Adams (and also supported Clinton).... These methods, operating at the State elections that were taking place even as the canal celebrations were under way, produced once more, in 1825, a strong majority of Clinton's adversaries in the Assembly. For Mr. Van Buren's new friendly spirit toward Clinton personally was not largely shared by his party. Samuel Young was in again from Saratoga, and Erastus Root from Delaware County, both strong, both relentlessly opposed to the Governor. Young became Speaker of this Assembly.

In dismissing such men somewhat briefly as enemies of Clinton, no intention exists of belittling them as apart from this enmity. Many of Clinton's most implacable adversaries were big men in their chosen paths, both public and private, making big contributions to their times. Their stature is indeed the measure for Clinton's own. They were big, but he was greater. He was forever in their way. And had he not been an obstacle worth their trouble, worth the hatred of their opposition, their time would not have been so largely spent in striving to humiliate and belittle him. It was largely in a loftiness that was above petty spite or futile jealousies that he towered over them.

One of Governor Clinton's chief contributions to the session of January, 1826, was a recommendation that normal schools be established for the training of teachers. This was a project long dear to his heart, but he was not to live to see it accomplished. He also urgently pleaded the necessity for supplying New York City with pure water. Further he recommended the construction of a State road from the Hudson to Lake Erie south of the canal, for which purpose a commission was already in existence following an earlier recommendation of his own. Also at this session his recommendations regarding the extension of the franchise and the appointment of justices of the peace by the people were brought before the Legislature in the form of a bill and passed, after being vigorously and somewhat acidly opposed by Erastus Root.

Mr. Van Buren was by this time evincing increasing anxiousness to keep on Clinton's right side. Clinton on his part was as anxious as ever for harmony in politics. But it was too much to hope that they would often see eye to eye, and indeed they did not. Mr. Clinton went his own way about men and their fitness for office, and Mr. Van Buren's representatives in Albany had to be given their orders to fall into line. For Mr. Van Buren was now getting ready to be a leader in support of Andrew Jackson as the next President. And Mr. Clinton, a Jackson man of new power and long standing, had become very much worth while. It was no mean task that Van Buren assumed when he undertook to make advances to the Governor. The enmity toward De Witt Clinton within the Tammany ranks was so deep-rooted that even a party leader could not feel confident of overcoming it. And the fear of Jackson on the part of those of Clinton's supporters who had long since pledged themselves to Adams was not to be overcome by mere overtures on the part of the Bucktails in the direction of the Governor. Mr. Van Buren found it politic also not to come out openly for Jackson until the State elections of 1827 were over.... He saw to it that the Bucktails did their part in carrying out his broad scheme; that they fell into line when the Regency indorsed Samuel Jones, son of Clinton's former law preceptor, and a Clintonian nominee, for the office of Chancellor; and that they did not dissent when other ardent supporters of Clinton were given minor offices. He managed to hold Root and Young and an untold legion of others in leash for the time being....

A Clintonian convention for the nomination of a Governor and Lieut.-Governor met at Utica that September; and Mr. Clinton, in spite of opposition from the anti-Jacksonian section of the former People's Party, was finally unanimously named. Lieut.-Governor Tallmadge's renomination was as unanimously rejected. Henry Huntington of Oneida County was the choice of the convention for his successor.

A Van Burenite convention also met, at Herkimer. Mr. Van Buren's following was not yet sufficiently tamed to abandon hope of electing a Governor more genuinely to its liking than Clinton, and this time it was for the leaders of the Bucktails to follow the common herd. But it was not a very formidable nomination that they made. It was artful, in that by naming an Adams man, William B. Rochester, as their candidate, an anti-Jackson as well as anti-Clinton portion of the Bucktails, urged largely thereto by Peter B. Porter of Black Rock, did manage to draw off some votes from among the strong Clintonian support. But Clinton's victory over such an opponent at such a time was a foregone conclusion, and the nomination that the Albany Regency took rather more seriously was that of a Lieut.-Governor. The benefits accruing from the presence in the Senate of a Lieut.-Governor friendly to the Regency had recently been effectively proven by Tallmadge.... They wanted to renew the benefits—and they succeeded. Their nominee, Nathaniel Pitcher, received a majority of four thousand votes over Mr. Huntington. Governor Clinton received a majority of three thousand, six hundred and fifty votes over Judge Rochester. The Van Burenites—and particularly the Jacksonian Van Burenites—triumphed almost generally throughout the State.

The campaign had been shot through with excitement, hatred and malice, however, by the circumstance that one William Morgan, of Batavia, in September, 1826, was abducted from a jail to which he had been confined, and apparently murdered; for no further trace of him was found. The story that arose and gained a horrified and country-wide credence was that the Masons had summarily disposed of him for publishing the secrets of the craft. Certain heads of Masonic lodges had undoubtedly placed him in jail, on vague and allegedly trumped-up charges. Certainly he was a printer and a Mason and intimate with the ritual. The story was that Masons had planned and committed both the abduction and the murder—more, that those supreme in Masonry had ordered them to do so....

Needless to say, the horror was worked for all it was worth against De Witt Clinton, long Grand Master of the highest Masonic order. To his death the enemies of Freemasonry were to hound him with the accusation that he had personally ordered Morgan "suppressed." The letters on anti-Masonry addressed by Colonel William L. Stone to President John Quincy Adams definitely dispose of this crowning calumny. So does Clinton's private correspondence, in manuscript in the Columbia University Library, which shows him tireless and unequivocating in trying to track the guilty parties down and in vowing that, friend or foe, adherent or enemy, they should be punished to the full extent of the law. So do the tenor of his life and the invariable nature of his ethics. But only the circumstance that Rochester was also a Mason prevented the vote in 1826 from being at least closer than it was. It was estimated that from twenty to thirty thousand people refrained from voting who would have been for Clinton had the scandal not arisen.

Erastus Root was chosen Speaker of the Assembly at the January, 1827, session. In his induction address he remarked:

> It is usual for the Speaker to assure the House that he will pursue an impartial course of procedure. If by impartiality is meant to throw aside the principles which distinguish the party to which I belong, it must not be expected that I will be impartial. I was elected to the Legislature by a political party, and it would appear that I am honored with this chair by the same party. When a committee is to be appointed on a question which may involve party considerations, it may be expected that I shall appoint a majority of that committee from the party to which I belong. And on a question of local bearing, involving interests to any considerable extent, it cannot be expected that I will refer it to a committee entirely opposed to it; I am not willing to put a child to nurse to be strangled.

Speaker Root was, however, both willing and anxious to perform that service, metaphorically speaking, for the Governor of New York. And the occasion was not to be lacking.

18

REWARD

1827-1828

GOVERNOR CLINTON in his January, 1827, message congratulated the New York Legislature on the adoption by general vote of those new amendments to the State Constitution which he himself had previously urged—the extension of the franchise to all citizens resident for more than a half-year in any one voting district, and the appointment by the voters of local justices of the peace. The temper of the people, and of the more honest legislators, was increasingly toward the destruction of the evils of patronage and of political control. The people, largely by grace of Clintonian insistence, had done what they could toward these ends. Compared with what had gone before, it seemed like full emancipation....

The Governor was also jubilant, in his more formal public manner, about the canals. The total canal income from all authorized canal sources for the year just past, he stated, would exceed a million dollars. The total debt was seven million, seven hundred and seventy thousand odd. He said:

> This State has derived great reputation from its enterprise in undertaking, and its perseverance in executing, a work of immense benefit, and it ought to set another example of the extinguishment of a great public debt. This precedent will be more beneficial in itself, and more animating in all its aspects and consequences, than any fugitive or even permanent advantages that can emanate from another course.

He adverted once more to the banks—the quite disproportionately multiplied banks of the country—which had lately been indulging in a perfect orgy of paper money, with a resultant instability in values in all quarters and in bank resources everywhere, and a failing of confidence and of a feeling of security on the part of the public. He preached against the money power, but still had faith enough in his own State's resources to advocate pledging them further in public improvements, including a system of feeder canals to extend the territory served by the great waterway; and notably, again, the transverse State road, which was then before the committees but was soon to be defeated largely by men from constituencies bordering the Erie Canal.... His canal schemes as now extended embraced both widespread and valiant measures. He was not only willing, but anxious, now, to bring Lake Ontario into the canal system by a feeder from Oswego, and he made a recommendation accordingly.

Considerable agitation arose in the course of this session over the filling of a State vacancy in the United States Senate. The Adams men in the Clinton ranks nominated Stephen Van Rensselaer. The Jackson Van Burenites, joined for the first time by a portion of the Clintonians—the Jackson Clintonians—nominated Martin Van Buren; and wooed, by the simple method of continuing rather noncommittal about Jackson, a number of Adams Van Burenites also. Van Buren it was, by a large majority—Van Buren and all the forces behind him that had formerly plumped for Crawford and now were for Jackson; Van Buren aided by the die-hard group who would never cease hating Clinton, and also by a Clintonian group which, for many reasons, they welcomed with considerable warmth. For Tammany never did lose hope of controlling Clintonianism, even though its hope of controlling Clinton himself had died many violent deaths. And Van Buren, while building up an ingenious and stealthy support for Jackson in the State, was able, by the devious means above described, to leave Jackson's other chief supporter in the State, De Witt Clinton, very much where he had been. It was a typically Van Burenite strategy, and like most Van Burenite strategies, it worked in a general atmosphere of the blandest apparent good will. The point was that Mr. Clinton was by no means out of the running for a Presidential nomination on his own account. He did not seek it, and he announced through the press and by private letters that he did not now desire it. Public meetings in Virginia, in Ohio and at Buffalo now nominated him for President; but Clinton was at one with Van Buren at least as to the person most desirable for that office.

January, 1828, saw Van Buren mighty in the halls of Congress, and mightier yet through a strong majority in the Legislature of his native State. January, 1828, saw Governor Clinton lamenting the fires that raged about the Presidential contenders, fanned by political acrimonies and maneuverings for position in State elections. He said again that the Presidential electors ought to be chosen by districts throughout the United States, by popular vote, and that the Constitution should so provide. He said that the President of the United States should be ineligible for a second term. He also drew the fire of the Canal Commission by stating that they were not living up to their duties, but were neglecting to keep the canals clear of ice and obstructions for at least eight months in the year. (The Commission retorted to this that they had too much respect for the public funds to "waste" them in clearing ice from the path of any individual canal-boat man who might complain.) He insisted that the proposed system of subsidiary canals ought to be built by the State, and gave it as his firm opinion that only the ultimate pecuniary and other profit of the State, and not the immediate canal revenue from tolls, should govern the question of the desirability or otherwise of the extension of the system of improvements. (Samuel Young, now at the head of the Canal Commission, hotly disagreed with him, and said that immediately related profit by revenue on the canals themselves was all that should decide the question.) The Governor recommended the raising of tobacco and hemp in the new lands to the west. The northern States, he said, ought to be able, with these two staples, to rival the cotton-growing States of the South. He referred to the courts of law. He wanted the circuit system, and the system by which one court tried a case on the law and another on the facts, abolished.

Meanwhile the admiration between Andrew Jackson and De Witt Clinton remained mutual. As Jackson's shadow fell stronger and stronger upon the White House, the direction in which Governor Clinton's career would next develop seemed to his friends to grow more and more obvious. As the General's chances grew, with his lieutenants disdaining no weapon which could by any odds get him safely to Washington this time, so did De Witt Clinton's amplified band of faithful followers intensify their efforts in his behalf. With the entire country now aware of this great New Yorker through his supreme accomplishment, the canal; with the man himself committed to the popular candidate for President; some signal reward, some certain advancement toward a greater eminence in the future seemed already pigeon-holed for him—Van Buren and his own particular aspirations, of course, permitting.... De Witt Clinton had never stood higher, or soared more loftily in spirit. Still a patron of the arts, the sciences, of religious denominations widely diversified, of medicine and of education, in May, 1827, he had made his famous address to the alumni of his alma mater, Columbia College. Before three generations of former students he had traced that institution's beginnings, which were also, educationally, his own; had gone farther back, to the royal college called King's, and to students thereof: John Jay, Robert R. Livingston, Gouverneur Morris, Alexander Hamilton, Peter Van Schaick, Robert Troup. He recalled the words of the English Chatham on the correspondence from America at the outset of the Revolution, in which certain of these alumni had had an active hand:

> When your Lordships look at the papers transmitted to us from America, when you consider their decency, firmness and wisdom, you cannot but respect their cause and wish to make it your own. For myself, I must declare and avow, that in all my reading and observation, and it has been my favorite study... that for solidity of reasoning, force of sagacity, and wisdom of conclusion, under such a complication of difficult circumstances, no nation or body of men can stand in preference to the general Congress at Philadelphia.

Jay and his fellows had gone unheeded, and the King's College had closed its doors to learning while the King himself tried, and failed, to teach his colonies a lesson in autocracy. De Witt Clinton told his fellow-alumni how, when the fighting was over, King's College had become Columbia College, and he its earliest student. He was prouder than ever of the distinction, for from that time onward the story of Columbia was his, so near had he remained to her doors, so close, regardless of politics, to her interests. He could tell her story at first hand, tying it up with his abiding love for the cause of education, his enduring friendship among students and faculty. He traced the College's tree of life through all its branches. He followed the ups and downs of finance and of numbers as they related to the succeeding classes. He harped on his pet obsessions: science, knowledge as applied to everyday life; and quoted that far-distant kinsman of his mother's, the Dutch Pensioner John De Witt, who when asked scornfully of what use his early deep studies in mathematics had been in the active and somewhat violent scenes of his subsequent career, replied that the scientific way of calculating had "passed from his memory to his judgment." Governor Clinton damned the school of ignorance which held that the less a man read, the more he thought (a very numerous school in his day); that education was allied to aristocracy; that the true statesman should rely exclusively upon his own experience, since "experience was the only good school." Clinton told the assembled ex-students that knowledge was light, that education was liberty, that culture was national glory, and above all that college days were the golden days of life. . . .

But there was a golden hue over these days, too. He had the felicity of seeing slavery abolished—the final consummation of the legislative enactment of Tompkins' last administration—in New York State on July 4th, 1827. He had the peace of feeling old enmities apparently at rest. Honor was his from far and near; and what his political friends still wished for, worked for, in his behalf was a more worldly, more practical honor. The indications were increasingly that it would soon be his.

Whether the wily Van Buren would have furthered the hopes of these Clintonians can only be conjectured. He had sagacity and he also had patience. He could always see the way the political breezes were likely to veer, and since the President's House undoubtedly was and had always been his own lodestar, he was not averse to being carried thither on any breeze whatsoever. For this he had given his support to William H. Crawford. For this, when Crawford's health removed him from the race, he had switched his aid to Jackson. For this he might either have fought or, failing, helped De Witt Clinton.

But all this is speculation. The facts present the year 1828 opening on a rising wave of Jacksonian expectations. And on many men's lips at any rate there was the certainty of the Secretaryship of State—the "succession"—for De Witt Clinton if he desired it. Perhaps he did not. Perhaps the popular favor of the State of New York—his earliest aspiration and his earliest love—would have continued to satisfy him. Or perhaps, as many have said, it would now have been, with him, the highest place, or none. . . . Whichever may have been the truth, Jackson's gratitude and approval, notwithstanding the agency in Jackson's behalf of Martin Van Buren, must have placed De Witt Clinton in a stronger position than ever before in regard to the Presidential future. Clinton's ambitions had never stood so close to the pinnacle of their sometime desire. His worth, above all, had never come so near to due recognition.

It was not to be. Ever since his accident in 1818, he had been debarred from the exercise that had up to that time been a part of his daily existence. He had grown a little flabby and considerably plethoric as a result. In December, 1827, he suffered a severe attack of influenza, which left him exceedingly weak and depleted. His doctors—and particularly his lifelong close friend, Dr. Hosack—increasingly feared for him. Indeed, seeing him on a day in early February, 1828, after an absence of some weeks, Hosack was alarmed to the point of despair. Clinton had seemed to be choking. He had had difficulty in rising, in moving at all, and his color was purple where always it had been healthily ruddy.

"I shall never see Clinton again," the Doctor wrote to a medical friend on the eve of another brief journey. And he never did.

Not that the Governor thought of giving way to the alarming state of his health. Not that he even seemed to notice it, save for the precautions which had been forced on him from time to time. In the first week of February, 1828, he was devoting his mind and his legal bent, in his official capacity, to a question of right which had arisen between the Courts of the State. In January of that year, one William Miller had been sentenced to death for murder. In conformity with his unfailing anxiety to see justice done in a matter of so grave an import as the right of a State to take a human life, the Governor, approached for a pardon, had spent a great deal of time on the papers and on depositions and relevant statements in the case. But as it happened it was a clear case, and the verdict was confirmed by Governor Clinton.

On January 27th, the Court of Oyer and Terminer of New

York County handed to the Governor a letter stating that on reviewing the case that Court had "considered it their duty" to reprieve the man until February 16th. De Witt Clinton was not to be any longer among his fellow-men on that date; but on February 5th, 1828, he wrote a letter to Judge Edwards, presiding over the New York County Court of Oyer and Terminer, in which, with a discernment and an ability at the peak of their powers, he showed that the Constitution bestowed on the Governor the final power over reprieves and pardons, and illustrated the mischief that must arise if each of the fifty-six Courts of Oyer and Terminer (one for each county) had the power to overthrow the Executive's decisions. He canceled the reprieve, with the hope "that the Court's action might be without future imitation."

It was his last public act—a contribution to the law and to the stability of his State. His ill-health, his failing looks, continued. On February 8th, Josiah Ogden Hoffman—prominent lawyer, practiced legislator, father of that ill-fated sweetheart for whom Washington Irving mourned his life through—was writing beseeching the Governor to try a new prescription which he enclosed, and expressing "ardent wishes" for the Governor's health and prosperity. The letter, five days on its journey, never came before the eyes for which it was intended. On February 11th, 1828, which was a little less than three weeks short of the completion of his fifty-ninth year, Governor Clinton went to the Senate to deliver his usual message. He spoke it in a clear and powerful voice, and later pressed the hands that were offered him in friendship. He saw visitors, as usual, all day, dealt with State papers, wrote innumerable letters and his never-failing entry in his diary. After dining, which he was wont to do at four in the afternoon, he retired to his library, accompanied by his son Charles. They discussed, in the capacity of principal and secretary, a few matters of personal business. He gave, it is likely, a few moments to the details of a discourse he had been requested to make to the Literary and Philosophical Society on the recent death of his friend Thomas Addis Emmett. Then, of a sudden, he sat back in his chair, complaining of a stricture in his chest. Charles ran for water, for aid, and returned with both.

It was already too late. De Witt Clinton would pronounce

no discourse on the departed Emmett. De Witt Clinton himself was dead, in harness, as he must always have hoped he would die. At peace, as he wished no less. "I do not know that I have a hostile feeling against any human being," he had written to his devoted friend Pintard only the day before....

What followed was a blot on the page of New York's history. True, the State, as the country over, was stunned and grieved beyond words, and there was no lack of superficial evidence of that grief. As the word ran through the city of Albany, people came thronging to the Governor's house, incredulous, grief-struck, mourning unashamed. On February 12th, all city and State business was suspended, and the newspapers, sable-bordered, sang their pæans and added their lamentations. New York City likewise became a place of mourning and of tribute. On February 15th, all New York turned out to do honor to the funeral rites. Army, navy, the Church, the professions, the mercantile interests and the State were represented in the massed and impressive cortège. Newspapers, homesteads, streets resounded with the name of Clinton. Schools, colleges, learned societies, hospital staffs wore mourning bands, and men of the utmost eminence pronounced noble eulogies. When the news reached Washington, the shock, the sorrow, of Albany, of New York, were repeated. The New York representation in Congress met without party distinctions, to laud Clinton, to bewail the passing of Clinton. Martin Van Buren, addressing the meeting, spoke in praise of Clinton. He said:

> ...The triumph of his talents and patriotism cannot fail to become monuments of high and enduring fame. We cannot, indeed, but remember that in our public career, collisions of opinion and action, at once extensive, earnest and enduring, have arisen between the deceased and many of us. For myself, sir, it gives me a deep-felt, though melancholy satisfaction to know, and more so to be conscious that the deceased also felt and acknowledged, that our political differences have been wholly free from that most venomous and corroding of all poisons, personal hatred.
>
> But in other respects it is now immaterial what was the character of those collisions. They have been turned to nothing, and less than nothing, by the event we deplore, and I doubt not that we will, with one voice and heart, yield to his memory the well-deserved tribute of our respect for his name and our warmest gratitude for his great and signal services. For myself, sir,

> so strong, so sincere, and so engrossing is that feeling, that I who whilst living never, no, never, envied him any thing, now that he has fallen, am greatly tempted to envy him his grave with its honors. . . .

Nevertheless, the general sentiment did not strike very deep, in one important if more worldly direction. Mr. Clinton had left a widow and four minor children, as it transpired, without the means of support. He had left, moreover, an unpaid obligation in the sum of six thousand dollars. He had followed, all his life, the highest financial principles. He had been scrupulous in meeting financial indebtedness of every kind. But he had lent, lavishly, being totally unable to say no to distress or, most often, to refuse aid for far less pressing needs. He had gone on countless notes, and inevitably had had to help meet a number of them. And he had fairly poured out his resources in aid of the innumerable charities and public movements in which he had been interested. All his life long, ambition or no, he had poured out his means for his country—for government causes, for political funds, for schools and fortifications and canal expenses and propaganda. And now he was dead, so suddenly, so totally unprepared. And when he was dead, no such charity as he had practiced was vouchsafed his memory through his dependent kin. The creditor to whom the six thousand dollars was due promptly obtained a judgment and fetched the sheriff; and the Legislature of the State of New York, when it had finished expressing itself suitably in official meetings and adjournments and eulogia, stood by while De Witt Clinton's possessions, from his carriage horses down to his beds and chairs, went under the hammer and barely satisfied the judgment.

In the Legislature of New York State, in the halls he had so recently graced, a bill awarding full salary for his services as Canal Commissioner to his needy next-of-kin was thrown out with malice and with venom. So much for De Witt Clinton, great Governor, great benefactor, great figure of New York State; "the Pericles," as George Griffin called him, "of our Commonwealth . . . (who) for nearly thirty years . . . exercised without stooping to the little arts of popularity an intellectual dominion in his native State scarcely inferior to that of the illustrious Athenian—a dominion as benignant as it was effective."

Peter B. Porter of Black Rock, in opposing the bill, said that

Clinton would have been the last man in the world to wish such a thing.... There was recalled with artful effect the indubitable fact, not always so highly appreciated in the same quarter, that Mr. Clinton had made it a practice to refuse compensation for his work on the canal.

Erastus Root, in the Assembly, loudly opposed any grant at all; and a gentleman named Mann said that the State would do better to pay the public debt and stabilize the currency, than to make a reward so "unwarranted." Porter asserted that Mr. Clinton had been dismissed from the Canal Commission because his services were unsatisfactory.... No one, said Porter, was readier than he to admit that Clinton was a great man, an able writer, an ardent worker for public welfare and improvement. But of course, said the advocate of the faulty Black Rock adjunct to the canal, referring to the advocate of the Buffalo exit and the harbor works at that point, of locks versus inclined planes, of hard cement versus porous foundations—of course, De Witt Clinton was no engineer....

Meanwhile this public servant's effects had gone under the hammer, and his family actually faced want. What was more to the point for the gentlemen of the Legislature, the public was up in arms about the affair. Peter Porter, it transpired, was willing to present a bill calling for a grant of ten thousand dollars to Clinton's minor children, together with the remainder of his salary as Governor for the current year. The children's education, said Porter, was already started. Ten thousand dollars should be ample to complete it.... But indeed, he said, he would make it twenty, did he not have assurance that no such sum would be passed by the membership of the House....

The press now loudly gave tongue. The Clintonian papers literally burst forth in condemnation once again. They held up to everlasting obloquy a State that could treat the memory of its outstanding figure thus. They called down imprecations on the heads of those who had styled themselves Clinton's friends. And the latter took heed. It made them, in effect, strong where they had been weak. It gave them the impetus, the incentive, to push their demands, to support them, to cite the public and journalistic wrath, till no majority, certainly, in that body of men could completely withstand them. But Porter's ten thousand dollars was all they could get. It remained the official valuation of Clinton's services to his State....

So it was that his heirs wrested a heritage of bread and butter to sustain them in their pride for the spiritual heritage their father had handed down. His mortal remains were rather less well treated. He had been given, at the expense of the State, a magnificent, gorgeously panoplied funeral—but no grave. The family burying-ground, like the ancient homestead itself, in Little Britain had long since passed into other ownership. Clinton graves now had to be bought where they might, and in this case the wherewithal was lacking. For years, therefore, De Witt Clinton's bones were to repose in the vault of Dr. Stringer, a sympathetic friend, in Albany, while memorial tablets were erected in the New York City Hall and elsewhere describing the high lights of his career....

At the end of March, 1829, Charles A. Clinton, who had acted for a time as secretary to Mr. Pitcher, the new Governor *pro tem.*, but had later taken up the practice of law, wrote to General Peter Gansevoort, one of his father's former secretaries. Gansevoort had, indeed, stood as spokesman for the family in the hour of their sorrow, when they were inundated with expressions of sympathy. Now he and Simeon De Witt Bloodgood, another of Clinton's former secretaries, wanted to procure a vault at their own expense, and a lengthy correspondence ensued between Gansevoort and Charles Clinton, who was too proud to allow it but at the same time too poor to do it adequately himself. Young Clinton, a year before his father's death, had married a niece of Philip Hone, but in the midst of earning a livelihood and raising a family was not too busy to think about the simple honors that were still owing to his father. He did not want charity, or a field-day for the morbidly curious. With reluctance he consented to allow obviously privileged groups to subscribe. It is not, however, until June 21st, 1844, that an Albany newspaper bears the announcement: "The remains of De Witt Clinton, which had been deposited in the cemetery in Swan Street, were removed to New York for interment under a monument created by the family." It was his former friends, the merchants of New York, who helped to pay for the ground he hallowed,—a plot in Greenwood Cemetery, Brooklyn,—and to set up over the place a few years later a colossal statue of their hero in heroic bronze. The Freemasons had already added their final tribute by purchasing the silver vases which had been presented to Clinton by the merchants of Pearl Street, but had been sacrificed in the sale of his property. The Masons presented them anew to his heirs for ever. The Clinton vases later justified this benevolence on the part of the secret fraternities by constituting the difference between independent subsistence and dependence for Clinton's last surviving child. They now repose, appropriately enough, in the great hall of the Chamber of Commerce of the State of New York.

The Clinton heirs, to the third generation, numbered men who worked in the cause of inland navigation—the cause that had made De Witt Clinton's own fame. His grandson, George,[1] son of George, was to earn the title of "Father of the Barge Canal" for his eminent services in securing the larger and more modernized New York State waterway which, begun in 1899 and following in part the original Canal, still bears the commodity wealth of a mighty West to the markets of the world.

[1] Who survives.

BIBLIOGRAPHY[1]

Manuscript Sources

Diary of De Witt Clinton, in Library of New York Historical Society.

Correspondence and Private Papers of De Witt Clinton in New York Public Library; Columbia University Library; State Library, Albany, N. Y.; Library of Congress; New York Historical Society; Pierpont Morgan Library; State Museum, Newburgh; and in private collections.

Correspondence of James and George Clinton in New York Public Library; Library of Congress; State Museum, Newburgh; Pierpont Morgan Library, etc.

Correspondence and Private Journals and Papers of John Pintard.

Correspondence of General Peter Gansevoort, Jr., and

Housebook, private papers and letters of Catherine Gansevoort Lansing, both in Manuscript Division, New York Public Library.

De Witt Clinton: Letters to his son George W. Clinton at Hamilton College, N. Y., in State Library, Albany, N. Y.

Correspondence of Thomas Jefferson, James Madison, Robert Fulton, Andrew Jackson, James Kent and others, in Library of Congress.

Printed Sources

Life of De Witt Clinton, by James Renwick. New York, Harper & Bros., 1840.

Life and Writings of De Witt Clinton, by William W. Campbell. New York, Baker & Scribner, 1849.

Memoir of De Witt Clinton, by David Hosack. New York, J. Seymour, 1829.

De Witt Clinton and the Origin of the Spoils System in New York, by Howard Lee McBain. New York, Columbia University Press, 1907.

De Witt Clinton as a Politician, by John Bigelow (in Harper's *New Monthly Magazine,* Vol. L). New York, Harper & Bros., 1875.

Speeches, scientific essays, newspaper and other writings of De Witt Clinton, as indexed in New York Public Library and elsewhere.

Contemporary Files of the New York *Journal;* New York *Evening Post; American Citizen; Spectator;* New York *Morning Chronicle;* Albany *Argus;* Albany *Register;* and other newspapers too numerous to mention.

[1] See Foreword.

Genealogical Sketch of the Clinton Family, by Charles A. Clinton.

Diary of John Quincy Adams, edited by Charles Francis Adams. Philadelphia, J. B. Lippincott & Co., 1874-77.

Annals of Albany, by Joel Munsell. Albany, J. Munsell, 1849-59.

Collections on the History of Albany. Albany, J. Munsell, 1865-70.

Articles in *Dictionary of American Biography, Encyclopedia of Social Sciences,* and other collective works.

John Jacob Astor, Business Man, by Kenneth Wiggins Porter. Cambridge, Harvard University Press, 1931.

A Chronicle of One Hundred and Fifty Years: The Chamber of Commerce of the State of New York, 1768–1918, by Joseph Bucklin Bishop. New York, Chas. Scribner's Sons, 1918.

Report on the Practicability of Obtaining Pure and Wholesome Water for the City, by De Witt Clinton, Jr. New York, 1832.

Correspondence on the Importance and Practicability of a Railroad from New York to New Orleans, with a Report on the Subject, by De Witt Clinton, Jr. New York, 1830.

Public Papers of George Clinton, published by the State of New York. New York and Albany, 1899-1914.

History of Columbia University. New York, Columbia University Press, 1904.

Common Council, New York City, Minutes of.

Decline of Aristocracy in the Politics of New York, The, by Dixon Ryan Fox. New York, Columbia University Press, 1919.

Delaplaine's Repository, Vol. I. Philadelphia, Joseph Delaplaine, 1815-16.

De Witt Family of Ulster County, New York, by Thomas G. Evans. New York Genealogical and Biographical Record, October 1886.

Tjerck Classen De Witt and Some of His Descendants, by Rev. Wm. Walsh. Historical Society of Newburgh Bay and the Highlands. Historical Papers No. 9, Newburgh, N. Y., 1902.

Discourses and Eulogia on the Death of De Witt Clinton, Various.

Educational Views and Influence of De Witt Clinton, The, by Edward A. Fitzpatrick. New York, Teachers College, Columbia University, 1911.

Electioneering, political and miscellaneous pamphlets for and against De Witt Clinton, as indexed in New York Public Library and elsewhere.

Erie Canal, Memoir prepared at the request of the . . . Common Council, by Cadwallader D. Colden. New York, W. A. Davis, 1825.

Erie Canal history and other records in Buffalo Historical Society Publications.

Five American Politicians, by Samuel P. Orth. Cleveland, The Burrows Bros. Co., 1906.

Frontier in American History, The, by Frederick Jackson Turner. New York, Henry Holt & Co., 1921.

Governors of New York State, Lives of the, by J. S. Jenkins. Auburn, Derby & Miller, 1852.

Speeches of the Different Governors to the Legislature of the State of New York. Albany, J. B. Van Steenbergh, 1825.

Fitz-Greene Halleck, by Nelson Frederick Adkins. New Haven, Yale University Press, 1930.

History of American Economic Life, A, by Edward C. Kirkland. New York, F. S. Crofts & Co., 1932.

History of the Bench and Bar of the State of New York. New York, New York History Co., 1897.

History of the United States of America, 1801–1817, by Henry Adams. New York, Charles Scribner's Sons, 1921.

Histories, Standard, General.

Diary of Philip Hone, The, edited by Bayard Tuckerman. New York,, Dodd, Mead & Company, 1899.

Iconography of Manhattan Island, by I. N. Phelps Stokes. New York, Robert H. Dodd, 1915-1928.

Correspondence and Public Papers of John Jay.

Jefferson and Hamilton, by Claude G. Bowers. Boston and New York, Houghton, Mifflin Co., 1925.

Johnson's Law Reports.

James Kent, Memoirs and Letters of, by William Kent. Boston, Little, Brown & Co., 1898.

Rufus King, Life and Correspondence of, by Charles R. King. New York, G. P. Putnam's Sons, 1894-1900.

Long Island, History of, by Benjamin F. Thompson. New York, Gould, Banks & Co., 1843.

History and Reminiscences of Lower Wall Street, by Abram Wakeman. New York, Spice Mill Publishing Co., 1914.

Military Minutes of the Council of Appointment of the State of New York. Albany, published by the State of New York, 1901.

Gouverneur Morris, Diary and Letters of, edited by A. C. Morris. New York, 1888.

National Portrait Gallery of Distinguished Americans, Vol. 2, by E. A. Duyckinck. New York, Johnson, Fry & Co., 1861.

Native Stock, by Arthur Pound. New York, The Macmillan Co., 1931.

Newburgh, New York, History of the Town of, by E. M. Ruttenber. Newburgh, E. M. Ruttenber & Co., 1859.

New Windsor, New York, History of the Town of, by Edward M. Ruttenber. Newburgh, N. Y., Historical Society of Newburgh Bay and the Highlands, 1911.

New York Genealogical and Biographical Record.

New York as Washington Knew It After the Revolution, by William Loring Andrews. New York, Chas. Scribner's Sons, 1905.

The City of New York in the Year of Washington's Inauguration. New York, Anson D. F. Randolph & Co., 1889.

New York Historical Society, The, 1804–1904, by Robert Hendre Kelby. New York, New York Historical Society, 1905.

New York Historical Society Collections.

New York, History of the City of, by Martha J. Lamb. New York and Chicago, A. S. Barnes & Co., 1877-80.

New York, Memorial History of the City of, edited by James Grant Wilson. New York, New York History Co., 1893.

New York, by Ellis H. Roberts. Boston and New York, Houghton, Mifflin & Co., 1897.

New York State: Senate and Assembly, Journals of the.

New York in the American Revolution, by Wilbur C. Abbott. New York, Chas. Scribner's Sons, 1929.

New York Civil List and Constitutional History, The.

Olde Ulster. Kingston, N. Y., Benjamin M. Brink, 1905-6.

Orange County, New York, An Outline History of, by S. W. Eager. Newburgh, S. T. Callahan, 1846-7.

Pageant of America, The, Vol. 4: The March of Commerce, by Malcolm Keir. New Haven, Yale University Press, 1927.

Political Parties in the State of New York, History of, by Jabez D. Hammond. Syracuse, N. Y., Hall, Mills & Co., 1852.

Political History of the State of New York, by De Alva Stanwood Alexander. New York, Henry Holt & Co., 1906.

Public School Society of the City of New York, History of the, by William Oland Bourne. New York, G. P. Putnam's Sons, 1873.

Centennial Memorial of the A. R. Presbyterian Church of Little Britain, New York, edited by Archibald C. Niven. New York, Robert Carter & Bros., 1859.

New York During the Last Half Century, by John W. Francis. New York, J. F. Trow, 1857.

Annual Reports of the State Engineer, New York: Canals.

Scotch-Irish in America, The, by Henry J. Ford. Princeton, N. J., Princeton University Press, 1915.

Tammany Hall, History of, by Gustavus Myers. New York, Boni & Liveright, 1917.

Tammany Hall, by M. R. Werner. New York, Doubleday, Doran & Co., Inc., 1928.

Taverns of New York, Old, by W. Harrison Bayles. New York, Frank Allaben Genealogical Co., 1915.

Daniel D. Tompkins, Public Papers of. New York and Albany, Wynkoop, Hallenbeck, Crawford Co., 1898.

Tribute to the Memory of De Witt Clinton, by a Citizen of Albany (Cuyler Staats). Albany, Webster & Wood, 1828.

U. S. Senate, Journals and Records of.

U. S. Senate, Recollections of the, by C. J. Ingersoll.

Valentine's Manual of the City of New York.

Autobiography of Martin Van Buren (in American Historical Society: Annual Report, 1918, Vol. 2). Washington, Government Printing Office, 1920.

An Epoch and a Man: Martin Van Buren and His Times, by Denis Tilden Lynch. New York, H. Liveright, 1929.

Washington, George, Writings of, edited by Worthington Chauncey Ford. New York, G. P. Putnam's Sons, 1889.

History of the . . . Western Canals in the State of New York, by Elkanah Watson. Albany, D. Steele, 1820.

Thurlow Weed, Life of. Boston and New York, Houghton, Mifflin & Co., 1883-4.

Further standard lives, papers, etc., of Aaron Burr, Martin Van Buren, Andrew Jackson, Thomas Jefferson, John Jay, Robert R. Livingston, Gouverneur Morris, Ambrose Spencer, Daniel D. Tompkins and other noted contemporaries of De Witt Clinton.

INDEX